D0367491

MOVING OUT OF EDUCATION

THE EDUCATOR'S GUIDE TO CAREER MANAGEMENT AND CHANGE

RONALD L. KRANNICH *and* WILLIAM J. BANIS

PROGRESSIVE CONCEPTS INCORPORATED
2541 Lakewood Lane
Chesapeake, Virginia 23321

1981

Dedicated to CARYL *and* REBECCA

MOVING OUT OF EDUCATION: The Educator's Guide to
                        Career Management and Change

Copyright © 1981 by Ronald L. Krannich and William J. Banis

Second Printing, January 1982.

Library of Congress Catalog Card Number: 81-81663

ISBN 0-940010-00-3

TABLE OF CONTENTS

LIST OF TABLES

LIST OF FIGURES

PREFACE

This book represents a new attempt to deal with the problems facing educators and education. Its title and purpose are the same: help educators *move out of education* and into more rewarding careers. If read and practiced by many educators, this book may help ease one major problem now besetting American education at all levels--too many educators for too few jobs. Central to the purpose of this book is our belief that it is time to approach this problem in a more systematic, informed, and humane manner than previously attempted.

This is a different book for most educators and career planners. It is the product of the collaborative efforts of two educators--a political scientist/public administrationist and a program manager/practitioner--who have direct experience with the career problems of educators at all levels. At the same time, the book is a critical examination of career planning approaches in general and the career problems of educators in particular.

The impetus for this book began when we decided to do something different about how we educate students. We collaborated in designing a career planning teaching module for students in traditional social science and humanities courses. In so doing, we learned a great deal about each other's fields and expertise. However, in the process of implementing the teaching module, we observed an interesting phenomenon: faculty indicated more interest in career counseling than students! Indeed, career problems appeared to be more pronounced among faculty than students. This was not surprising. Higher educators were experiencing problems similar to those of elementary and secondary educators as they began scrambling to avoid the effects of retrenchment, inflation, and stalled careers. Although cognizant of their problem, most educators did not seem to know how to cope with career problems and many sought assistance through individual counseling or weekend career planning workshops. While many entertained the idea of moving out of education, few knew what to do, where to go, or how to make the move.

We found the problems of educators and education both interesting and challenging. We were interested because we were involved in the problem, yet we had done nothing about it. It was challenging because so little is known about how educators can make satisfying and rewarding career changes. These concerns were further reinforced by our experiences with educators and our knowledge of general career counseling practices and behavioral science theories. We felt there were better ways to help career disturbed educators than to have them spend thousands of dollars on the services of employment "experts".

The result of our collaborative thinking and synthesizing is this essentially self-directed career management book which recognizes the unique problems educators face when attempting to move out of education. We began with a commitment that, above all else, this book must be honest, comprehensive, intelligible, systematic, integrated, and of high quality and proven effectiveness. We especially were concerned with quality and effectiveness. As educators, we also have a professional responsibility to tell the truth and to do so based upon reliable data and reality-tested theory and logic. The book also is designed to be intelligible without being trite. We have purposefully avoided the jargon of career counselors, behavioral scientists, and our respective fields as well as attempted to maintain the credibility of the subject by extensively documenting the text. Finally, the book is comprehensive and integrated. Taken together, the chapters represent a critical synthesis of several career counseling and social science perspectives, approaches, theories, research, and findings. Although we recommend a few supplementary readings, most everything you need to know about developing an effective job search is included in the following pages. The chapters, in turn, are integrated with one another. We begin with a statement of the problem, relate it to important career considerations, and develop a step-by-step practical job search campaign involving setting objectives, identifying skills, writing a resume, researching organizations, networking, interviewing, and negotiating the job. Except for the specialized information on government employment and targeting Washington, D.C. and other communities, each chapter builds upon each previous chapter. Therefore, you should read the chapters in their proper sequence.

We have incurred our share of personal and professional debts in writing this book. We dedicate it to Caryl and Rebecca--two very understanding and patient wives who tolerated the abnormalities of our endless hours of writing, conferring, revising, typing, and proofing. Caryl Krannich made valuable editorial suggestions, proofread the manuscript several times, and corrected many of our errors. In addition, we want to thank each other for working so well together. We learned a great deal about how to destroy and rebuild each other's ideas, sentences, and paragraphs without affecting our egos or threatening our friendship. Above all, we consistently discovered the opposite of Murphy's Law. For us, it was usually "If anything can go right, it will!"

Our other debts are acknowledged in the references. Most career planning literature owes a debt to Bernard Haldane, especially to his pioneering work on skills identification and referral interviews. We gratefully acknowledge his contributions; we have incorporated many of his ideas both knowingly--for which we note--and unknowingly. Relating to Haldane's contributions is Arthur Miller's and Ralph Mattson's work on Motivated Abilities Patterns; we present a detailed examination of this in Chapter V. If you desire further information on their work, write to Miller and Mattson at the following address: People Management Incorporated, 10 Station Street, Simsbury, Connecticut 06070.

We are concerned with results as well as improving on past experience. Thus, we expect you to get positive results when you put this book into practice. Please let us know about your experiences so that we can continue to provide you and others with effective guidance for moving out of education.

Ronald L. Krannich and William J. Banis
Chesapeake, Virginia
April, 1981

CHAPTER I

FACING TRUTH ABOUT GOING NOWHERE

This book is about facing reality and doing something about it. It is designed for educators who are contemplating doing what does not come natural to them--moving out of education. We see several negative trends in education which need to be approached in less conventional and more systematic, personal, and professional manners than heretofore attempted. The problem we address is both personal and professional: many educators are locked into increasingly unrewarding jobs. As their careers plateau prematurely, many lack opportunities for career advancement and increased job satisfaction. Moreover, their future in education looks even bleaker over the coming decades.

What should educators do in an increasingly unrewarding career situation? Some educators call for professional renewal: more faculty perseverance, unity, and participation in decision-making (*Today's Education*: 59GE). Other educators have changed careers for the better. Most, however, remain in education where they jockey for fewer promotions and smaller salary increments. Many of these educators would like to get out of education, but they are either afraid to risk the unknown or don't know how to make the break.

We don't tell educators what they should do. After all, individual needs and situations differ. Instead, we provide one perspective on this problem which has not been adequately presented to educators before. We outline in detail the most advanced methods for moving out of education into new and rewarding careers and jobs. Our perspective may disturb--indeed anger--many educators who are fervently committed to their profession, who call for professional renewal, and who disdain status, money, and material pleasure. Education needs such people; we admire their dedication and spirit and wish them well. On the other hand, we address the concerns of many educators who believe they deserve better.

This is a very different book for educators. We intend to tell the truth about why many educators are going nowhere. We outline why and how they can move into more rewarding and satisfying careers. Above all, we attempt to take the fear and frustration out of thinking and doing the unknown--leaving education. In the end, our goal is to help educators as well as improve education.

BUSINESS GONE BAD

Nearly 3 million educators run a $100 billion a year business of teaching 60 million students in over 175,000 public and private institutions of elementary, secondary, and higher education. The sheer size, cost, and diversity of the educational establishment is staggering.

While once a growing, dynamic, and promising industry, education is in trouble these days. Declining enrollments, inflation, and increasingly restrictive budgets have created several depressing scenarios for educators. As the post-World War II baby boom generation completed its education in the 1960s and 1970s, elementary and secondary teachers have found fewer students to teach. In many communities--especially in the large urban centers of the northeast and north central United States--declining student enrollments have resulted in closing schools and firing teachers.

The downturns in elementary and secondary education are now impacting on higher education. The great expansion of programs, faculty, and facilities in the 1960s is over. Institutions are retrenching with leaner budgets and anticipating the coming bad years of declining enrollments. Programs and faculty in education, the social sciences, and the humanities--lacking a ready market of future elementary and secondary teachers to train--have been hit the hardest. Individual scenarios may differ, but the overall prognosis is the same: bad years ahead for institutions, faculty, staff, and administrators. Accordingly, educators face two career futures: stay in education and cope with retrenchment, or move out of education in order to advance their careers.

Business is bad these days in education. Regardless of creative efforts to ward off the worst effects of retrenchment, business is not likely to get better within the next two decades. Only elementary education will experience a resurgence in enrollment in the late 1980s, but this will not necessarily result in improved careers for teachers. Educators will need to lower their expectations and live with less status and financial security. Many have done so already. For example, elementary and secondary schools discourage new teachers with low wages. Older experienced teachers receive disincentives such as increased workloads, inadequate wages, and threats of job loss. Many teachers cannot support a family on an educator's salary nor can they find adequate opportunities to supplement their incomes. These teachers need to face the truth about going nowhere as well as learn how to avoid an even more depressing future in education.

Moving up within education by getting an M.A. or Ph.D. degree to teach in junior colleges, colleges, or universities is a sure way to further depress one's career. After all, higher education already is experiencing similar difficulties. As with elementary and secondary education, faculty and administrators in colleges and universities are securing the hatches for the coming bad years.

What happens to educators in such situations? For elementary and secondary education, one frequent outcome is tensions and conflicts among school board members, parents, teachers, and administrators. Young teachers are terminated in order to keep tenured, and sometimes less able, teachers. Superintendents become immersed in crisis management, and many get fired (Keough: 334-335). Overall, many people are unnecessarily hurt in such situations. Others survive with a few scars. Hardly anyone gets by without some damage.

We invite you to examine two scenarios in higher education from the perspectives of individual faculty members. If you change the cast of characters and the institutional settings, these scenarios are similarly pertinent to elementary and secondary education. If you think you can improve your career by moving into higher education, you should take a hard look at several realities relating to retrenchment.

JUST STARTING OUT

You receive your M.A. or Ph.D. You're proud of your achievement and excited about your future as an academician. You think you're going somewhere. Now, on to your first job. You hope it's with a good university, maybe not as good as the one you graduated from, but good nonetheless. You want to teach bright students; publish in major scholarly journals; go to conferences and present thought-provoking papers before your peers; make an impact on your profession; get tenured and promoted to full professor; take long vacations; work with interesting people; and thoroughly enjoy your work. You are joining the ranks of a noble profession of respectable individuals who seek to advance knowledge and discover truth. Status and promotion rewards go to those who work hard, are dedicated, and produce quality work. You are convinced a cruel world exists outside education.

But reality disturbs your idealism and optimism. You begin your first teaching job at an undistinguished and pretentious medium-sized university located in a small town that boasts a Kmart, McDonald's, Taco Bell, and a condominium. You start at $14,000 a year--it's better than the $3,000 a year you made as someone's assistant in graduate school and, after all, money is not important. The faculty and administration claim this university is really going places--the big league--and they need people with your credentials to help build the institution. So you're important to their future--that's flattering. You take the job with the expectation of eventually moving on to a really good university, once you've made your mark here. You need to start somewhere. This is the best offer you have in today's tight job market; indeed, you're lucky you got this job!

With a heavy workload of teaching four courses a semester, plus advising and committee work, you feel you are a jack-of-all-trades. They want you to teach everything in sight, regardless of your training and interests. You work 70-hour weeks as a dedicated teacher, researcher, community servant, and emerging scholar in your field. You're good at what you do, even though you are doing too much. But after three years, unexpectedly you are told that you will no longer be retained, because you don't measure up to the high standards of your mediocre department, school, or university--although no one knows exactly what those standards are. You sense something went wrong, but you're not sure what it was. You now know this isn't what you expected when you were in graduate school planning your bright future in academe.

You know you deserved better. You are one of the most productive and competent faculty members around this institution. In fact, you are a rate-breaker who makes others envious of your professional accom-

4

plishments. Your superiors--men of limited achievement outside this institution--do a great deal of university politicking; they curry favor with their superiors; they attempt to impress their subordinates with the number and quality of committee assignments and social invitations they receive; and they talk a lot about what a great university they're building. Too bad you won't be around for the self-congratulatory speeches that come at the beginning and end of the academic year. These people are politically entrenched with tenure, seniority, and the right set of survival and promotional relationships. You have been dealt with unjustly and unprofessionally, but your only way up in the academic career game is to get out of your present institution without making too big of a fuss; these people may be vindictive if you fight them. Lawyers cost more money than your job is worth. You're a realist, so you go job-hunting--most likely for a similar position at another academic institution--where this scenario may or may not be repeated again. Maybe this was just an unlucky first job. Or perhaps your problem is not unique? You begin hearing more and more stories, with similar themes, from friends and colleagues at other academic institutions. Can this be true elsewhere?

Sound familiar? If not, let's try a second scenario.

STAYED AROUND TOO LONG

This time you receive tenure and are promoted to associate professor. However, you soon discover this long sought-after security has unanticipated costs. Younger academicians, just out of graduate school and with low salary expectations, are eager for work. Since the administration prefers hiring such Ph.D.s, if it weren't for the security of tenure, you would probably lose your present job to one of them.

You have mellowed with age. Your research and publication productivity has declined. You are less marketable today as a secure tenured associate professor than when you were an insecure nontenured assistant professor. Teaching and administrative duties are now routine; they lack the challenge and excitement they had when they were new and unfamiliar. Your salary continues to decline in the face of increasing inflation and meager salary increments. Your 25-year old former students, who graduated with bachelor's degrees four years ago, are now making $6,000 a year more than you--and they will more than double your salary in another four years. While you would like to send your two children to an outstanding college, you can't afford $8,000 per child on your $20,000 annual salary. Maybe you could move into university administration? But few if any opportunities are available for you, since other faculty members are eager to do the same. Besides, you're not sure you would like the life style of an administrator. Best to stay where you are and, in the meantime, maybe things will improve at the university.

But let's face it, nothing's getting better. Enrollments are declining, the budget must be cut by 10 percent, and the university administration is talking about re-examining the tenure policy; actually they need to make internal personnel "adjustments" in light of new economic realities. However, 75 percent of the budget already goes to personnel, and pruning the budget usually means cutting personnel. This time it means terminating both tenured and nontenured faculty. Faculty morale declines accordingly; the once collegial atmosphere of trust and mutual respect leads to distrust, suspicion, envy, and vindictiveness as petty politics take center stage in the drama of *retrenchment* (Levine; Levine and Rubin). Changes in administrative personnel--dean, vice-president, and president--are supposed to result in more productivity. However, "productivity" is really a euphemism for "retrenchment."

The name of the game is "survival" and "holding your own ground." Retrenchment politics become somewhat ruthless and unprofessional. You sense the new administrators are rearranging the deck chairs on the Titanic. Within three to five years they will probably move on to other institutions where they will convince another governing board that they can save another sinking ship by being hard-nosed about financial and personnel matters. They talk about quality, but they are experts at cutting budgets and firing faculty. They--along with their well groomed administrative entourages and consultant-friends--constitute a new breed of pragmatic administrators in higher education. They are the middle-men supposedly saving colleges and universities from the axes of politicians and from the unrealistic demands of discontented, self-centered faculty members.

You discover you're trapped with tenure. You want out, but you don't know what to do or where to go. At times you have second thoughts, because your low paying job looks relatively good in the face of a tight job market and compared to the plight of nontenured faculty members these days. Worst of all, tenure may not be as secure as you thought since more and more tenured faculty are being terminated.

You are lucky to have tenure. But are you? Compared to whom and what? Your options have been limited by tenure. You have security--for now--but this security has psychological and material costs. Contrary to what many people think, you are not deadwood. You feel underemployed, over-worked with trivia, and unappreciated and neglected by your superiors and colleagues. You look forward to those long vacations that you were told were rewards of academe--even though you work without compensation during most vacations. You often think of retiring at age 65. Retirement comes with a complimentary university rocking chair; hand shakes and pats on the back from administrators and fellow faculty members for your "great contributions"; testimonials from your more appreciative former students; a small pension; and lifetime access to the university library, faculty dining room, and perhaps your department's Xerox machine. You take pride in the fact that so many of your students became successful in their careers--moreso than you--and you take some of the credit for their successes--justifiably or not. You occasionally wonder how different life would have been had you not received tenure. What ever happened to your former colleagues who were denied tenure?

LIVING IN THE REAL WORLD

These and other comparable scenarios are found throughout higher, secondary, and elementary education (Perron; McGuire; Shawn). This is not to say that all educators are unhappy or suffer from a bad case of "false consciousness." Many are happy, satisfied, and productive and wouldn't trade their present positions for anything or any money. They thrive in educational environments; some work in a few of the remaining growth institutions. A few others are even financially well off due to a combination of early promotions, seniority, book royalties, and consulting activities.

We believe the happy, enthusiastic, and prosperous educators are a vanishing breed. For the trends are unmistakable and believable. With few exceptions, colleges and universities are beginning to show signs of a sick and dying industry which seeks survival at any cost--grade inflation, lower admissions standards, reducing the percentage of tenured faculty, increasing the number of part-time teachers, abolishing programs, intensely lobbying state legislators and the federal government. The double whammy for educational institutions during the 1980s and 1990s is declining enrollments and rising costs (_CHE_, January 28, 1980: 1, 9). The triple whammy for faculty members is heavier workloads, decreased job security, and higher costs of living attendant with inflation and low salary increments.

The effects of retrenchment on institutions and individuals are already evident. Programs and departments are being eliminated in many colleges and universities. Several small colleges have closed and many others will do so in the near future (_CHE_, June 9, 1980: 1, 8; June 30, 1980: 7-8). Nearly everywhere faculty have lost influence in university governance; greater erosion of faculty influence is expected in the coming decade. Indeed, the 1980 Supreme Court Yeshiva ruling is a devastating blow to faculty influence. It further legitimizes the pre-eminent decision-making role of administrators and governing boards vis-a-vis faculty members: as managerial employees, faculty are not entitled to collective bargaining rights. Because of this ruling, several colleges and universities have refused to engage in collective bargaining with their faculties (_CHE_, June 9, 1980: 2).

Personnel problems and debilitating internal politics are also disturbing trends. University presidents admit that next to financial problems, personnel problems are their biggest headache (_CHE_, August 25, 1980: 6). The case of Charles Stastny, a tenured associate political science professor at Central Washington University, is perhaps indicative of future trends in university politics and job insecurity. Mr. Stastny was fired in 1979 for "insubordination." The circumstances surrounding this case, as well as the possible precedent it sets for tenure policies nationwide, are shocking for many educators. The Stastny case provides strong evidence that firing for "insubordination," or some other equally vague charge, is one way administrators handle personnel problems relating to retrenchment. Instead of reducing faculty on justifiable economic grounds, reductions are made on questionable personal and professional grounds which directly damage the careers of faculty members (_CHE_, May 27, 1980: 3-4).

Such an environment breeds the very evils that academicians have long associated with the "cruelness" of the nonacademic world. Viewed from the offices of the American Association for University Professors (AAUP), colleges and universities appear to be under seige with internal personnel and political problems. A new trend--or perhaps a new awareness--of academic vindictiveness and intolerance is evident in this era of retrenchment. Survival is "in" and quality and excellence is "out" (CHE, January 28, 1980: 1). AAUP's files overflow with "mean little cases." According to Jordan E. Kurland, associate general secretary of the AAUP,

> The issues are largely matters of conflicting personalities or life styles....Punitive action is taken against faculty members not because they are regarded by their peers as unproductive or inferior scholars, but because they are "on the outs" with people who can influence decisions about whether they will be tenured, promoted, or granted salary increases.
> "Mean little cases," is how Mr. Kurland describes the controversies. "The subject is mean, the people are mean, and the whole thing leaves a bad taste in your mouth." (CHE, April 28, 1980: 1).

Such behavior is known to occur outside academe. Many experienced educators, however, are familiar with this behavior in academe, although it has never been reported to AAUP in such volume or talked about so openly in public. Indeed, Kennedy reports that approximately 75 percent of all firings are "political assassinations" rather than legitimate cases of incompetence (Kennedy, 1980a; Irish: 181). Eisen puts this figure at 100 percent (Eisen: 26). Hence, it increasingly appears that universities approximate many other institutions in terms of the personnel politics of hiring, promoting, and firing.

Stripped of the idealism, mythology, and mysticism that insulates education from the "other" world, educators, too, have "dirty laundry" in their closets, and it is increasingly being aired in public. Academicians, like normal people, experience the "Killer Bs": blockage, boredom, and burnout (Kennedy, 1980b: 13). They go through job stress and mid-career crises; many have ulcers and problems with nerves; and some work with superiors and colleagues who are entrenched incompetents. Many educators are treated unfairly, but, like most poor people, they lack the power and influence to do something about it. Most educators are returning to the "good old days" when teachers constituted an economically marginal class in society. Educators also are involved in all kinds of internal politics that inequitably distribute the decreasing rewards their institutions have to offer. Indeed, academic politics may be more complex and debilitating than politics in other institutions (Kennedy, 1980a; Dubrin).

THE CAREER DISTURBED

An increasing number of educators are becoming career disturbed and anxious about their futures. Career disturbed educators have one or more of the following characteristics:

* are being terminated for every conceivable reason, from budgetary cuts to "insubordination" and "incompetence."
* are increasingly aware of receiving disincentives such as low salary increments and heavier workloads.
* are dissatisfied with their jobs due to disincentives, interpersonal problems, dull work, and failed expectations.
* have established achievement and monetary goals which cannot be met within education.
* want more challenging and rewarding careers but do not know how to move out of education.
* enjoy their work but can't make ends meet if they continue in education.

While many educators want out, they are caught in the academic trap of being over-specialized in particular disciplines, uncertain what they can do besides teaching and research, or are afraid to abandon the seeming security of tenure.

Several new activities of professional associations and universities are indicative of a new mood to "get out." Responding to the demand for career advice on alternatives to academe, as well as declining membership, many education, social science, and humanities associations are publishing more career-oriented literature, organizing career planning workshops and seminars, and re-orienting placement services to include both academic and nonacademic jobs.

Some of the most popular seminars, workshops, and panels at professional conferences deal with career planning for educators. For example, at the 1979 annual meeting of the Association for Asian Studies in Washington, D.C., two of the most attended sessions--standing room only--were a roundtable on "Non-Academic Careers in Asian Studies" and a workshop on "Job Search for Asianists Seeking Non-Academic Career Alternatives." Specialists from university career planning and placement offices and individuals in government and business positions assisted interested faculty and students in identifying career alternatives and in writing nonacademic resumes. At the 1980 annual meeting of the Speech Communication Association in New York City, members paid $20.00 to attend a six-hour short course to learn strategies and gain "inside" information on "Shifting Gears: How to Make a Career Change from Academe to Business and Industry." This was a shorter version of two three-day conferences held during the summer of 1980 in Malibu, California and Washington, D.C. on "Careers in Communication." The conferences were designed to "better understand the changing job market and the skills required for a variety of jobs in business, industry, government, and other non-academic settings" (SCA, April 1980: 1).

The American Sociological Association has undoubtedly initiated the most interesting response to the career problems of educators. At the annual conference in 1980, ASA members passed a controversial resolution to use CETA funds to train unemployed sociologists:

The American Sociological Association has voted to

seek funds from the Department of Labor for
"sociologists and useful sociological projects"
under the Comprehensive Employment and Training
Act.

In a lengthy debate at the association's
annual meeting, opponents charged that participation
in the CETA program, enacted in 1973 to provide job
training programs for the "economically disadvantaged"
would lower the esteem of the profession.

Its supporters argued that proposed projects,
conducted by community organizations and sociological
societies, would aid unemployed and underemployed
sociologists. They noted that the government had
sponsored similar projects for unemployed artists
(*CHE*, September 8, 1980: 2).

Several universities have begun developing specialized career
planning programs for academicians. One of the most comprehensive programs is found at the University of Virginia. During June and July of
each year, the Career Opportunities Institute at UVA sponsors a six-
week summer institute on "Career Opportunities for Ph.D.'s in the
Humanities and Social Sciences." For $2,217 per person (includes room,
board, and subsidized tuition), Ph.D. recipients can study how to get a
job outside academe. Limited to 40 participants, the institute teaches
students how to organize a career development plan, conduct career research for identifying career alternatives, write job-winning resumes,
develop job contacts and conduct job interviews. In addition, participants receive basic training in business administration. Within two
weeks of completing the first institute, students found positions with
government agencies, international construction firms, major stock
brokerage houses, and a multi-national petroleum company.

Not surprisingly, many professional associations and universities
are repeating this pattern of providing formal training programs for
acquiring jobs outside education. The reason is simple: a growing
number of faculty and students are career disturbed, anxious, and dis-
tressed. They want out of educational professions that no longer provide expected opportunities and rewards.

GOING SOMEWHERE FROM HERE

The time is right for this book. Thousands of career disturbed
and anxious educators need practical career assistance. Elementary
and secondary teachers, many facing termination, perhaps have the greatest needs at this moment; many are becoming even more disturbed as they
fail to advance within education by acquiring more graduate degrees.
Many tenured and nontenured faculty members, who already moved into
higher education, are seeking a way out of their present jobs. Many
university administrators, who formerly held academic positions, also
are looking for a way out of education. Many graduate students contemplating academic careers seek information on the job market as well as
job search techniques. All of these individuals need assistance. Our
goal is to help them as much as possible.

We have purposefully written a no-nonsense "how to" book for educators. We designed it to be simple and jargon-free. However, educators normally do not read this type of material, because they are suspicious of simplistic "yes/no" or "how to" answers to complex questions, and because they prefer aesthetic, descriptive, explanatory, and theory-building literature in the specialized languages of their disciplines. However, we see no alternative way to address this problem. Other "how to" career planning literature is not designed to deal with the unique problems of moving out of education. Therefore, our approach is applied and prescriptive; it is a mixture of empirical research, experience, intuition, and common sense. We explain the problem of educational careers and outline proven methods for identifying and finding rewarding careers outside education.

This is a nuts and bolts book about a problem and how to solve it. We provide no magical formulas nor demand skills other than those most educators already possess and enjoy utilizing. Many of our methods are validated in the social science research findings of psychologists, sociologists, economists, and political scientists. Individuals in these disciplines will find that this book transforms several of their explanatory theories--especially role and social network--into prescriptions for conducting an effective job search.

We begin with some basic facts and assumptions about the nature of careers and the educational market place and outline a few rules for getting you started on your job search. First, most individuals entering the workplace now experience many career and job changes throughout their lives. Since jobs and careers are dynamic, changing, and unpredictable, you should view your present job and career as temporary. Educators who begin and remain in a single educational position throughout their lifetime are anomalies in today's dynamic job market.

Second, you should be prepared to change jobs and careers with the minimum amount of psychological and financial trauma. A job change--voluntary or forced--should result in a healthy career advancement. Since a career consists of a series of related jobs, the best way to advance your career is to plan for job changes. Unfortunately, most people become victims of the job market. For example, it is a national tragedy to find highly skilled Ph.D.s, who have a great deal of time and money invested in their educations, performing jobs ill-suited to their motivations, abilities, and skills. There is no reason--other than short-sightedness--for these people to be driving taxi cabs, pumping gas, or selling insurance, unless they really desire such career alternatives. You should take charge of your future by finding jobs and careers that are _right for you_.

Third, a high percentage of the labor force is unhappy as well as underemployed in their present jobs. When was the last early Monday morning you couldn't wait to get to the office to begin working? When was the last Friday afternoon you became depressed, because you had to leave your job? If you can't answer these questions with recent dates, chances are you belong to the ranks of the unhappy workers who experience the "Monday morning blues"--knowing they have five more days to go--and the "thank-God-it's-Friday joys"--two days before the "Monday morning blues" begin again. Some estimate that the leading cause of health problems in this country is job unhappiness, stress, and depression (*HEW*, 1974). If you belong to this group, you should seriously consider learning all you can about how to get out of your present job and into one that is more satisfying. We urge you to start right now; set a firm date when you will start your new career. Keeping this date in mind, follow our advice in the next 12 chapters for developing and implementing your own career plan.

Fourth, assuming you belong to a troubled industry, it is best that you get out rather than stay in. If you believe education is in serious trouble, then Eisen's advice may be important for you:

> there is nothing worse than to be in a dying
> industry....Dying industries usually fail slowly,
> with weak companies failing and strong ones cutting
> back. Highly qualified employees are continually
> being cut loose, and many of them continue to hang
> around, competing fiercely for the few remaining
> openings in other companies. Don't be one of
> them! (Eisen: 23)

If this describes your present job situation, you need to do something soon.

Numerous educational institutions provide ample evidence that people who stay around get hurt unnecessarily. You should not become another victim of such an institution. Analyze your situation; consider getting out before it's too late and before the damage is too extensive. There are immediate advantages to getting out. You will improve your chances of realizing your potential as well as achieving both personal and professional success. Ironically, you may actually improve education by releasing some of the personnel pressure that is so central to its present decline.

Fifth, since you are well educated, we assume you can learn on your own when information is presented in a clear, concise, and self-directed format. For the cover price of this book, you should be able to do most of what you would learn through an expensive workshop, institute, seminar, or consulting organization. The costs of these structured learning experiences range anywhere from $100 for a workshop to $5,000 or more for the services of a professional organization. However, depending on your needs, you may want to utilize some of these services. This book will help you evaluate which are best for you.

Sixth, in order to benefit directly from this book, you must put it into practice. We know, based on others' experiences in writing "how to" books and from our own clients, that only a small percentage of individuals who seek career assistance ever follow through in implementing it. If you practice the principles and strategies outlined in this book, consider several prerequisites for making them work for you:

1. *You must develop a positive mental attitude about yourself and your capacity to succeed* in finding a job that is right for you. If you are negative or pessimistic, you are heading for failure.
2. *You must continuously ask questions about jobs*

and careers. You will learn the most from others. Keep thinking about job alternatives. Talk to successful and positive people. People generally like to be helpful and give advice. However, some of the worst people to consult may be fellow educators; you may threaten their sense of security and create conflict for them by considering to move out of education.

3. *You must set goals and plan accordingly*. Your goals should be periodically reassessed in light of new information, knowledge, and interests. This is a learning experience, and thus you should be open to new information and willing to change your thinking if necessary. Without goals you will be going nowhere. Plan your job search and work your plan.

4. *You must be committed to working hard at finding a job*. Finding a good job may be the hardest work you ever do. A successful job search requires time, commitment, and persistent effort. Devote time each day to your job search. We know of no shortcuts in this process.

5. *You must like to meet and work with people*. Job hunting is a social process. If you lack initiative or are an academic recluse, this book will disappoint you. If you are shy, our approaches will help you; they are neither "pushy" nor "aggressive" for making new contacts. Overall, our approaches should help you develop productive relationships.

6. *You must not be discouraged in your job search*. You will succeed if you have a positive self-image and a "can do" attitude and if you approach your job search with the understanding that rejections and disappointments are a normal part of the process. When you get discouraged, talk to positive people and think about the following:

> If you sometimes get discouraged, consider this fellow: He dropped out of grade school. Ran a country store. Went broke. Took 15 years to pay off his bills. Took a wife. Unhappy marriage. Ran for the House. Lost twice. Ran for the Senate. Lost twice. Delivered speech that became a classic. Audience indifferent. Attacked daily by the press and despised by half the country. Despite all of this, imagine how many people all over the world have been inspired by this awkward, rumpled, brooding man who signed his name simply

> A. Lincoln (*Washington Post*, December 21, 1980: F8)

These prerequisites are further explained and detailed as a set of 20 "principles" in Chapter III.

APPROACHES TO GETTING AHEAD

What is new about this book is its focus on the educator. Much "how to" literature is available on career planning. Indeed, the field has proliferated with books, articles, and training groups. Most of this literature is redundant, geared toward a general audience, based more on common sense than research and experience, lacks sensitivity to the needs of specific occupational groups, and is best suited for individuals pursuing sales careers. Based on sales strategies used by insurance and real estate agents, much of the literature exhorts you to "sell yourself."

While some of the career planning literature is very useful, much of it lacks credibility because it has a questionable research and experience base, it over-generalizes, and it is too aggressive for educators. However, several books are foundational and we acknowledge these accordingly.

The work of Bernard Haldane Associates remains the most influential in the career and job search counseling field. Most career planning authors owe numerous professional debts to Bernard Haldane's concepts and techniques, although many fail to credit him. Richard Germann's and Peter Arnold's *Bernard Haldane Associates' Job and Career Building* (New York: Harper and Row, 1980) outlines the basic Haldane methods and strategies. Their skill identification and referral strategies remain outstanding contributions to the career counseling field. In addition, we find their applied strategies to be surprisingly credible when related to social science research on role and social network theories.

Richard Nelson Bolles' *What Color Is Your Parachute?* (Berkeley, California: Ten Speed Press, 1980) remains a classic for job seekers of all ages and occupations. Bolles' major strengths lie in challenging myths about the job market and the job search, identifying individual goals and skills, and outlining a general strategy for initiating a job search campaign. Since Bolles aims at all audiences simultaneously, he lacks a sensitivity to different professional and career cultures. Educators should be particularly cautious with his advice to volunteer solutions to organizational problems of potential employers, which is frankly presumptuous.

Richard Lathrop's *Who's Hiring Who* (Berkeley, California: Ten Speed Press, 1977) should be read as a companion piece to Bolles' book. Targeted at a general audience, Lathrop's book is particularly outstanding on resumes (he prefers the term "Qualification Brief"), cover letters, and interview skills. Educators will find this book useful, but they should be careful in utilizing what we consider to be overly-aggressive strategies. For example, Lathrop advises you to "come on strong" with your future supervisor by boasting what a terrific person you are for a yet undetermined job (Lathrop: 37). Don't take this too seriously, unless you plan to sell used cars! Like Bolles, Lathrop advises you to propose solutions to employers' problems--assuming they want to hear such things from prospective candidates.

Richard Irish's _Go Hire Yourself an Employer_ (Garden City, N.Y.: Doubleday, 1978) represents years of experience in career counseling and a great deal of common sense. The book is written in a lucid style and is enjoyable to read. Its question/answer format addresses nearly all important concerns you may have relating to the major dimensions of the career planning and job search processes.

Marcia R. Fox's _Put Your Degree to Work_ (New York: W.W. Norton, 1979) is a useful guide for graduate students entering the job market. She introduces her graduate student audience to important career planning considerations.

CREATING A NEW REALITY

Moving out of education and into new careers requires the use of specific concepts, methods, strategies, and skills. Learning how to use these is the central concern of this book. In the following chapters, we analyze the problems of educational careers, examine basic concepts of career management, and outline proven methods for finding new jobs.

Our concept of the career planning process is adapted from the Ferrini and Parker career development model (Ferrini and Parker: 10). It is a comprehensive and integrated four-step process involving career assessment, exploration, skill development, and implementation. This model is illustrated in Figure 1. The following chapters further integrate and relate each sequential step to your ultimate goal of initiating a new job and career. Chapter IV translates this process model into an integrated set of specific career planning activities within a temporal framework.

Beginning in Chapter II, we analyze the career environment of educators by outlining present and future problems facing individuals who plan to get into or stay in education. If you are familiar with the problems of education, you may wish to skip this chapter altogether. It concludes by examining survival and advancement strategies for those who choose to remain in education.

Chapter III examines basic job search myths as well as myths relating to education and the marketability of educators. It outlines various approaches for achieving success in general and an effective job search in particular. After examining the role of faith, planning, and luck in the career planning process, this chapter concludes with a discussion of 20 "principles" for conducting an effective job search.

Chapter IV provides the overall framework for initiating an effective job search campaign. It outlines alternatives to conducting your own job search, cautions you to the world of frauds and hucksters, and stresses the importance of using library resources and getting organized. The chapter concludes with a discussion of the importance of creating contingencies and redundancy throughout the job search process.

FIGURE 1

CAREER DEVELOPMENT PROCESS

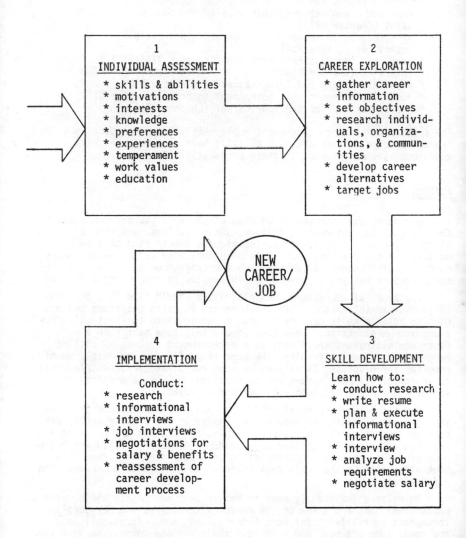

The remaining chapters examine individual job search steps and provide information on how to:

* identify your motivated abilities and transferable skills (Chapter V)
* develop a functional job objective (Chapter VI)
* write a resume for outside education (Chapter VII)
* research organizations, individuals, and communities (Chapter VIII)
* prospect, build networks, and conduct informational interviews (Chapter IX)
* conduct a long-distance campaign (Chapters VIII/XII)
* interview (Chapter X)
* negotiate salary and fringe benefits (Chapter X)
* acquire employment with government agencies (Chapter XI)
* start your new job and your career (Chapter XIII)

The special chapters on government employment (XI) and conducting a job search campaign in Washington, D.C. (XII) have been included because educators have an interest in these subjects.

AUDIENCES AND USERS

Our major audience should consist of career disturbed and displaced educators at the university, college, junior college, and secondary and elementary school levels. These individuals should find this book most useful. At the same time, we anticipate that many satisfied and happy educators will examine this book. We encourage them to, because in another five or ten years they may be interested in conducting a job search.

Two types of educational administrators should find this book useful. Many administrators left teaching and research positions but now wish to advance their careers further by moving into administrative positions outside education. This book should help them make such a move. Other administrators are directing a retrenchment process of cutting budgets and releasing faculty. We hope they will develop outplacement programs for displaced faculty based upon our strategies. Outplacement is an infinitely more humane and professional way of terminating personnel and it benefits both employer and employee.

Our final audience consists of would-be academicians who are finishing graduate school or leaving government or the private sector for colleges and universities. The strategies for getting _out_ of academe are also effective for getting _into_ academe. However, if you are beginning graduate school and contemplating an academic career, read this book along with Martha Fox's book in order to put academic careers into perspective.

We believe individuals need to better plan and manage their careers. Educational jobs are a few of the career alternatives you may sample throughout your life. Like most alternatives, some educational jobs are good, some are bad, and most have their ups and downs. We wish you good luck in whatever you do, and we hope this book will assist you in taking charge of your future.

CHAPTER II

SURVIVING THE COMING BAD YEARS

Recent headlines in leading educational journals tell a story about some new educational games few educators have ever played:

Abandonment of the Public Schools
Grave National Decline in Education
Teaching: Why I Got in, Why I Got Out
Teacher Burnout
Teacher Job Security vs. Declining Enrollments
Should Teachers Go Down With the Sinking Ship?
58 Degree Programs to be Eliminated at Louisiana's Public Universities
Colleges Still Living in Yesteryear, Futurists Charge
The Firing of Charles Stastny: A Test for Tenure
200 Small Colleges Could Close in the 1980's
New York Universities See 1981 Budget Costing Many Jobs
Questioning the Unquestionable: Should All Colleges Survive?
When Will Academicians Enter the Ranks of the Working Poor?
Carnegie Panel Says Enrollment Decline Will Create a 'New Academic Revolution'

These articles raise serious questions about the health of elementary, secondary, and higher education as well as the future of careers in education.

The facts are clear and the implications are evident. But many educators are unaware of the facts, oblivious to the implications, or engaging in wishful thinking about their futures. In this chapter we review the facts and discuss the implications for educators at all levels. The most important fact we address is the end of growth in American education due to major demographic and social changes which began a decade ago and will continue over the next two decades (Abramowitz and Rosenfeld). Elementary school enrollments peaked in 1969 and have been declining ever since. While these enrollments will increase again in 1985, they will not return to their former levels. Secondary school enrollments peaked in 1976. After a steady decline, secondary enrollments will begin to increase during the 1990s. The Golden Era in higher education--when student enrollments were increasing, budgets were adequate, new faculty were being hired, and universities were trying to become research centers of excellence--is over. High expectations generated during the 1950s and 1960s among educators have been dashed by the realities of enrollment declines, budget cuts, and a scramble for institutional and individual survival.

Today, educators find themselves in environments of insecurity, uncertainty, and shared poverty--and their futures look no better.

Little wonder many educators desire to change environments. Indeed, moving out of education is increasingly viewed as a necessary and raional act of self-preservation.

BAD TIMES FOR ELEMENTARY AND SECONDARY EDUCATION

Much has been written on the coming bad years in general. According to Howard Ruff in *How to Survive and Prosper in the Coming Bad Years*, the U.S. economy will soon collapse as we enter into a depression; therefore, prepare for the future by putting your money into silver and gold and moving away from big cities. Other "crises writers" reach similar conclusions and stress the need to learn techniques for surviving and prospering during the coming economic disaster (Casey; Abert; Smith).

If you believe such doom and gloom writers, you may as well stay in education and prepare for the worst. Changing careers or jobs will make little difference under such circumstances. In fact, you probably purchased the wrong book! If you truly believe in a coming apocalypse, you should become a survivalist. Put your paper money into silver and gold coins (small denominations), buy some guns, stock a year's supply of freeze-dried and canned foods, sell your home in the city, and move to a town or into the hills. If and when everything around you collapses, you can tell your ill-prepared friends "I told you so." You may be right, but chances are you will make a fool of yourself believing in and acting upon the advice of such soothsayers who are making fortunes with best-selling disaster books.

However, the coming bad years are predictable for education, and our soothsayers have credibility. For we are already in the bad years, and we have sufficient data to predict likely outcomes over the next two decades. In addition, the data enables us to outline a range of alternative futures for educational institutions as well as for educators.

Elementary and secondary education have disproportionately experienced bad times during the past decade. Higher education has begun reeling from the impact of changing demographic patterns previously experienced at these other levels. The post-World War II baby boom generation entered and exited elementary and secondary schools during the 1950s and 1960s. Enrollment increases were dramatic, but so were the declines. Between 1950 and 1970, elementary school enrollments increased from 22 million to 37 million; secondary school enrollments went from 6.5 million to 15 million. During this same period, expenditures for elementary and secondary education increased from $6 billion to $40 billion as more schools were built, materials purchased, programs initiated, and teachers and administrators hired. Instructional staff alone increased from 960,000 to 2.2 million during this time (Davis and Lewis: 19). On all fronts education was a growth industry. Not surprisingly, teachers and administrators entered education with optimistic career expectations.

The downturn in elementary and secondary education began as demographic and social changes occurred on two major fronts. First, fertility rates declined in the 1950s and 1960s as more women entered the workforce, couples married later, and having children became more expensive. Furthermore, the post-war baby boom generation completed elementary and secondary schooling by the 1970s. As illustrated in Table 1, enrollments in elementary schools peaked in 1969 and began a steady decline in 1970. These enrollments are expected to decline 18 percent by 1985 (Fishlow: 49). Secondary school enrollments peaked in 1976 and began declining in 1977. They are expected to fall by 25 percent during the 1980s. As illustrated in Table 2, elementary school enrollments will begin to increase in 1985 as children of the previous baby boom generation start entering elementary schools. These enrollments should increase by 20 percent from 1985 to 1995 (Fishlow: 61). Similar enrollment increases will be experienced in secondary schools. Between 1990 and 1995, secondary school-age children will increase by 19 percent and by another 10 percent in the 1995 to 2000 period. High school graduates will continue to decline from 2.8 million in 1978 to 2.1 million in 1991; by 1995 2.3 million will be graduated (_CHE_, January 7, 1980: 8).

The second demographic change is the internal shift of population from central cities to suburbs and from northeastern and north central metropolitan areas to the Sunbelt and western regions. The combined impact of both demographic changes on many school districts of northeastern and north central United States has resulted in sharp enrollment declines, major budget cutbacks, and drastic reductions in staffing levels of teachers and administrators. Only elementary and secondary education in the South seems to have weathered the worst effects of these demographic changes. However, as illustrated in Figure 2, the South has experienced a decline in enrollment, although not as great as the rest of the country. From 1975 to 1985, school-age population in the South will decline by 8 percent, compared to 13.7 percent for the United States as a whole (Galambos: 8-10).

The projected increases in elementary and secondary enrollments during the late 1980s and early 1990s mean more jobs for teachers. A teacher shortage may even occur, because universities are producing fewer teachers, and many teachers are leaving education. However, this does not necessarily mean educational careers will improve. Teachers' salaries will most likely remain low, because educational budgets will continue to be restrictive. As job opportunities improve, career rewards will not increase enough to make education an attractive career alternative. Hence, bad years still lie ahead for elementary and secondary teachers.

DOWNTURNS IN HIGHER EDUCATION

Recent studies of higher education are pessimistic about its future. Economic and demographic changes passed on from elementary and secondary education are creating serious problems for higher education. As illustrated in Figure 3, the number of 18-year olds, which traditionally provided the bulk of new college enrollments, is declining. Even the most optimistic scenarios for the 1980s and 1990s are depressing. As illustrated in Figures 4 and 5, the 1980s will be a decade of declining enrollments and rising costs; the effects of these trends will be felt way into the 1990s. With the end of the baby boom era and the subsequent

TABLE 1

PROJECTED ELEMENTARY AND SECONDARY ENROLLMENTS,
1964 to 1984 (in 000's)

Year	K-8	9-12	K-12
1964	35,025	12,691	47,716
1965	35,463	13,010	48,473
1966	35,945	13,294	49,239
1967	36,241	13,650	49,891
1968	36,626	14,118	50,744
1969	36,797*	14,322	51,119
1970	36,677	14,632	51,309*
1971	36,165	15,116	51,281
1972	35,531	15,113	50,644
1973	34,953	15,277	50,229
1974	34,419	15,337	49,756
Projected			
1975	33,800	15,500	49,300
1976	33,300	15,600*	48,900
1977	32,600	15,500	48,100
1978	31,800	15,400	47,200
1979	31,100	15,100	46,200
1980	30,900	14,600	45,500
1981	30,800	14,100	44,900
1982	30,900	13,600	44,500
1983	31,200	13,300	44,500
1984	31,500	13,300	44,800

* Peak year.

SOURCES: U.S. Department of Health, Education, and Welfare, _Projections of Education Statistics to 1984/85_: 18; and Fishlow: 49. Numbers include public and non-public schools.

TABLE 2

PROJECTED SCHOOL ENROLLMENTS FOR SELECTED YEARS,
1974-1990

Grade	Enrollment in Year (in thousands)			
	1974	1980	1985	1990
K	2,672	2,431	2,950	3,172
1	3,527	3,179	3,783	4,200
2	3,540	3,194	3,579	4,095
3	3,691	3,416	3,462	4,074
4	3,793	3,546	3,250	3,902
5	4,036	3,611	3,226	3,879
6	4,045	3,485	3,124	3,677
7	4,092	3,447	3,181	3,519
8	4,108	3,487	3,330	3,353
TOTAL, K-8	33,504	29,796	29,885	33,871
9	4,034	3,552	3,480	3,191
10	3,964	3,657	3,409	3,050
11	3,653	3,501	3,083	2,765
12	3,669	3,619	3,108	2,870
TOTAL, 9-12	15,320	14,329	13,080	11,876

SOURCES: U.S. Bureau of Census, *Current Population Reports*, Series
P-25, No. 601, "Projections of the Population of the United
States, 1975 to 2050" (Washington, D.C.: U.S. Government
Printing Office, 1975); U.S. Bureau of the Census, *Census
of Population: 1970*, Subject Reports, Final Report PC(2)-5A,
"School Enrollment" (Washington, D.C.: U.S. Government
Printing Office, 1973): 119; and Davis and Lewis: 21.

22

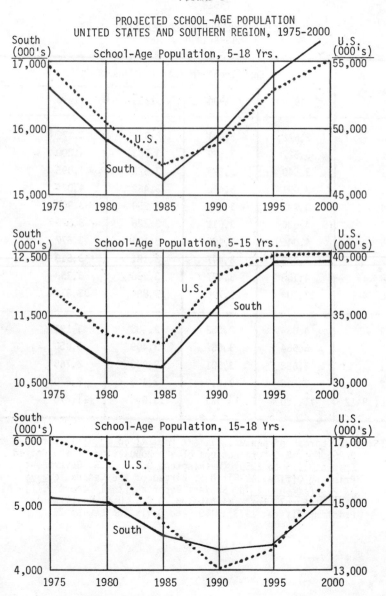

FIGURE 2

PROJECTED SCHOOL-AGE POPULATION
UNITED STATES AND SOUTHERN REGION, 1975-2000

School-Age Population, 5-18 Yrs.

School-Age Population, 5-15 Yrs.

School-Age Population, 15-18 Yrs.

SOURCE: Galambos: 9.

FIGURE 3

NUMBER OF 18-YEAR-OLDS AND 18-24-YEAR-OLDS
1960-2000

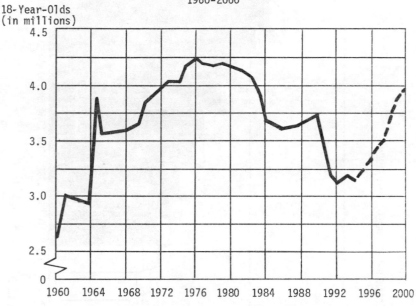

18-Year-Olds
(in millions)

——— Estimated

– – – Projected (Intermediate Projection)

18-24-Year-Olds (in millions)	1960=16.1	1970=24.7	1980=29.5
	1990=25.1	2000=24.7	

SOURCES: *Today's Education*: 55; U.S. Department of Commerce, Bureau of the Census, *Estimates of the Population of the United States, by Age, Sex, and Race: April 1, 1960, to July 11, 1973*, Current Population Reports, Series P-25, No. 519; *Estimates of the Population of the United States, by Age, Sex, and Race: 1970 to 1977*, Current Population Reports, Series P-25, No. 870; and *Projections of the Population of the United States: 1977 to 2050*, Current Population Reports, Series P-25, No. 704 (Washington, D.C.: the Bureau, April 1974, April 1978, January 1980, July 1977).

24

FIGURE 4

HIGHER EDUCATION PRICE INDEX, 1970–1988

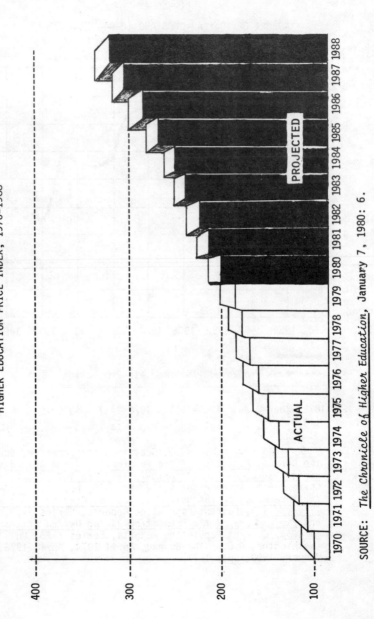

SOURCE: *The Chronicle of Higher Education,* January 7, 1980: 6.

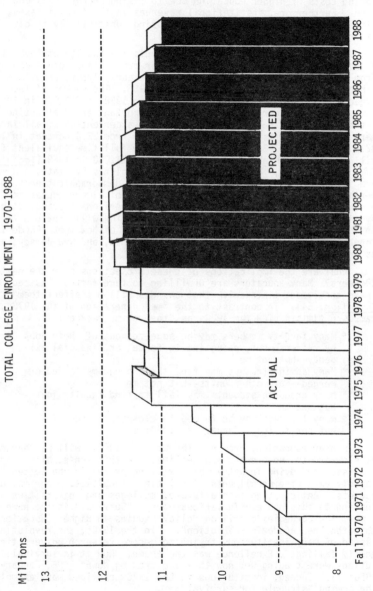

FIGURE 5

TOTAL COLLEGE ENROLLMENT, 1970-1988

Millions

13 ----
12 ----
11 ----
10 ----
9 ----
8 ----

PROJECTED

ACTUAL

Fall 1970 1971 1972 1973 1974 1975 1976 1977 1978 1979 1980 1981 1982 1983 1984 1985 1986 1987 1988

SOURCE: *The Chronicle of Higher Education,* January 7, 1980: 6.

"demographic depression" of fewer 18-21 year olds entering college, undergraduate enrollments will decline from 5 to 15 percent over the next two decades (_CHE_, January 28, 1980: 1). Equally problematic are the soring costs of higher education due to rising energy costs and inflation. Furthermore, institutional revenues in the form of taxes, tuition, gifts, and investments, are not increasing substantially to offset these rising costs (_CHE_, January 7, 1980: 6).

The statistics on student enrollments and faculty employment in higher education are not encouraging for present and future educators. From a high of nearly 12.0 million in the early 1980s, enrollments are expected to decline to 11.0 million by 1988. The number of faculty will steadily decline from a high of 647,000 in 1978 to 612,000 in 1988. However, these figures conceal another important trend affecting faculty --the use of more part-time teachers. As a percentage of all faculty, part-time faculty is projected to increase from 22.4 percent in 1968 to 32.2 percent in 1988. The demand for new full-time equivalent faculty will fall from a high of 81,000 in 1975 to 21,000 in 1988 (_Today's Education_: 56-57). Projected enrollment declines by states and regions are illustrated in Figure 6. Following the demographic trends in elementary and secondary education, the future of higher education is less bleak in the southern and western states of Arizona, Nevada, Utah, Wyoming, Idaho, and Texas. The worst scenarios will continue to occur in the northeastern and north central states of New York, Rhode Island, Connecticut, Massachusetts, Ohio, Pennsylvania, and New Jersey, as well as in the District of Columbia.

What are the implications of these projections over the next 10 to 20 years? Many educators are unwilling to face facts. Instead, they "have concluded--mistakenly--that changes will not affect them" (_Today's Education_: 54). In contrast to the "me" generation of the 1970s, these campus optimists view the 1980s as "the not-me decade":

* Many faculty members may be squeezed out of their jobs
  by retrenchment, reduction in force, or financial exi-
  gency--but not me
* Many administrators may find their programs folded or
  merged--into other units--but not me
* Many graduate students may fail to find faculty jobs--
  but not me
* Many trustees may be forced to close their schools--
  but not me (_CHE_, January 7, 1980: 6)

Higher education, from now through the 1990s, will be characterized by slow-growth, no-growth, and decline. In this sense, higher education is a sick and dying industry which will never regain the Golden Era of rapidly expanding enrollments, facilities, faculties, programs, and budgets. Anticipating such a future, colleges and universities are adjusting to this new era in various ways. "Survival" is the name of the game. The Carnegie Council on Policy Studies in Higher Education calls this the "new academic revolution": "In the 1970s, the revolution consisted of many institutions trying to become research universities and mostly failing....Excellence was the theme. Now it is survival. Institutions were trading up; now they are trading down" (_CHE_, January 28, 1980: 1). Indeed, institutions in the 1970s provided many examples of the coming "struggle for survival":

FIGURE 6

PROJECTED CHANGE IN NUMBERS OF PUBLIC HIGH
SCHOOL GRADUATES BY STATES

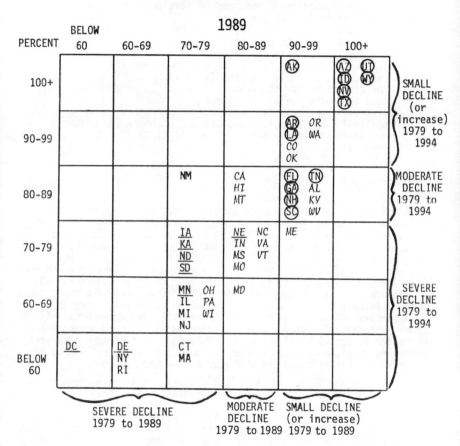

NOTE: The classes of 1984, 1989, 1994 are percentages of class of 1979.

LEGEND:
* *States with severe early decline: class of 1984=70-79% of class of 1979* (underlined)
* *States with moderate early decline: class of 1984=80-89% of class of 1979*
* States with small early decline: class of 1984=90-99% of class of 1979 (circled ◯)

SOURCE: *Today's Education*: 55.

28

* The lowering of admissions requirements.
* The search for non-traditional students, who in the
  past have been least preferred.
* The increased emphasis on retention of students.
* The rising level of grades to attract and retain
  students in courses and departments.
* The turn toward vocational and professional subjects
  following student demand.
* The introduction of new fields and courses that are
  highly popular with students.
* The faculty interest in collective bargaining to
  protect tenure and real income and sometimes, to
  resist the impacts of affirmative action.
* The effort to find top leadership which is good at
  cost accounting or at recruitment of students or at
  fund raising or at all three; to find managers for
  survival...instead of innovators and planners for a
  different--hopefully better future (_CHE_, January 28,
  1980: 11).

JOINING THE WORKING POOR

The impact of these changes on individual faculty members is relatively predictable. Educators in the more vulnerable disciplines of
education, the humanities, and the social sciences are seeing their programs and departments geared-down or abolished. Continued support for
programs is justified by producing students or external funding. As
budgets get cut, faculty members face zero-sum situations in which some
programs and departments gain at the expense of others; winners and
losers are evident. At the same time, faculty members "are going to be
in as difficult a period as has happened in the twentieth century. It
is extremely unlikely that their salaries will keep up with salaries in
other professions. There will be little new hiring, and promotions will
be harder to get" (_CHE_, January 28, 1980: 11). The pattern of poverty,
evidenced in elementary and secondary education, will most likely be
repeated for higher educators who stay around too long.

Although the 1950s and 1960s saw a substantial improvement in educators' living standards, historically educators have been on the economic margins of society. The financial status of faculty looks dismal by
any standards. With thousands of dollars invested in their educations,
academicians are now returning to their former economic status. According to Abbott, they are quickly joining the ranks of the working poor.
Using academic salary trends for the 1970-1977 period in projecting
faculty income to the year 2000, Abbott's most optimistic projection is
that the lower ranking academicians will join the working poor in the
1980s. Furthermore, by the year 2000, faculty at the higher ranks will
receive an income comparable to the poverty threshold of today's assistant professors. The implications of these projections for faculty
members are alarming:

The first--and most probable--is that academic families
with a single income must adapt to a lower level of

income. Although the present generation of academicians may consider themselves to be in an income
bind, later generations may look to these as the
"good old days"....it is also unclear whether the
relatively high prestige academicians now enjoy
will continue when academicians enter the ranks of
the working poor.

Second, entry into the academic profession in
the future may be based on access to supplementary
sources of income. There are several forms this
could take. Some professions rely on family sources
of support at the entry (i.e., assistant professor)
level. Banking was formerly such a case. This has
the unfortunate effect of making such a profession
selective by social origins. An alternative source
of supplementing income is part-time employment,
which may vary from extra teaching, and consulting,
to a non-professionally-related occupation. Since
the academic role requires a full commitment of
time, being forced to divert time for other purposes,
especially at the assistant professor level, would
add additional strain to the academic role....future
academic families will increasingly be career families, and thus supported by joint incomes.

Finally, there are countervailing forces that
could operate to reverse the dismal projections. As
the reality that academic salaries are approaching
the poverty level becomes more apparent, there may
be spontaneous sources of support to counteract, at
least partially, the declining economic state of the
profession. It is also unclear whether college
faculty will generally resort to collection bargaining on the trade union model. The prevailing professional ideology probably does not support this....
The era in which academicians can collectively neglect
their economic interests is now over (Abbott: 352-353).

The dismal economic state of academicians is further confirmed in
our experience with assisting students and faculty in career planning.
Many students with B.A.s in the humanities and social sciences are acquiring entry-level positions in the $12,000 to $18,000 range. These
salaries are at least equivalent to or higher than salaries received by
most beginning assistant professors with Ph.D.s. This point is aptly
illustrated by examining a job listing which appeared in _The Chronicle
of Higher Education_ during the summer of 1980. It was for a faculty
position with a small college in a town of 12,500 in South Dakota:

POLITICAL SCIENCE/PRE-LAW ADVISOR: Instructor or
Assistant Professor, tenure track, beginning Sept.
1980. Teach 12 hrs. per semester plus interterm.
Generalist with broad emphasis in political and
administrative theory. Other areas include Federal
State, and Local government. Ph.D. required, teaching experience preferred. Salary range $12,000-
$13,000.

Admittedly the cost of living is lower in South Dakota than in many
other places, and there may not be much to spend one's money on in this
small town. But $12,000-$13,000 per year and a 12-hour teaching load
for a Ph.D. would be an insult to most professionals in non-academic
occupations. Furthermore, to make the insult worse, competition was
probably great for this position. In the end, this college offered
someone an opportunity to voluntarily enter the ranks of the working
poor.

With some basic typing skills and a pleasant telephone voice, the
academician in South Dakota could have become a secretary or reception-
ist in Houston, Texas for $14,000 a year--and with much higher benefits,
job security, and career advancement opportunities. The same individual
would probably qualify for a GS-13 position with the federal government.
Beginning salary at this level is $32,088, with generous benefits and a
better retirement plan than most colleges and universities. Within
three years, this person could advance to $42,000 per year. Moreover,
as a federal employee, this individual would probably work directly in
his or her area of expertise--unlike the jack-of-all-trades job in South
Dakota.

ALTERNATIVE FUTURES

So far we have outlined what we consider to be a realistic appraisal of the present and future state of education. The Carnegie Report
on Higher Education goes further. It outlines two scenarios--one pessimistic and one optimistic--which constitute alternative futures for
higher education (_CHE_, January 28, 1980: 9). Pessimists see our worst
fears being realized. They project:

1. Enrollments will decline by 40-50 percent because
   the glut of college graduates in the labor market
   will drive down salaries of college graduates and
   therefore make college education less attractive.
2. The financial status of institutions will decline
   markedly due to a combination of tax revolts, inflation, and declining endowments.
3. The struggle for survival will result in more
   destructive competition within and between institu-
   tions--even more false advertising, grade inflation,
   easy credits and courses. Public confidence erodes
   and more controls are placed on higher education.
4. Faculty members refuse to face reality and become
   rigidly defensive through collective bargaining and
   attacks on university administrators. Tenured-in
   faculty are mainly white males who are becoming
   older and further removed from the students.
5. Increasing difficulty to recruit quality administrators because of the difficulties surrounding university administrative roles, such as harrassment.
6. Students enter a Golden Age of influence over faculty
   and administrators; standards are lowered as students
   drop in and out.

7. Increased public intervention and control over the details of institutional life. Greater quantitative and qualitative management over the decline in enrollments.
8. Private institutions will be economically decimated because they cannot compete with high tuitions; they seek public subsidies in competition with public institutions.
9. Institutions no longer control their futures.
10. Research activity declines because younger scientists are not hired and older scientists are less productive.
11. All institutions become less dynamic; they are torn by internal strife in a Hobbesean world of "every man against every man"; and they become bureaucratic mechanisms rather than self-governing entities.
12. More competition and mistrust in campus governance.
13. The new teaching technology of cassettes, TV, and computers displaces the traditional classroom; colleges fight the new technology and thereby drive it into commercial channels.

Some of these projections already have become realities in many colleges and universities. The question is: To what degree will they become realities in the more than 3,000 junior colleges, colleges, and universities in this country? After all, several higher education institutions have closed their doors: 46 in 1968, 102 in 1973, 63 in 1978, and perhaps 200 in the 1980s (*Today's Education*: 57; *CHE*, June 9, 1980).

Optimists see a different but related future. American higher education is at best resilient and capable of adjusting to the new era:

1. Enrollments may actually increase by 25 to 40 percent as more older people and foreign students replace the missing traditional 18-21 year old students.
2. The federal and state governments come to the aid of higher education in not reducing resources as much as enrollment declines.
3. Higher education has enough political influence to hold its own; unemployment results in increased enrollment. More federal and state subsidies for students to attend colleges and universities.
4. Academic integrity is maintained through new codes of fair practice.
5. With the end of expansion, increased attention is given to quality in teaching, research, and public service.
6. Faculty members develop more realistic expectations and become more public interest-oriented. A small flow of high-quality young faculty members and minorities is assured through new imaginative personnel policies.
7. Trustees choose better administrators who are good

> leaders and fund raisers.
8. Students demand quality education by shopping around for the best institutions and programs; they face a better job market.
9. Public authorities exercise self-restraint by not intruding into the details of institutional life.
10. Only the weakest public and private institutions will collapse; this will improve the overall system of higher education.
11. The federal government, as well as private industry, increases support for basic research.
12. Colleges and universities remain flexible.
13. Colleges and universities reshape their educational philosophies and organizations in line with the realities of the present and the challenges of the future.
14. The new technology is used along with more traditional forms of instruction.
15. Higher education plays a central role in the revitalization of the nation.

The outlook for individual faculty members over the next twenty years is not good in either scenario. Expanding personal incomes, career opportunities, and rewards of the 1950s and 1960s have all but ended; they are not expected to substantially improve in the foreseeable future. The best scenario for educators is surviving without losing too much ground. For we have entered into an educational era of hard times, limited opportunities, and lowered expectations.

COPING WITH THE 1980s AND 1990s

The real survivors in education, at least within the next five years, will be found in today's growth fields. In elementary and secondary education, math, science, and special education teachers will find numerous opportunities; but career rewards will be disappointing when compared to alternatives outside education. Thus, having a teaching job will mean a continued low level of survival.

In colleges and universities, business, computer science, and engineering are the growth fields within the next few years. With the shift in student interests to more practical and job-oriented subjects, the internal organization of colleges and universities has been substantially altered (*CHE*, October 20, 1980: 56). Stressing FTE (Full-Time Equivalent) productivity measures, internal resources are being redistributed to fields demonstrating high student demand. The losers are programs, departments, and faculty members in education, the humanities, and the social sciences. While faculty in these areas decry their loss of influence, stress the importance of their subjects for the enlightenment of mankind, and scramble to make their courses part of the university distribution requirements as well as more "relevant," hard times lie ahead nonetheless.

Take, for example, what is happening in several colleges and universities across the country. In 1979 the State of Louisiana eliminated

58 degree programs. Most of the programs had proliferated during the growth years of the 1960s. Faced with declining enrollments, such programs could no longer justify continued support. Fifty-five of the 58 eliminated programs were in education; eight were doctoral programs; and most were designed for school teachers (CHE, January 14, 1980: 6).

Several universities have developed long-range plans and instituted "retrenchment policies" for coping with the 1980s and 1990s. Duke University's plan for the 1980s will determine whether six units of the university should survive: department of education, school of forestry and environmental studies; department of health, physical education, and recreation; the marine biology laboratory at Beaufort, N.C.; the school of nursing; and the department of sociology. The university president also plans to reduce the faculty by 15 percent, which means eliminating 80 positions (CHE, January 7, 1980: 7).

The Wisconsin and Michigan university systems are facing similar realities. The Wisconsin state legislature expects public university enrollment to decline by 15 percent, or by 150,250 students, by 1993. Since funding formulas link enrollments to financial support, the Wisconsin university system must reduce its instructional budget by 4 percent, or $12.5 million. Major cuts will be made in existing programs and faculty positions (CHE, January 7, 1980: 7). At the University of Michigan and Michigan State University, studies are underway to eliminate tenured faculty and abolish departments and programs due to an impending "state of financial crisis" (CHE, March 2, 1981: 5).

Columbia University's Commission on Academic Priorities in the Arts and Sciences has recommended a program of "selective excellence." This means a limited number of programs--deemed the best--will receive continued support. It also means an internal redistribution of resources: eliminating 12 faculty positions in the humanities and creating 17 new positions in the natural and mathematical sciences (CHE, January 7, 1980: 9).

Other colleges and universities are developing similar planning processes and retrenchment policies for the 1980s and 1990s. The immediate future of faculty in the growth fields appears to be relatively secure. However, faculty in education, the humanities, and the social sciences are most likely to be the targets of retrenchment policies over the next decade. Consequently, they especially need to consider alternatives to careers in education.

SURVIVAL STRATEGIES WITHIN EDUCATION

While the remainder of this book assists you in moving out of education, you may choose to stay in education or re-enter at a later date. If so, you can do certain things to increase your job security. Always remember that a job means giving your time and talents in exchange for position, status, money, and other resources. You are an expendible commodity; educational institutions can survive without your services. They rent your labor, and they are not obliged to love you. Therefore, approach educational jobs in as realistic and objective a manner as possible.

Given the depressed nature of the educational job market, you need to organize a job search campaign which focuses upon particular communities and institutions. Begin by analyzing educational trends, especially demographic and enrollment patterns. For elementary and secondary education, few opportunities are available in schools of northeastern and north central urban areas. Look toward the growth states in the Sunbelt and western regions, such as Arizona, Texas, Nevada, Utah, Louisiana, Colorado, Idaho, Florida, and Arkansas. Florida should be the fastest growing state in the 1980s (Sivy: 76). Also, within each state, identify communities which are experiencing population increases. Most of these cities have populations over 100,000 but under 2,000,000. The 20 fastest growing cities, in rank order, are Las Vegas, Austin, Tucson, Fort Lauderdale, Houston, Phoenix, Oxnard, Calif., Tacoma, San Diego, Annaheim, Tulsa, Salt Lake City, Portland, Ore., Seattle, Oklahoma City, Tampa, West Palm Beach, Baton Rouge, Riverside, Calif., and Orlando. Even within communities, school enrollments will differ according to internal population shifts. New housing developments for medium-income families on the periphery of communities will have more new schools than the older central city schools which normally experience enrollment declines.

After completing your regional, state, and community research, target particular schools by using our job search methods in subsequent chapters. Our advice on writing resumes, conducting research, prospecting, establishing networks, and doing informational interviews should result in a successful job search.

If you seek a position in higher education, you need to follow a similar job search strategy. You should first analyze educational trends and the financial soundness of individual colleges and universities. For example, consider the American Council of Education's predictions of future regional growth and decline patterns in higher education:

1. Six states can be expected to have higher college enrollments in 1985: Arizona, Colorado, Delaware, Florida, Idaho, and Utah.
2. The largest number of states, thirty-three, will not experience significant enrollment declines, because the immigration of students will offset the normal population decline. These thirty-three states enrolled 62 percent of all freshmen in 1975.
3. Eleven states will experience a decrease in enrollment: Arkansas, Connecticut, Illinois, Iowa, Kentucky, Minnesota, New Jersey, New York, North Dakota, Ohio, and Pennsylvania. These states, which enrolled 28 percent of 1975 freshmen, will experience a decrease in the college-age population and, with the exception of Iowa and Kentucky, they have traditionally exported more students than they have imported (_Academe_, February 1980: 17).

Based on this data, you should investigate institutions in Arizona, Colorado, Delaware, Florida, Idaho, and Utah.

However, do not neglect other states. Each state will have some institutions which are experiencing more or less positive growth patterns.

The same is true for programs and departments within individual institutions. Some institutions may have rapidly developing criminal justice programs; other institutions may have failing criminal justice programs but successful and growing public administration and technical writing programs. There is no substitute for knowing the internal patterns of state educational systems as well as individual institutions. National, regional, and state trends are not necessarily true for individual institutions, schools, departments, and programs. You should occasionally examine the pages of _The Chronicle of Higher Education_ and other educational publications. For example, enrollment figures for all colleges and universities are published each year in _The Chronicle_; annual percentage increases and decreases in enrollment are included so that you can identify particular institutions with promising growth patterns.

Once you have identified institutions for job targeting, you should acquire information on whether the institutions are financially sound, have established reputations, are located in a growing urban area, have a substantial number of majors in your field, and include your subject matter in the university distribution requirements. In analyzing individual programs and departments, you should consider the percentage of tenured faculty; promotion and tenure policies, patterns, practices, and problems; stability of administrative leadership and the general internal political and interpersonal environments.

If you are intent upon staying in elementary, secondary, or higher education, you will probably find a job, especially if you work hard and persevere in targeting your job search. Even in a tight job market, jobs are available in your field. As long as individuals in educational positions practice your specialty, you have a potential job opening. People do move out of education, resign, get fired, retire, move into administrative positions, and die. You need to develop a systematic job search campaign in which you identify potential job openings, make contacts prior to formal job listings, and thus increase your chances of getting the job you want.

Moreover, in tight job market situations, you should place greater reliance on informal and personal strategies. Even though institutions are supposed to hire according to affirmative action, equal opportunity, and merit considerations, many positions are filled on the basis of personal relationships. Do not waste time waiting to react to formal job announcements. Seize the initiative by developing a systematic job search campaign for targeting institutions and uncovering pre-advertised opportunities. You can accomplish this by following our recommended targeting procedure :

1. Identify where it is you would like to work--a region, state, city, and/or institution.
2. Conduct a market survey to identify several viable schools, colleges, or universities. Pay particular attention to changing demographic and enrollment patterns.
3. Target the institution by checking with people in your network of contacts, such as former professors, fellow graduate students, friends, professional acquaintances, family, former students. Ask your

contacts for information on the institution, including names of any individuals who work there or
know someone who may.
4. Write a resume in a professional and functional
format (see our chapter on resume writing).
5. Write letters, telephone, and make appointments to
meet with your contacts. Give them a copy of your
resume. If you have no contacts, write a letter
to key people, such as a department chairperson,
superintendent, or dean, and request a meeting to
discuss your mutual interests.
6. Research the institution more closely (enrollments,
financial status, majors, distribution requirements,
politics) and ask your contacts for suggestions
about employment at this or any nearby institutions,
as well as names of additional people who would be
good to talk with.
7. Send thank-you notes expressing your gratitude for
the meetings and advice. Ask to be remembered for
future reference, if and when your contacts hear of
any positions for someone with your qualifications.
8. Submit a formal application if a vacancy opens in
your targeted institution. Call your contacts for
additional information as well as to let them know
you have applied.
9. Repeat steps 1-8 for all other institutions you
wish to target.
10. Interview according to our advice in the chapter on
interviewing.

Your chances of finding an educational position of your choosing
will be enhanced greatly if you follow this strategy. As will become
evident in subsequent chapters, the least effective way of getting a
good job is to compete with 100 or more other applicants by only applying to formal job listings in professional newsletters and newspapers.
You should understand and utilize the dynamics of the informal system in
order to maximize your chances of getting a good job.

COMPETING FOR LOW STAKES

While *high competition* characterizes the employment picture for
many educators, *low stakes* characterize many jobs in education. Educators continue to fiercely compete for decreasing rewards. For example,
in higher education big decisions often involve nickle-dime stakes which
affect few people other than some petty players of academic politics.
Academicians sometimes spend hours arguing in committee meetings over
how to best divide $300 in travel funds among eight faculty members, or
how to divide $2,000 in research money among 18 competing faculty
members. On a larger scale, some national research funding groups
attempt to allocate, for example, $40,000 to seven out of 80 competing
academic research proposals.

Given such a situation, the question for many educators today is:

Can I really afford to play the new educational game of high competition and low stakes? If your answer is "no," you should begin considering career alternatives.

However, moving out of education is not an easy task. Indeed, some people envision a new frustrated class of unemployed, underemployed, and displaced educators selling insurance, pumping gas, or driving taxi cabs. But maybe educators are too removed from reality to understand who is really underemployed and career displaced. Take, for example, the life of the "Ph.D Cabbie" outside education.

The Ph.D. Cabbie: 'I Don't Miss It, Not Anymore'
(Perron: 31)

It was only a 10-block walk to the convention center, but the rain changed my mind about exercise. I climbed in a cab at the hotel entrance, gave my destination, and settled back. We didn't move. Cars jammed the streets in the morning rush hour.

"You with the teachers' convention?" the cabbie asked over the noise of slapping windshield wipers. I nodded at the eyes in the rearview mirror.

"Used to be a teacher myself."

"Is that right?" I smiled, more interested in watching the umbrellas play bumper car along the sidewalk.

"Yeah. Lasted about four years." He nosed the cab into traffic and hit the first of several halts before the end of the block.

"Why'd you quit?"

"I didn't. I was squeezed out in the money crunch. Things got a bit tight at ol' Plimpton College."

"College? You have a doctorate?"

"Yeah, Indiana. Class of '74."

"No kidding. How long you been driving a hack?"

"About six months."

Unemployment Abounds

"The way things are going, I might be joining you. A lot of underemployed Ph.D.'s running around."

"Underemployed? Yeah, well, I'm fully employed."

"I don't think I'd be happy not teaching."

"It's all relative. I'm happy when I'm feeding my family."

"I guess." I looked at my watch. "I'm due to speak in about 20 minutes. Think I'll make it?"

"You'll make it. This jam won't last much longer."

I watched the rain squiggle down the side window. Different openings for my speech ran through my mind. Maybe I should start with a reference to the weather.

"I don't miss it, not anymore," he began again. "I never could get used to grading people."

"Really? Haven't you tried to find another teaching job.?"

"I did at first. Hell, I sent letters all over the place. All I ever got were polite responses requesting a pound of documentation."

"I finally figured it out: games. It's all who you know."

"Well, you're probably right." In fact I knew he was right. I had gotten my job through the chairman of my doctoral committee.

"I didn't know anybody."

"Must have been rough."

"I won't bore you with the details. My wife made enough for us to get along, but the old life style went out the window. One day I ran across an old friend and he got me this job."

"Doesn't sound like a long-term solution, though," I said.

"I have to admit one thing. I do miss the spotlight. As a professor you are somebody. It's an incredible high. Like with you, now--going to a conference, giving a speech, earning the praise. I loved that part. When I think of it, I forget all the hassles--the committee doldrums, the paperwork, the grades, even the publish-or-perish junk."

"I don't mind all that stuff. Helping students learn is what it's really all about--watching them develop, seeing them put ideas to work. It's worth it."

"Well, that, too, I guess. But being content is the big factor, no matter what you do."

Life 'No Five-year Plan'

"I know," I said. "I sure enjoy what I do.
I think most people enjoy their work--or they don't
stick around long. It's got to be meaningful."

"It gets meaningful when you can eat. The rest
is pride. I had to work that out. I saw myself as
a breed apart--officially registered by my Ph.D. I
had to learn."

"But you're wasting years of training."

"Maybe. Maybe not. Life's not a five-year plan.
And, hell, it's really not too bad driving. You meet
some weirdoes, but most of the time people are a riot."

"Must be a shock when they learn you're a Ph.D."

"Hey, I don't usually tell people. They'd think
I was some kind of a nut. That's one of the first
things you learn: Never tell anyone but an academic."

The traffic started to break.

"Think you'll ever teach again?"

"I doubt it. I don't think many teachers would
go back if they knew it's less of a hassle outside--
and the pay's better."

"For myself, I prefer summers off. I couldn't
face the grind of a 9-to-5 job."

"That's a myth. You're working more than a
40-hour week--preparing for classes, grading papers,
doing research."

"For sure."

"So there you are. Hey, I've got more time in
this job than I ever had in teaching."

I caught sight of the convention center looming
out of the rain. When we were directly across from the
main entrance he pulled a quick U-turn and stopped at
the curb.

"Good luck on your speech--and holding onto your
job," he said as I paid. I tried to add a dollar tip,
but he refused it. "Keep it. You need it more than
I do. I've already made last year's teaching salary
in the few months I've been driving."

'I'm a Survivor'

"No, take it. Think of it as a kind of rebate
on your degree, compliments of my university." It just

popped out.

He smiled. *"I'm a survivor. What the hell, life's full of surprises. Who knows? Maybe I've got a new teaching job already--right here in the driver's seat."*

I kept my dollar and went off through the rain. I found the room and took my place on the panel just as the first speaker began with a reference to the weather.

I opened with a story about my Ph.D. cabbie. People didn't know whether to laugh or take it seriously.

CHAPTER III

TAKING ANOTHER LOOK

It is time to take another look at the careers of educators as well as the information and advice available to help educators change and advance their careers. Thus far no literature has addressed the problems of educators by providing practical guidance on how to move out of education and into more rewarding careers. Instead, educators have had to rely on popular and general career planning literature which does not deal directly with their career problems.

Indeed, much general literature has been written on how to change jobs and careers. However, a critical examination of this literature raises serious questions about its credibility and usefulness. Educators especially should be suspicious of "how to" advice on changing jobs and careers. For most of the popular career planning literature is simplistic, flippant, excessively aggressive, and requires an unusual amount of faith. Taken too seriously, this literature may be counterproductive for some people. Nonetheless, some of this literature is useful, and we attempt to place it in perspective for educators.

In this chapter we take another look at the career planning literature and the advice--both good and bad--it may give you. We analyze, critique, and synthesize the state of the art, science, or religion of career planning. We do this by reviewing the literature on selling success and career planning as well as outlining myths that constrain career planning initiatives. Furthermore, we define our assumptions, specify our approach, and identify major "principles" for beginning an effective job search campaign.

SELLING SUCCESS ON FAITH

Much of the "how to" career planning literature is based upon the assumptions and principles evident in the evangelical "success" literature. This is understandable since many career planning writers have little or no behavioral science backgrounds. Many authors are trained in sales, marketing, and religion, and some lack a background in anything. Most share one general assumption: since career planning involves selling yourself, you must learn good sales techniques. Not surprisingly, many of the sales techniques are plagiarized creatively from the "how to succeed" in the insurance, real estate, and other direct-sales businesses.

Packaging and selling success is big business today. The curious, the hopeful, the insecure, and the desperate may pay $200 or more to attend a short "success seminar," which often doubles as a "get rich

quick" seminar. Combining Dale Carnegie, Amway, and evangelical preach-
ing methods, these seminars teach one simple recipe for achieving success:
believe in yourself; you have the inner power of self-transformation.
Releasing this inner power involves practicing several principles of positive thinking:

1. You must have vision, a dream, or *goals*!
2. You must *think big*!
3. You must have *self-esteem*--get rid of your guilt
   and inferiority and believe that *you are somebody*!
4. You must *work hard* at achieving your goals!
5. You must be single-minded and *persistent* in
   achieving your goals. Perseverance is a must!
6. You must be *committed* to achieving success!
7. You must not be discouraged as you encounter some
   failures on the path to success. *Be optimistic*!
8. You must associate with others and spread "good
   will" in your relationships. *Associate* with
   successful people!
9. You must be *honest* to yourself and others!
10. You must be positive and *enthusiastic* in your
    approach! (Yeager and Wead)

Without a doubt, when dramatized in a seminar setting, this advice
gives many participants a "seminar high" and helps build the self-confidence and self-esteem essential for practicing the new faith. We do not
reject these principles, because we know they work for some people who
have become born-again Christians and entrepreneurs. Anyone in direct-
sales businesses, such as insurance, real estate, or Amway, know these
are principles of good salesmanship.

But no one knows what percentage of people experience self-transfor-
mations based upon such principles. Other people may be disappointed,
especially after discovering they lack other important ingredients for
getting ahead--intelligence, expertise, and ability. Sellers of success
seldom talk about these other ingredients.

The same "success through self-transformation" principles are
packaged and re-packaged in the booming market of "how to" successfully
invest in real estate, tackle the stock and bond markets, lose weight,
make friends, improve appearance and dress, and play corporate politics.
One prophet gives an all inclusive formula for acquiring a higher income,
financial security, a prestige job, power and influence, and greater
happiness: THINK BIG! His $3.95 book will do 63 things for you. Among
these:

* Win Success by Believing You Can Succeed
* Plan a Concrete Success-Building Program
* Overcome Your Fear of Other People
* Learn the Five Positive Steps to Build Confidence
  and Destroy Fear
* Look Important, Because It Helps You Think Important
* Prevent Small People from Holding You Back
* Go First Class in Everything You Do
* Grow the "You-Are-Important" Attitude
* Achieve Positive Results Through Persistence and
  Experimentation

* Whip Discouragement by Finding the Good Side to
  Every Situation
* Learn the Four Rules of Leadership
* Think Progress, Believe in Progress, Push for
  Progress (Schwartz: 10-12)

Still others have written best-selling books on how to get ahead by using intimidation (Ringer) and power politics (Korda). These writers belong to the Machiavellian "me" school of the 1970s. Korda, for example, advises you to tell yourself:

* It's O.K. to be greedy.
* It's O.K. to be ambitious.
* It's O.K. to look out for Number One.
* It's O.K. to have a good time.
* It's O.K. to be Machiavellian (if you can get away
  with it).
* It's O.K. to recognize that honesty is not always
  the best policy (provided you don't go around
  saying so).
* It's O.K. to be a winner.
* And it's _always_ O.K. to be rich. (Korda: 3).

Moreover, you have the motivational patterns to succeed, if you answer "Yes" to these questions:

* Are you ambitious?
* Are you willing to work hard when you have to?
* Are you willing to put your interests first?
* Are you willing to take risks?
* Do you sincerely want to be rich?
* Have you got the guts to accept change? (Korda: 5)

All of these success writers claim their methods and strategies work. However, other than testimonials from a few born-again individuals (Conn), no evidence validates their claims. Faith, which cannot be tested, is the single most important method.

Therefore, you should be cautious of these prophets. While their prescriptions may work for some people, they may fail or be harmful or counter-productive for others, particularly when incorporated into a job search campaign. Perhaps much of the success literature and seminars should contain consumer warnings: "Be careful--what you learn may be dangerous to your future!"

Since no one knows why some people are more successful than others, there is no single valid method or magical formula for achieving success. We do know that birth order, intelligence, and goal setting are not good indicators of early success. Studies of young successful people have found that the most important quality explaining success is the need to achieve or _drive_. The young achiever and the entrepreneur have similar characteristics: "possesses a high energy level, restless, a willingness to work hard and take risks, a desire to escape from insecurity" (Kellogg: 38). Overall, studies of leadership, success, and the entre-preneurial and executive personality remain inconclusive:

One study says originality, popularity, sociability,
judgment, aggressiveness, the desire to excel, humor,
cooperativeness, liveliness and athletic ability are

factors essential to successful leadership. Another
gives the following recipe for success: intelligence,
verbalization skills, integrity, self-acceptance,
leadership (defined as the ability to get things done),
adaptability, such "accidental" factors as good health
and good luck. Good grief--one study of successful men
and women merely lists talent, luck and persistence.
Another heralds hard work, period....Elsewhere, a more
traditional study tells us that successful people set
goals, make lists and believe in the American Dream.
Another tells us that the ability to seize and recognize
opportunity is important, that creativity, self-reliance,
and willingness to accept responsibility are keys to
success. The sea of speculation, however ill or well-
defined, is vast (Kellogg: 32-33).

Contrary to the advice of books and seminars on how to succeed, no
studies indicate that "thinking big" will do the trick. Good luck still
appears cheaper and more effective for attaining success than faith in
such books and seminars.

Nonetheless, we do not reject the "how to" principles altogether.
While most do not fit into our scientific and rational modes of thinking,
we recognize that the proof is in the pudding. Faith does produce
results, as many preachers and salespersons will verify. Lives have
been transformed based on belief in such principles. Since some of these
principles may be helpful to you, we outline several "principles" in the
final section of this chapter; there we link faith to planning and
serendipity.

QUESTIONING FACTS, MYTHS, AND REALITIES

The standard works on how to change careers and jobs borrow heavily
from the principles of the success sellers. Based on the "do your own
thing" philosophy of the 1960s, many books proclaim that you can conduct
all aspects of a job search on your own. Materials usually are presented
in self-directed formats which enable you to identify your transferable
skills and relate them to your objective, resume, and job targets.

The more we review the literature, the more we are unable to identify validated facts, methods, and results. Writers make broad claims
and fictionalize facts for effect. The result is a seemingly authorita-
tive body of career planning knowledge. For example, the most popular
career planning writer makes the following claims:

* There are 79,000,000 job markets in the U.S.
* The average worker today will change careers three
  to five times and have an average of 15 jobs in his
  or her lifetime.
* 80 percent of the population is underemployed
  (Bolles, 1978a).

Such "facts" should be qualified as follows:

* The job market is extremely decentralized, fragmented, and chaotic; it confuses and frustrates

people who expect it to be centralized and organized.
* It is normal to change careers and jobs these days.
  Some people may have as many as four or more career
  changes and 15 different jobs during their lifetime.
* Many people are unhappy with their jobs and feel
  underemployed.

Although many writers exaggerate facts, they have contributed
greatly to challenging myths about the job market and the career planning
and job search processes. For example, Bolles (1978b) identifies several
myths and realities which affect the job search:

Myth	*Reality*
In a tight job situation there are few jobs available.	There are about 2 million job vacancies listed at any given time. Another 6 million are not advertised.
Most people know how to find a job.	Most people use the most ineffective methods--resumes and employment agencies.
Several places will assist job-hunters.	Several will, but they lack information and are more interested in serving employers.
Employers know what they want.	Some do, but most have problems and are uncertain how to hire good employees. Help them.
Experience and credentials are the most important considerations to employers in screening and hiring.	Employees also screen employers and should concentrate on their future rather than their past.
The best qualified person gets the job.	The person who knows how to best get the job, gets the job.

Bernard Haldane Associates identify several additional myths relevant to most beginning job searchers (Germann and Arnold: 1-11):

Myths	*Reality*
Careers are accidental.	Careers are a series of planned and lucky accidents.
You should go only into a growing field.	Bad strategy which will lead to job dissatisfaction. Go after what *you* want to do.
People who *have* contacts get good jobs.	People who know how to *make* contacts get good jobs.
The best qualified persons get hired.	Employers hire people they *like*; technical competence is of secondary importance.
It is difficult for someone over 40 to find a good job.	It is actually easier if they plan and conduct a well-organized job search campaign.

You must be an aggressive person in your job search.	Aggressive people tend to be offensive people. You need good human relations skills as well as a _purpose_ in mind.
Personnel departments hire people.	Few personnel departments hire--most only screen. The boss usually hires.
Do a lot of research on an organization or interviewer before the interview.	This may be a waste of time. Get information and establish rapport by asking intelligent questions and listening.
Education and religion remain outside the rat race of corporate politics.	These fields are more suscept-ible to such problems because of the highly interpersonal nature of the jobs.

Richard Irish, using a question/answer format, attempts to further dispel many myth-based fears which impede effective job searches:

Question	_Answer_
What is the purpose of education? (9-10)	Education does not train people for jobs. Schools mainly give employment to educators--not students. Educators still train students in "disciplines" which are irrelevant to the job market. Educators need to adapt "discipline" training to other "fields": -Librarians to become Information Retrieval Experts -Political Scientists to become Policy Analysts -Journalists to become Technical Writers and Proposal-Developers -Foreign Affairs Specialists to solve domestic problems
What is the revolution in the job market? (1)	Changing jobs and careers fre-quently due to the fluid nature of the job market.
Is it good to job-jump? (157)	Of course. As soon as you find a job, start looking for your next one. Your first loyalty is to yourself.
Why focus on your skills in the job search? (187-188)	People change jobs and careers frequently. Their skills, abilities, and talents are transferable from one setting to another.
Why do people succeed in judgment jobs? (14)	They know how to relate to people--lead, enlighten, praise,

chastise, judge, accept, reject, understand.

Is it easier to find a job as a "specialist" or as a "generalist"? (18-19)	Depends on the demand at the time. Specialists often lack imagination in understanding their skills and feel "locked into" their training.
Is there less job competition at the top? (23)	Yes. Most people seek job security at the lower levels rather than risk being fired at the top.
What should we know about the job market? (75)	-The most "qualified" people for a job are those who know how to find the job.

-Focus your job search on particular employers rather than broaden it to many employers.
-Most employers are like most job seekers: they don't know what they want.
-Avoid personnel agencies, career guidance counselors, and executive-search firms. They work for themselves and employers --not you.
-A resume will not get you a job--it only gets an interview.
-Most judgment jobs are not advertised.
-Employers have difficulty finding truly _effective_ people to fill judgment jobs.

Irish goes further by assigning grades to various strategies commonly used in finding judgment jobs (Irish: 109):

* Cold-turkey interview with strangers in key positions: A-
* Interview with important friends in key positions: B-
* Broadcasting hundreds of functional resumes within your "field" and following up with a telephone call: A-
* Selectively sending obituary resumes with a standard cover letter: D
* Completing application forms and interviewing with people in personnel: F
* Returning for another advanced degree and using the college placement office: C
* Doing informational interviews with the expectation someone will give you a job because they like your looks: F
* Talking a lot about your job campaign and gathering names of people to see: B
* Quiting your job search for a grunt job in anticipation that prosperity will return: F

* Joining a job club, such as "Forty Plus":   B+
* Selling your ideas and proposals to others: A
* Using the U.S. Employment Service: F
* "Blitzing" company presidents with letters: A
* Taking a "stop-loss" job while continuing your search
  for a judgment job: A

LOOKING OUTSIDE EDUCATION

We agree with many of these myths, realities, and "insights" concerning the nature of the job market and job search, even though most lack empirical referents. At the same time, we have found several additional myths and realities pertinent to educators:

Myths	*Reality*
It is unprofessional to use "connections" in getting a job, particularly in education.	Only ineffective job seekers believe this. Research shows that most educators got their jobs by using the ubiquitious "connection"; indeed, as a group academicians are major users of the "old boy network," "connections," "patron-client" relations, and the informal system (Brown, 1965, 1967; Granovetter). Since educators' job hunting practices are similar to those of the general population (Germann and Arnold: 65), they should have little difficulty adapting their informal strategies to finding positions outside education.
Educators cannot find jobs appropriate to their backgrounds outside education.	Only if they don't look in the right places. There are numerous opportunities for educators. You must first think about marketing your *transferable talents* rather than your discipline or subject specialties. The higher-level judgment jobs stress the type of skills educators possess-- analytical, communication, interpersonal, and leadership skills.
Money is not important to educators.	This myth is one reason why educators are so poorly paid. In fact, one study found that the most important correlate of job satisfaction among educators in the humanities was money (Solmon, Ochsner, Hurwicz: 181)! There is nothing wrong in making a lot of

Educators are the nicest and most humane people to associate with.

money and enjoying it. Educators who leave education and double or triple their incomes seem to enjoy their work as well as the money.

There are many types of educators, as there are many types of bankers, insurance agents, government officials, and lawyers. You will probably find just as many mean, vindictive, jealous, and back-stabbing educators as you will find counterparts in other professions. Experience outside education will quickly dispel this myth.

Educational institutions are the most intellectually stimulating environments to work in.

It depends on which institution, school, department, or community you work and live in. Some have intellectually stifling environments. There are numerous challenging and stimulating environments outside education.

Educational positions are the most secure, once you get tenure.

Tenure is being eroded by financial considerations. Elementary, secondary, and higher education institutions have learned how to reduce forces in spite of tenure. Security is when you are wealthy and have no superiors. As long as someone else pays you wages, your security is subject to the whims of your boss and the ups and downs of economic cycles. Educators may get three, six, or nine months notice before termination compared to the usual short-term notice outside education. Also, as long as educators remain relatively unorganized, they will lack security. The security of tenure also tends to keep salaries low and encourage deadwood. If your boss doesn't like you and you have tenure, he or she can always get rid of you by other means: heavy teaching and advising loads, numerous and useless committee assignments, no promotions, insulting salary increments, no travel funds, or bad office location and space. The security of tenure is tenuous.

There are less politics in education than in other organizations.	Education probably has _more_ politics due to the highly interpersonal nature of educational work (Germann and Arnold: 9). Politics in education can be just as vicious and debilitating as politics elsewhere. However, it differs in one major respect: in education politics often is played for _low stakes_. Elsewhere politics have greater meaning and impact and may be worth playing.
Educators have more freedom to "do their own thing."	Many educators have flexible time schedules, but unless they are deadwood, educators also have little free time to "do their own thing." When they do have free time, they keep busy on job-related matters or work to supplement their incomes. Educators often follow Parkinson's Law: work expands to fill the time available for completion.
Educators have more status than professionals in other occupations.	Maybe. At least educators still believe this. However, you can't eat status; you can't take a trip on status; you can't buy a new home, car, or boat on status; and you can't send your kids to college on status. Worst of all, as educators enter the ranks of the working poor, their future social status is very much in doubt (Abbott: 352).

We believe educators need to do more reality-testing than they have to date. In the absence of information on alternative realities, like other groups in society, educators tend to develop myths about their occupational benefits and importance vis-a-vis others. For as one recent study of academicians concludes, "Present students should learn from those with job experience that many nonacademic jobs _are_ satisfying, rewarding, and productive. Once this realization occurs, students' perspectives and, perhaps, their preparation, job search methods, and preferences will change" (Solmon, Ochsner, Hurwicz: 7).

PROGRESSING BEYOND STANDARD APPROACHES

Our approach to the job search is moderate to conservative in tone. We make no claims that a single approach is best for all job search situations. We utilize a multi-faceted or contingency approach: different individuals need to use different approaches for different situations. Since people differ, you must first know yourself and your audience before you decide on methods and strategies.

Perfecting a single method for every job seeker and for one generalized audience disregards reality as well as common sense. Yet, most of the "selling success" and career planning literature continues to preach a single method for a stereotyped audience. Indeed, employers are often portrayed as dumb, but interviewees are coached to be clever. For example, job searchers are often told how to dress, sit, listen, and answer questions. Intelligence, abilities, talents, and qualifications seldom are considered. In short, job searchers are being told to substitute *form* for *substance* as if their good looks, charm, dress, and cleverness will get them a job.

Another assumption found in the standard career planning literature is that you can conduct the job search on your own by using self-directed methods. We agree but with one major qualification. Your job search can be enhanced considerably by utilizing professional assistance at critical stages, especially for identifying your skills and abilities. The major career planning literature stresses the importance of identifying your *skills*. Accordingly, it outlines several alternative self-directed exercises (Holland; Bolles, 1980; Haldane; Germann and Arnold; Figler; Crystal and Bolles) aimed at skills identification. While these are useful methods, we go beyond skills identification by including what we consider to be the most advanced, comprehensive, and useful technique for assessing motivational patterns: System for Identifying Motivational Abilities (SIMA). We have used this technique with much greater success than the self-directed skills exercises. However, this technique requires professional assistance in interpreting the critical motivational patterns for all subsequent steps in the job search process.

SPECIFYING OUR ASSUMPTIONS

We make certain assumptions about our audience and the nature of the tasks before us. First, for the most part we are addressing educators who are both suspicious and sophisticated. Being *suspicious* means questioning the credibility of those who try to provide a quick-fix to the serious business of changing careers and jobs. Educators expect hard work as well as no easy formulas or short cuts to success. Therefore, our goal is to present you with the best reality-tested methods available for moving out of education.

Educators also are *sophisticated*. As highly educated individuals, they know reality is structured in more complex terms than simple right/wrong and yes/no alternatives. Faith is fine, but facts make more sense and lead to more valid and reliable results. Our approach is based on such an understanding of the structure of reality. In addition, we assume educators are at least average or above average in intelligence and thus capable of comprehending and learning on their own. Excepting the SIMA technique, this is a self-directed career planning book.

Our methods are built upon the healthy suspicions and sophistication of our past clients. The competencies we require for implementing a successful job search are strengths educators already possess: communication (oral and written), interpersonal, research, organization, perseverance, and self-management skills.

Our second assumption is that educators have professional ethics and that job search methods must be designed with these ethics in mind.

Educators stress honesty, integrity, and forthrightness. However, many job search methods verge on deceptive sales techniques. There is absolutely no need to develop a rip-off mentality for getting a job. In the dog-eat-dog world, it's the dogs that get eaten. We stress the importance of being professional at all times in your job search. Never create a situation that would raise a question about your honesty and integrity. However, as we will note later, honesty and forthrightness should not create new liabilities for you, such as naivity and stupidity. Honest people sometimes say dumb things about themselves by confessing their negatives to others. Avoid being unethical *and* stupid!

Third, many educators are highly motivated to seek career changes. Educators are willing to put in time, effort, and some expense to reach their goals. Indeed, some educators are facing career crisis situations which demand immediate action. Since most educators receive relatively low salaries, their salary expectations should not pose serious problems in making career changes.

Fourth, educators, like many other professionals, need information on career planning and job search processes. Lacking a clear understanding of their marketable talents, they take a narrow view of alternative jobs and careers. Most important of all, they do not know how to most effectively identify their abilities and objectives, write a resume, conduct career and job research, interview, and negotiate a job. Since educators possess the key skills for conducting an effective job search-- communication, interpersonal, research, organization, and perseverance-- we expect to advise highly motivated and skilled learners.

Finally, we assume our audience is capable of conducting a successful job search. In fact, many educators possess one additional characteristic which is absent in many other occupations--flexible schedules. Most educators are not slaves to a 9 to 5 work routine, and they have long vacation periods during which they can conduct a highly effective job search campaign in more than one community. Few other professionals have such advantageous work schedules. Of course, other professionals also are being paid better than educators!

Our final set of assumptions relates to the nature of the job market and unemployment. The job market is decentralized, fragmented, and chaotic. As such, job seekers must create some structure and coherence for themselves. While they can pay hundreds or thousands of dollars to employment agencies to do this work, we know job seekers are better off doing their own structuring. We outline in subsequent chapters how to get a better handle on this disorganized job market.

The nature of unemployment is not well understood. Lathrop (1978: 5) identifies three types of unemployment: cyclical, structural, and frictional. Approximately 25 million people seek employment each year because of these three types of unemployment. Each type requires different job search techniques. Cyclical unemployment, created by fluctuating economic and business cycles, is the most widely known. For example, auto and steel workers as well as a professional Santa Claus, are displaced temporarily by economic and seasonal downturns in business cycles. These employees usually return to work when the economy improves.

Structural unemployment, the most permanent form, is created by changes in the nature of work. Workers' skills become obsolete because of technological advances. Street sweepers, buggy-whip makers, tailors, shoemakers, and aerospace scientists and engineers have become victims of such unemployment. In many communities throughout the United States educators have become the most recent victims of structural unemployment.

Frictional unemployment, the least understood form, may account for as much as 40 percent of all unemployment. This type of unemployment occurs due to a time lag between the time a job becomes available and the time it is filled. In this situation, job opportunities exist but are going unfilled because of poor communication within the job market. The problem is further exacerbated because job seekers lack crucial competencies for conducting an effective job search campaign.

Educators face both structural and frictional unemployment. Given the disorganized nature of the job market, educators need methods for identifying new opportunities outside education as well as for shortening the lag time. Our methods are designed to increase the occupational mobility of displaced educators by helping them cope with both structural and frictional unemployment.

HIRING AN EDUCATOR

Why hire an educator? This question is asked by many employers outside education, and thus you should be prepared to answer it. While educators make assumptions about the work world outside education, this other world also makes certain assumptions about educators. Many of these assumptions constitute stereotypes which support employers' objections to hiring educators.

Ask people outside education what they think about educators. While they may confer high status to the teaching profession, many people also have definite views on why they should not hire an educator. Here are some of the most frequent employer stereotypes and objections:

* Educators are too individualistic. They work in highly unstructured environments. Too used to "doing their own thing," educators are not good at being part of a team and taking directions.
* Educators are not entrepreneurial enough; they seek individual gratification and self-esteem, are too preoccupied with impractical ideas, and lack a sense of good business.
* Educators lack a sense of productivity and accountability. Teachers perform routines rather than set goals and measure results. They are rewarded for seniority rather than for productivity.
* Educators lack pragmatism, practicality, and common sense. They are idealists who don't live in the real world.

As with all stereotypes, there is some truth to these. Indeed, employers will point to examples of educators who couldn't make the transition to business or government.

However, we believe these stereotypes arise when former educators are misplaced in environments which are not conducive to their motivational patterns and work styles. Many ex-educators find the wrong jobs for themselves and their employers. Our methods are designed to enable educators to overcome such objections of employers. We recognize the importance of identifying job opportunities outside education which are most appropriate for each individual's abilities and motivational patterns.

ORGANIZING FOR SERENDIPITY AND LUCK

American culture tends to define a successful individual as one who achieves a certain degree of wealth, position, power, and fame. Our view of success in career planning is more subjective: achieving your own goals, however lofty or low. But how you achieve your goals is subject to considerable controversy.

Most people believe goals are achieved through rational planning. We tell ourselves and others to be rational by planning. Individual, scientific, and organizational decisions should follow a well-defined procedure: identifying a problem, setting goals, gathering data, out-lining alternatives, selecting the best alternative, implementing, eval-uating the results, and reconsidering to end or continue consideration of the decision. This procedure is known as "rational decision-making theory" in business and public administration. With a change in nomen-clature, it is also known as "the scientific method" in the hard sciences and "steps in a good research design" in the social sciences.

However, there is a tendency to confuse the _form_ or steps of ration-al decision-making, the scientific method, and the research design with the _substance_ or outcomes of decisions, science, and research. Indeed, most such prescriptions confuse myth with reality and thereby mislead individuals with a quick formula or recipe for solving problems and achieving goals. For example, research in business and public adminis-tration concludes that rational decision-making is an ideal model; in these fields reality best conforms to the logic of incrementalism (Wildavsky), muddling-through (Lindblom), "satisficing" behavior (Simon), reactive decision-making (Yates), and mix-scanning (Etzioni). Ironically, rational decision-making may be irrational in situations involving com-peting values and widespread participation (Yates: 252).

Several myths also relate to how science discovers "truths." For example, not all of science progresses along a linear path of increasing rationality (Kuhn) nor do all scientific findings follow the logic of the scientific method. In the social sciences, although academicians teach the highly acclaimed scientific research method to unitiated stu-dents, few researchers actually follow the method completely. Researchers in both the hard sciences and behavioral sciences jump around considerably; they follow some steps but by-pass others because intuition and luck tell them to move on to more productive activities. Serendipity, those chance occurances, is a frequent experience among researchers. In fact, seren-dipity may explain more scientific discoveries than scientists admit. Only those who continue to teach the scientific method, without doing research, believe that reality can conform to a rational method (Merton, 1968: 157-16

Similar observations and conclusions relate to planning in general, and individual success in particular. Luck plays an important role in everyone's life. Being in the right place, at the right time, can be infinitely more rewarding that all the well-crafted plans and rational decision-making. As Kellogg discovered,

> Certainly, luck and planning, in and of themselves, can only take you so far. There are an equal or greater number of factors too, that stop success: bad timing, a poor economy, an employer who doesn't believe in your talents or simply doesn't like you, being in the wrong field at the wrong time, being in the wrong field altogether (Kellogg: 69).

Chance factors, those you have little or no control over, are critically important to achieving successes and encountering failures. People tend to experience combinations of "good luck" and "bad luck," regardless of how rational they organize and plan their lives.

We do not mean to imply that rationality and planning are a waste of time. Our purpose is to understand their role in achieving success. Rationality and planning are *prescriptions*--not descriptions or explanations--of how to achieve future goals. They must be understood in relationship to luck and serendipity. Kellogg, in her study of successful individuals, identifies one key characteristic in this relationship:

> each [successful individual] was able to see opportunity and each was not afraid to grab it--or, if he or she was afraid, grabbed it anyway. Luck, planning and childhood trauma can only take one so far. The rest of the way depends on your *abilities, sensibilities and perceptions-- the awareness with which the whole package is put together. Each young success had the ability to shape the ball park around his or her talents, to know what those special talents and perceptions were so that when opportunity-- planned or lucky--came along it could be utilized* (Kellogg: 70, our emphasis).

Relating these findings to job search strategies, Jencks' and Granovetter's research further confirms the central importance of luck:

> [Luck is] chance acquaintances who steer you to one line of work rather than another, the range of jobs that happen to be available to a particular community when you are job hunting, the amount of overtime work in your particular plant, whether bad weather destroys your strawberry crop, whether the new superhighway has an exit near your restaurant, and a hundred other unpredictable accidents (Jencks, 1972: 227).

According to Granovetter's experience and research findings, "luck" in career planning is "having the right contact in the right place at the right time" (Granovetter: viii).

Ironically, these research findings strongly suggest that you should plan for luck. Plan to place yourself in many places, at many times, with many contacts, so that when opportunities arise, you will be in the best position to do exactly what Kellogg sees as characteristic of her successful subjects: see and grab opportunity; fully utilize your abilities, sensibilities, and perceptions; and shape the ball park

around your talents. Consequently, planning should not be viewed as
separate from luck. Rationality, planning, luck, and serendipity will
all play important roles in helping you move out of education. Recognizing this, our methods are designed to help you become sensitive to,
as well as receptive for, the experience of serendipity. We want you to
open your eyes to those chance occurances that may become your "good
luck."

FAITH, PLANNING, AND LUCK

Our understanding of the prerequisites for successful career planning is tempered by research, theory, experience, and common sense. We
present a checklist of factors which _may_ be important to achieving a
successful job search, and we suggest incorporating several of these
principles into your job search. Since our "principles" are not facts,
truths, or scientific findings, they must be approached with faith. As
such, we recognize that for every "principle," there may be an equally
valid counter-principle.

Principles, planning, and luck go together in a successful job
search campaign. We hope you will become incredibly lucky before spending hours in identifying your abilities and goals, writing a resume, and
contacting employers. Therefore, we outline several "principles" to
assist you in grabbing an opportunity when your time is right. You
should:

1. _work hard at finding a job_: Make this a daily
   endeavor and involve your family.
2. _not be discouraged with set-backs_: You are playing
   the odds, so expect disappointments and handle them
   in stride. You will have many more "no's" before
   uncovering that one "yes" which is right for you.
3. _be patient and persevere_: Expect three to six
   months of hard work before you connect with the
   right job.
4. _be honest with yourself and others_: Honesty is
   always the best policy, but don't be naive and
   stupid by confessing your negatives and shortcomings
   to others.
5. _develop a positive attitude toward yourself_: Nobody
   wants to employ guilt-ridden people with inferiority
   complexes. Focus on your positive characteristics.
6. _associate with positive and successful people_: You
   are in the people-business, and your success will
   depend on how well you relate to others. Run with
   winners.
7. _set goals_: You sould have a clear idea of what you
   want and where you are going. Without these, you
   will present a confusing and indecisive image to
   others. Set high goals that make you work hard.
8. _plan_: Convert your goals into action steps that
   are organized as short, intermediate, and long-
   range plans.

9. *get organized*: Translate your plans into activities, targets, names, addresses, telephone numbers, and materials. Develop an efficient and effective filing system and use a large calendar for setting time targets and recording appointments and useful information.

10. *be a good communicator*: Take stock of your oral, written, and nonverbal communication skills. How well do you communicate? Since most aspects of your job search involve communicating with others, and communication skills are one of the most sought-after skills in judgment jobs, always present yourself well both verbally and nonverbally.

11. *be energetic and enthusiastic*: Employers are attracted to positive people. They don't like negative and depressing people who toil at their work. Generate enthusiasm both verbally and nonverbally. Check on your telephone voice--it may be more unenthusiastic than your voice in face-to-face situations.

12. *ask questions*: Your best information comes from asking questions. Learn to develop intelligent questions that are non-aggressive, polite, and interesting to others. But don't ask too many questions.

13. *be a good listener*: Being a good listener is often more important than being a good questioner and talker. Learn to improve your face-to-face listening behavior (nonverbal cues) as well as remember and utilize information gained from others--if they need improving. Make others feel they enjoyed talking with you, i.e., you are one of the few people who actually listen to what they say.

14. *be polite and courteous*: If rejected by others, thank them for the "opportunity" they gave you. After all, they may later have additional opportunities, and they should remember you. Treat gatekeepers, especially secretaries, as human beings. Don't be aggressive or too assertive. Being courteous to others won't hurt you. A thank-you note can go a long way.

15. *be tactful*: Watch what you say to others about other people and your background. Don't be a gossip, back-stabber, or confessor.

16. *maintain a professional stance*: Be neat in what you do and wear, and speak with the confidence, authority, and maturity of a professional.

17. *be intelligent and competent*: Present yourself as someone who gets things done and achieves results--a producer. Employers generally seek people who are bright, hard working, responsible, can communicate well, have positive personalities, maintain good interpersonal relations, are likable, observe dress and social codes, take initiative, are talented, possess expertise in particular

58

areas, use good judgment, are cooperative, trustworthy, and loyal, generate confidence and credibility,
and are conventional. In other words, they like people
who can score in the "excellent" to "outstanding"
categories of the annual performance evaluation. In
short, they want God!

18. *not overdo your job search*: Don't engage in overkill
and bore everyone with your "job search" tales and
conversation. Achieve balance in everything you do.
Occasionally take a few days off to do nothing related
to your job search. Develop a system of incentives
and rewards--such as two free non-job search days a
week, if you accomplish targets A, B, C, and D.

19. *be open-minded and keep an eye open for "luck"*: Do
not become a victim of too much planning and goal-
oriented activity which can block out unanticipated
events. Planning can blind you to unexpected and
fruitful opportunities. Learn to deviate and re-
evaluate your goals and strategies. Evaluate new
opportunities; seize them if they appear appropriate
to your goals and intuition.

20. *evaluate your progress and adjust*: Take two hours
once every two weeks and evaluate what you are doing
and accomplishing. If necessary, tinker with your
plans and reorganize your activities and priorities.
Don't become too routinized and therefore kill
creativity and innovation.

Above all, you should not assume you must follow every "principle"
or piece of advice we and others present. Develop a healthy sense of
skepticism and initiative. We recognize that situations and individual
circumstances are diverse enough to permit modification, adaptation,
innovation, and experimentation in the process of conducting a job
search. Consider your job search to be a form of "creative field
research" which will have major outcomes for you, your family, and
others.

The following chapters outline the nuts and bolts of how to develop
and execute your job search. One "principle" stands out above all
others--hard work. We also believe the hard work will be a lot of fun
and enjoyment for you and your family. Most importantly, this should
be a new and exciting experience which will result in a new career and
renewed job satisfaction.

We present "how to" material on identifying your abilities and
objectives, writing a nonacademic resume, conducting research on individuals and organizations, networking and initiating informational interviews, and interviewing and negotiating for your new job. This is not
the "gospel," but we believe it is good solid advice for getting things
to happen for you. Again, we stress the importance of keeping your eyes
open for serendipity and luck. Feel free to vary our methods and
techniques as your understanding of *your* job market improves.

However, if you decide this is too time-consuming and frustrating,
then pay $3,000 and take your chances with a professional job search
organization. They may be better than doing nothing. But remember, the
bad times may come sooner than you think!

CHAPTER IV

INITIATING AN EFFECTIVE CAMPAIGN

A job search conducted on the bases of faith, planning, and luck can't possibly go wrong, unless you have an unusual amount of bad luck. In this chapter we outline how to avoid premature bad luck. We specify career planning alternatives to doing your own job search, warn you of possible pitfalls, and advise you how to best organize your resources and time as well as cope with the disorganized job market. Our philosophy and goals are straightforward: help you develop your own realistic and effective job search campaign which avoids several pitfalls encountered by others.

As an educator, you have two major advantages most professionals lack when beginning a job search. First, you do not begin with unrealistic salary expectations because your present salary is probably low. Your financial situation should improve in your next job; some educators even double or triple their salaries! Second, you are ideally situated to conduct your own job search campaign, because your occupation provides you with flexible working hours and certain on-the-job resources for conducting a job search. For example, you can use your school or campus library for conducting research on careers and organizations. Furthermore, during your lengthy semester or term breaks, you should be able to work full-time at finding a job. Use your time wisely since you may never again be in such an advantageous position to conduct your own job search campaign.

PLANNING FOR LUCK

Two important areas in everyone's life seldom get planned: choosing a spouse and choosing a career. While we can understand the emotional and chance nature of selecting a marriage partner, we have difficulty understanding why so many people continue to leave career decisions to chance, fate, or a combination of luck and rudimentary planning.

If you are the typical job-seeker without goals, plans, and purposeful action, you probably

* are uncertain about your job goals.
* don't understand the job-market revolution.
* are excessively concerned with titles, careers,
  and positions.
* fail to communicate your past experience into
  future occupational terms.
* are unclear about how to create job leads.
* lack expertise in negotiating a salary.

60

* are shy about approaching people you don't know
  and taking their time for an information gathering
  interview.
* are uneasy about using acceptable sales techniques
  to find a job.
* desire less authority and more co-operative
  decision-making.
* wish more information on where you belong in today's
  job market.
* worry about your lack of "experience" for entering
  other fields.
* are uncertain of your best abilities, skills, and
  talents.
* lack self-confidence for initiating an effective
  job search.
* hate being dependent on others but are afraid of
  being fired.
* envy others who love their work.
* think how you play politics is more important than
  how you perform on the job.
* don't know how to deal with the question of "experience"
  during an interview.
* are secretive about conducting your job search.
* believe interviewers are powerful people you should
  appease.
* believe being miserable on the job is normal
  (Irish: 21-22).

You should not become another such typical job-seeker.

Planning your job or career change has numerous benefits. Most importantly, you will become one of the few who ever conscientiously sets goals and systematically works at achieving those goals. You should set high goals and go after jobs requiring your highest level of skills and abilities (Bolles, 1980: 77). Most of these are "judgment jobs," such as general management, technical, entrepreneurial, and consultant positions. Judgment jobs require design, marketing, management, and evaluation skills (Irish: 20). In seeking these higher-level jobs, you will encounter less competition, higher salaries and benefits, and more responsibilities and risks. If you seek greater job security, these jobs may not be for you.

We, along with many others, recognize the important roles luck and faith play in finding a job. You probably "lucked into" your present job--perhaps you got it through a "contact" from a relative, friend, or college professor. But luck in career planning also means being in the right place, at the right time, with the right connections, to take advantage of new opportunities you ordinarily would not know about (Scheele: 10-15). You will improve your luck considerably by planning to place yourself in many places so that when the time comes, you will be in the right place to experience "good luck."

SEEKING "PROFESSIONAL" ASSISTANCE

This book is premised on the notion that the single best source for finding a job is you. We assume you are best equipped to achieve your goals: you are intelligent; you know yourself better than anyone else; you possess the necessary communication, interpersonal, analytical, and research skills for achieving success; you are independent and take initiative; and you have flexibility in your work schedule. At the same time, by conducting your own job search, you will learn much about yourself, others, and the job market. You will control the situation and be in a better position to know when "luck" comes your way.

This is not to say that alternatives to doing your own job search are useless and should be avoided. There are many highly specialized and excellent services you can use. However, it is still true that there is no such thing as a free lunch. You get what you pay for, and sometimes you get ripped-off in the process. Furthermore, the price can be staggering, especially compared to your present income. How does $3,000 sound? That is the average from a range of $1,500 to $10,000. At the same time, you may encounter a cruel world of frauds, hucksters, and rip-off artists who initially will make you feel good, but who eventually will make you feel stupid when they run with your money. You often can do better on your own. Of all occupations, we believe educators are in the best positions--considering their schedules and high-level skills and intelligence--to do as well as, or better than, the professional services.

What are the alternatives to conducting your own job search? Several types of organizations define the career planning and job search businesses. Remember, these organizations are in business, and businesses are supposed to show profits. These organizations will use all kinds of psychological sales techniques to get you to contract with them. Most will tell you that you cannot do your own job search, because you are not a "specialist"; thus, you need their expert services. They will tell you many success stories, show you their training materials and marketing strategies, impress you with biographical sketches of their staff members (some may have Ph.D.s) and charts and graphs, stress how much you need them, and make promises they won't put into writing. If you decide to use these services, check with the Better Business Bureau and talk to former clients (at least three of your choosing) as well as competing firms. Shop around and compare services, prices, and contracts. We suggest using these services as a last resort--and then choose the best. First try to do your own career planning and job search. You may surprise yourself by saving $5,000 and avoiding numerous frustrations and headaches.

There is no such thing as a "job market" where you can go for jobs. The so-called "job market" is a statistical construct based upon monthly employment and unemployment figures. If you believe there is something called a "job market," finding a job will be extremely difficult for you. Bolles dramatizes this point by stating that there are 79 million job markets, or non-farm payrolls, in the United States (Bolles, 1978a: 124). Elsewhere he identifies 14 million job markets, which constitute the total number of non-farm employers (Bolles, 1980: 122). Another estimate is that 90 percent of all jobs are found in a "hidden job

market." Since these jobs are neither advertised in newspapers nor
listed with employment agencies, they require personal investigative
strategies and techniques.

Following the structure of American business and government, the
employment process and so-called "job market" are extremely decentralized, fragmented, and chaotic. These characteristics should warn you
of possible pitfalls in engaging in activities that assume the existence of an organized market. You must organize your own job market.
Knowing this, the self-directed approach to finding a job makes good
sense.

The basic pitfall--one which may result in being victimized by
hucksters and rip-off artists--is to believe that there are organizations and services "out there" that can find you a job, because they
have access to the job market. Some organizations and services organize various segments of the market around certain specialties, but
most do what you should be doing--trying to bring some semblance of
logic, order, and structure to an inherently decentralized, fragmented,
and chaotic job market. These organizations and services will do the
following things for you:

1. teach you to organize the chaos, as this book
   does;
2. organize the chaos for you so you can select a
   job that is available on a particular day; or
3. combine 1 and 2.

ALTERNATIVE ORGANIZATIONS AND SERVICES

If you choose not to conduct your own job search campaign, you
will encounter twelve types of organizations and services which can
assist you. Each organization and service has a different approach to
the job market, and each requires different investments of your time
and money. Most are listed in the Yellow Pages of your telephone book
under Employment, Career Planning, Management Consultants, or Social
Services. None of these groups is organized to deal specifically with
the career problems of educators.

Public Employment Services

Public employment services usually are sponsored by state governments. They provide job vacancy information on a wide range of occupa-
tions--blue collar, white collar, unskilled, skilled, technical, managerial, and professional--for entry-level and experienced candidates.
However, a disproportionate number of their listings is for low-level
jobs in the $7,000 to $12,000 range. Public employment agencies also
offer varying degrees of support services, such as testing, counseling,
occupational information and educational workshops. For the most part,
the main emphasis is on making vacancy information available to job
seekers and referring candidates to employers. Some career planners
believe these organizations actually exacerbate unemployment because
they keep job seekers away from the most effective channel for finding
jobs--the hidden job market. Furthermore, public employment agencies

ment office to see what useful information and services are available
for you. Also, learn more about the career planning and placement office at your alma mater; ask if it provides alumni services or if it
may have any useful contacts for you. Be sure to talk to the personnel
in these offices. Let them know you are considering a career change
and you would appreciate their advice or assistance. If you work at a
college or university, this office should become part of your local network for gathering information and developing leads and contacts for
future informational interviews. Even though the personnel in this
office may be very busy working with students, they are some of the
best people to contact. Busy people are always your best contacts,
because they are involved and know what is going on in many different
directions (Germann and Arnold: 118).

Private Career and Job Search Firms

Private career and job search consulting firms work primarily with
executives and other professionals who need assistance in finding employment. These firms typically offer services such as individual assessment, career redirection counseling, and job search skills training.
In other words, these firms will teach you exactly what this book does
and much of what campus career planning and placement offices should be
doing.

These firms are in business to make a profit. Like most businesses, there are good ones and bad ones. You should shop around if you
decide to go this route. The firms market their services as a one-time
career investment which is tax deductible. Individual clients usually
pay for these services; fees are high, ranging from $1,500 to $10,000
and averaging about $3,000. For that amount you will learn how to plan
and conduct a job search or, in other words, how to better organize the
decentralized, fragmented, and chaotic job market. They do not find
you jobs; instead, they provide support and structure. Use this service
if you need a monetary incentive to get started on your job search. If
you pay someone $3,000 to train you, chances are you will be motivated
enough to follow-through.

A relatively new and growing aspect of these businesses is outplacement services. Employers who must terminate managers and professional staff may hire one of these firms as an external consultant to
orchestrate the termination process and to provide assistance for terminated employees. Many of the innovations in assessment techniques
and job search methods have been developed and tested by these firms.

Executive Search Firms

Executive search firms also are known as "management consultants,"
"executive recruiters," and "headhunters." These groups come in different sizes, orientations, and reputations.

Most executive search firms have four characteristics that separate
them from other types of job search organizations:

1. They are hired and paid by employers to find
   employees for specific critical positions in
   business and industry.

2. They initiate contacts with prospective employees.
3. They recruit individuals for higher level managerial or key technical positions in the $25,000 to $75,000 salary range.
4. They may specialize in particular technical or managerial fields.

While these firms are stereotyped as "flesh-peddlers" and "high rollers," they perform an increasingly critical function for organizations seeking top-level expertise. Many organizations prefer dealing with executive search specialists, because their own personnel departments are not capable of recruiting individuals for higher-level positions. In addition, these firms assure confidentiality to their clients as well as to prospective employees. Some, however, have sordid reputations. They sometimes engage in clandestine operations, such as bribing secretaries for a confidential company organizational chart or telephone directory, raiding the top-level management talent at a competitor's firm, or conducting secret interviews and negotiations in hotels (Noer).

You may want to contact some of these firms nonetheless. Let them know you are available, inform them of your qualifications and skills, and give them a copy of your resume, especially if you have a technical or business background. Make sure you contact several of these firms, because many are competing with one another in various specialized areas. Since these firms cost you nothing, you have everything to gain and nothing to lose. If they try to charge you a fee, you know you are in the wrong type of executive search firm.

Marketing Services

These firms combine the services of executive search firms and career planning organizations. They advertise in the professional section of newspapers, magazines, and journals. They will cost you plenty--$2,500 and up--and they stress the importance of being "professional" in your job search. Most services of this type tend to take a "shotgun" approach to placement by widely circulating client inquiry letters and resumes to large numbers of employers. This is accomplished by using high speed word processing equipment which merges directory information on corporations and their key personnel with clients' materials. While appearing to be "First Class," these firms actually do a slick sales campaign for you. They, too, will tell you that you can't conduct a job search on your own--especially by using this book.

Most of these firms specialize in marketing professionals who anticipate starting salaries of at least $20,000. However, many of these firms are more _form_ than substance. For an initial flat fee--perhaps $100--they will subject you to a battery of impressive psychological tests. After accepting you as a client and taking the rest of your money, they will organize a slick resume, conduct a market campaign of mass mailings and telephone calls, and schedule interviews for you. In other words, they do all the work for you; you only need to pay the fee and attend the interviews. This is easy and expensive; it is ideal for people who are either lazy or too busy to do their homework. Also, this approach will probably alienate many employers; it tends to be _too_ professional and _too_ slick; and it nonverbally communicates that you are

too lazy to find your own job. What will you do when you start working
for them? Find a surrogate employee? Not many employers want to hire
such people--but some do. Our best advice is: pay your money and take
your chances; you might do better with this book.

Women's Centers

Women's centers began to appear in growing numbers during the
1970s. Most centers were established to advance women's issues and
provide support services for women facing major life transitions--death
of a spouse, divorce, entry or re-entry into the workforce, and return
to school. Career development remains a central theme of these centers.
Typically, the centers provide individual career counseling, career
planning workshops, courses on job search, and training in job skills.
Some centers are independent and support their operations through direct
client fees; others are affiliated with colleges, universities or community agencies and support their operations through a combination of
funding sources.

Women's centers are useful to the uninitiated female job seeker. The
career planning workshops and courses are similar to the services provided by the private career and job search firms, although more superficial and less expensive. Some of these centers provide one invaluable
service which is not available through other sources--a job network consisting of women who are willing to give other women advice and contacts.
Women should investigate these centers in terms of the availability and
usefulness of such networks.

Testing and Assessment Centers

Testing and assessment centers usually are staffed by licensed psychologists who develop personality profiles on clients with a series of
testing instruments and techniques. These services may be requested by
individual clients who need assistance in making career choices or by
employers who want profiles on job candidates for use in the selection
and placement process. Most centers are independent and operate on a
profit basis. Their fees vary, depending on the extent of the assessment; they usually average $400 to $600 per individual. Some centers
operate on a non-profit basis in affiliation with service or church
organizations. Their fees are lower, usually ranging from $200 to $300.

We do not recommend using these services. The standard tests and
assessment devices are of questionable reliability, validity, and predictive value. Use them if you believe in magic but are too embarrassed
to see a traditional fortune teller. In the next chapter we outline
the SIMA technique which we feel is the best assessment device available
for identifying and relating your motivated abilities to your future
lifework objective.

Hiring and Career Conferences

Hiring or career conferences are a variation of the employment
agency concept. Conferences are organized by employment agencies to
bring employers and job seekers together for one or two days in hotel
or conference centers. The conference is scheduled and publicized far

in advance. After identifying and inviting employers to attend, the sponsoring agency recruits and prescreens candidates according to the employers' needs. Employers then review resume books and identify specific candidates to invite for interviews.

The conference usually begins with a combined orientation session for employers and candidates. Next, each employer gives a brief presentation on their organization and the positions available to the assembled candidates. Following the presentations, candidates approach the employers of their choice. The employers, in turn, schedule interviews with their selected candidates. Attendance and placement fees are paid by employers.

Such conferences have become increasingly popular with employers. They are also an excellent means for job seekers to get an overview of specific labor markets, meet employers, practice interviewing skills, and develop networks. Since candidates are not obligated to pay for these services, you have everything to gain by getting yourself "screened into" such conferences through an organizing employment agency.

Rehabilitative and Remedial Programs

Rehabilitative and remedial programs concentrate on assisting marginally, hard core, or structurally unemployed persons who lack work experience, marketable skills, or a basic education. Included in this general category are those programs which deal with persons who have prison records and physical, mental, or emotional handicaps. Most rehabilitative and remedial programs are publicly funded, although some are independent and support their operations with a combination of grants, contributions, and generated income. Hopefully, you will not need to use these services.

Professional Associations

Professional associations usually offer some type of placement assistance for their members. Providing a clearinghouse function, their common service is to list job vacancy information in the association's newsletter. In addition, many professional associations organize a placement center at their annual meeting. Organized from traditional "job market" and employment perspectives, most of these services allow employers and candidates an opportunity to meet for interviews. The quality and usefulness of these services varies. We have not been impressed with any of them. Job vacancy listings in the association's newsletter are similar to the "Help Wanted" ads in the newspapers. The placement centers at annual meetings are noted for promoting a "meat market" approach to the employment process. Don't expect great results from these services.

Special Career Services

Special career services sometimes emerge to deal with specific problems and needs. For example, during the recession in the aerospace industry in the 1960s, special programs were designed to help unemployed aerospace engineers find new jobs. Such programs tend to have low visibility and a short life span, but they may provide useful models which can be adapted to other situations. Indeed, in some communities special career planning services may be organized on an ad hoc basis for displaced educators affected by declining enrollments and severe budgetary cuts.

FRAUD, HUCKSTERS, AND MONEY

Would you select your spouse through a spouse-finding agency? Of course not, except out of desperation. If you are desperate and cannot find a job, seek help. But you will be a beggar, and beggars tend to be losers. You should never beg for a job. You have abilities, skills, and talents that are marketable, and you can learn how to market yourself.

However, if you choose to pay someone to do your work, beware of frauds and hucksters. The fields of career planning, job search, and employment are big businesses involving millions of dollars each year. These businesses have high attrition, as well as high employee turn-over, rates. You will encounter both effective and ineffective firms. The effective ones have good reputations and have been around the longest. Our best advice is to shop around, compare, and only sign a contract after thoroughly researching the organization and reading the fine print. Better still, try doing the job search based upon our suggested strategies. Doing it in this manner will be infinitely more rewarding and more fun.

ADVERTISING FOR FRIENDS

Another way to make life easy for yourself is to take out an ad in a newspaper or professional newsletter informing the world you are available for work. With this method, you don't have to rely on others to make job contacts--just check your mailbox for friends.

However, let's face it; this is a form of professional prostitution. You will probably be disappointed by the type of clients that visit you. You are fooling yourself if you think someone will knock on your door with the right job. Chances are you will buy several ads and receive numerous phone calls and letters from representatives of the private employment agencies and executive marketing firms. What do they want? They, of course, want to sell you their services. After all, you adver-tized the fact that you need help in finding a job. After paying the bills for your disappointing ads, you will realize you would have been wiser beginning with one of these organizations. Placing an ad may initially make you feel good; but it creates a false sense of making progress in your job search. Save your money for more productive job search activities.

JOINING OTHERS

While our strategies help individuals develop their own job campaigns, we also recommend linking these strategies to other individuals and groups. Outlined in subsequent chapters, our methods stress the central importance of developing and utilizing interpersonal networks throughout the job search process.

In addition to creating your own job search network, consider joining similar groups. For example, over the past few years "networking groups" have been organized in many cities for the purpose of helping women advance their careers (Welch). These groups come in different forms and sizes--from highly organized groups with computerized resume and data-banks to informal on-the-job groups. Men should also become involved in such groups.

Networking groups, job search cooperatives (Haldane), and job finders clubs (Azrin and Besalel) are nothing new. They have been given special attention because of the particular labor market problems associated with women and the hard core unemployed. We strongly urge you to form a job search support group. This can consist of your spouse and two or three friends and their spouses who are interested in exploring career alternatives and conducting a job search. Meet regularly--once every week--to share information, pool resources, critique each other's progress, suggest improvements in individual campaigns, share contacts, and provide support. If you do this, you should greatly improve your chances of finding a job. Furthermore, you will form lasting and rewarding personal relationships; you will lessen your frustrations by sharing them with others who understand; and you will find the process to be more enjoyable. In addition, the support and encouragement you receive from others will keep your motivation and self-esteem high as well as help you handle the psychological bumps and bruises associated with the job search. And don't forget to take care of your homefront by involving your spouse in the job search. For example, have your spouse assist you in writing letters, taking phone messages, conducting research, and evaluating your progress. If not, you may find that our idea of a "spouse-finder" wasn't funny after all!

Finally, you should consider linking your job search campaign to a few of the groups we mentioned earlier. Contact a few employment firms, placement offices, and professional associations. At the same time, become involved with a job search support group. Our basic principle is: never pay for something you can do just as well yourself, but always keep your options open.

BEGINNING WITH QUESTIONS

Assuming you will organize your own job search campaign, you should be aware of alternative ways of finding a job. Your first impulse may be to look at the want ads in the newspapers, professional newsletters, and journals. Be careful. Such ads should be given low priority in your hierarchy of job search strategies. Research shows one of the least effective ways of getting a job is to respond to such ads. As illustrated in Tables 3 and 4, the most effective ways of getting a job are informal--apply directly to an employer or ask friends, relatives, and acquaintances for assistance.

TABLE 3

USE AND EFFECTIVENESS OF JOB SEARCH METHODS

Method	Usage*	Effectiveness Rate**
Applied directly to employer	66.0%	47.7%
Asked friends about jobs where they work	50.8%	22.1%
Asked friends about jobs elsewhere	41.8%	11.9%
Asked relatives about jobs where they work	28.4%	19.3%
Asked relatives about jobs elsewhere	27.3%	7.4%
Answered local newspaper ads	45.9%	23.9%
Answered nonlocal newspaper ads	11.7%	10.0%
Private employment agency	21.0%	24.2%
State employment service	33.5%	13.7%
School placement office	12.5%	21.4%
Civil Service test	15.3%	12.5%
Asked teacher or professor	10.4%	12.1%
Went to place where employers come to pick up people	1.4%	8.2%
Placed ad in local newspaper	1.6%	12.9%
Placed ad in nonlocal newspaper	.5%	***
Answered ads in professional or trade journals	4.9%	7.3%
Union hiring hall	6.0%	22.2%
Contacted local organization	5.6%	12.7%
Placed ads in professional or trade journals	.6%	***
Other	11.8%	39.7%

* Percent of total jobseekers using the method.
** A percentage obtained by dividing the number of jobseekers who found work using the method by the total number of jobseekers who used the method, whether successfully or not.
*** Base less than 75,000.

SOURCE: Bolles, 1980: 34; based on survey conducted in 1972 and published in the Winter 1976 issue of *Occupational Outlook Quarterly* involving 10 million jobseekers.

These figures are even more pronounced in the case of higher-level jobs. The higher the level of the job, the more reliance you should place on informal and personal strategies, such as the use of professional and business acquaintances and direct contacts with employers. You increase your odds at getting a good job at a high level by shifting your attention to the informal system. This does not mean you should neglect formal job listings. On the contrary, monitor these listings. Apply for these jobs knowing that you are playing the odds, and often for low stakes. Don't spend an inordinate amount of time on such activities or anxiously wait to be interviewed and given job offers based

TABLE 4

EFFECTIVE METHODS OF FINDING A JOB, BY OCCUPATION*

Method	Professional and technical workers	Managers	Sales workers	Clerical workers	Craft workers	Operatives, except transport	Transport equipment operatives	Laborers, except farm	Service workers, except private household
Applied directly to employer	xx	xx	xx	xx	xx	xx	xx	xx	xx
Answered local newspaper ads	x	xx	xx	x	x	x	xx		xx
Asked friends about jobs where they work			x	x	xx	x	x	x	xx
Asked relatives about jobs where they work						x	x	x	x
Union hiring hall					xx	xx	x	x	
School placement office	xx			x					x
Private employment agency		xx		xx					
Asked friends about jobs elsewhere	x								
State employment service						x			
Contacted local organization									x

* One "x" indicates that the method was successful for 20%-24% of the people using it. The "xx" indicates that it was successful for 25% or more.

SOURCE: Bolles, 1980: 35; based on survey conducted in 1972 and published in the Winter 1976 issue of *Occupational Outlook Quarterly* involving 10 million jobseekers.

on such sources. We recommend, as others do, that you "invest" your job search efforts proportionately. Approximately 75 percent of your effort should go into developing direct contacts; 25 percent of your time and effort should cover the formal, published sources.

Your initial energy should be focused on thinking about jobs, careers, and your future. Where do you want to be five years from now? Ten? Twenty? Where would you like to work? San Francisco? Miami? Butte, Montana? What would you like to be doing? Writing? Managing a small research and consulting firm? Making important foreign policy decisions? Retiring? How much would you like to be making per year? $25,000? $50,000? $200,000? What is your potential beyond your present position? Address questions to yourself, your spouse, friends,

and acquaintances. Keep asking job and career-oriented questions until
you feel confident you know what it is you want to do. If you lose your
job, forget it; you may find that someone did you a favor. Avoid historical questions about what you should have done, those battles you
fought and lost, or how life might have been different if you hadn't
gotten into education. Don't worry too much. Worrying will not get
you anywhere. Be positive in your thinking as you concern yourself with
the future.

As you start asking new questions, you should begin exposing yourself to new people and different reading materials. If most of your
professional acquaintances and friends are educational colleagues, it
is time to meet new people in other organizations and occupations. Talk
to your banker or your minister or make an appointment to meet a successful individual in your community; talk to these people about your research on career and job alternatives. Ask for advice. Most people
will be happy to talk with you; many will be flattered you chose them
as your research subject. Most people also like to talk about their
work and give advice. However, they don't like being asked for a job.
Avoid asking for a job or a job lead. You first need to learn about
the world of work outside education. You are learning through new
friends and acquaintances; never exploit friendships.

REDISCOVERING THE LIBRARY

As you begin making new acquaintances, you should also start exposing yourself to new reading materials. Use your school or campus
library, especially the reference and documents sections. Start reading
The Wall Street Journal and the business sections of _The New York Times_
and _The Washington Post_. Occasionally look at newspapers from San
Francisco, Los Angeles, Houston, Dallas, Atlanta, Chicago, or Boston.
Get a better feel for what is going on in other communities. Keep an
eye on Houston, Phoenix, Fort Lauderdale, Miami, Salt Lake City, and
Denver. These are growth communities for people with your type of
skills.

Thumb through trade journals of different fields. Start skimming
articles in _Business Week_ and _Fortune_ magazines. Begin reading sections
of newspapers and magazines you ordinarily skip, especially if they are
the business and financial sections. Your goal is to expose yourself to
new information that will generate new questions and job directions.
Carry a small notebook so you can jot down names, ideas, and questions
you need to further research. Be particularly sensitive to names of
people who seem interesting, perhaps leaders in their fields. You may
want to write letters to these people and make appointments to see them
for career advice.

The reference section of libraries has numerous useful sources for
generating ideas. Look at some of these sources:

* _Yellow Pages of telephone books on different cities_:
  gives community profiles in terms of government agencies, businesses, and associations.
* _Encyclopedia of Associations_: lists approximately

15,000 associations in every field with names
of officers, telephone numbers, and brief descriptions of orientations and activities.
* _Encyclopedia of Business Information Services_:
  lists source materials on businesses.
* _Guide to American Directories_: describes 3,300
  directories by 400 topics.
* _The Standard Periodical Directory_: describes
  50,000 periodicals and directories.
* _Standard Rate and Data Business Publications
  Directory_: lists names and addresses of
  thousands of trade publications.
* _Geographical Index_: lists companies by cities
  and towns.
* _Dun and Bradstreet Million Dollar Directory_:
  lists names and addresses of thousands of trade
  publications.
* _Dun and Bradstreet Middle Market Directory_:
  lists companies with assets between $500,000 and
  $1 million.
* _Poor's Register of Corporations, Directors, and
  Executives_: gives names and addresses of 260,000
  leading executives by company and product.
* _Standard Directory of Advertisers_: lists 50 major
  industries with names, addresses, and telephone
  numbers.
* _Thomas' Register of American Manufacturers_: lists
  100,000 manufacturers by location and product.
* _Who's Who in Commerce and Industry_: names and
  biographical sketches of top executives.
* _State Directories_: each state has a directory
  of trade and industry. If not in your library,
  contact your local or state Chamber of Commerce
  or write to U.S. Chamber of Commerce, 1615 H
  Street, N.W., Washington, D.C. 20006.
* _Regional and community magazines_: most large
  cities and metropolitan areas have community
  magazines which focus on business, industry,
  education, the arts, and politics; states and
  regions also have their own magazines.

The documents section of libraries will have other useful source
materials, particularly on government agencies. The U.S. Department of
Labor issues several publications pertinent to job searchers. The major
ones are:

* _The Dictionary of Occupational Titles_
* _Occupational Outlook Handbook_
* _Occupational Outlook Quarterly_

If you are interested in working with the federal government, consult
the _Federal Yellow Book._ It outlines the organization of all executive
agencies and gives the names, addresses, and phone numbers of key officials. The _Congressional Yellow Book_ is a companion volume on congressional agencies and personal and committee staffs in the House and

Senate. These volumes are up-dated every six months. Three other sources, although more general, may be useful:

* *United States Government Manual*: gives organizational charts and summaries of structures and
  functions of agencies.
* *Congressional Directory*: lists names, addresses,
  phone numbers, and biographical sketches of
  Congressmen, Senators, and staffers.
* *Washington Information Directory*: general information covered in other directories.

For a sampling of the political and governmental cultures in Washington,
D.C., examine a few issues of the *National Journal*, *Washington Monthly*,
and *The Washington Post*.

The documents section should also include materials on state and
local governments and international organizations. These may be in the
form of staff directories, telephone books, or organizational charts and
handbooks. If you are interested in international-related fields--such
as volunteer organizations, banks, trade, finance, international organizations, and agencies in the U.S. government--one of the best sources
is Eric Kocher's *International Jobs: Where They Are, How to Get Them*.
This book gives a comprehensive listing and summary of organizations,
including names, addresses, general job search strategies, and expected
qualifications.

*The general problem you will face is the lack of a single informa-
tional source on any particular occupational category.* Because the job
market is decentralized, fragmented, and chaotic, you must take the initiative in organizing those aspects of the market that interest you.
This process is time consuming; no one can do it for you. By doing it
yourself, you will learn a great deal about career options, and you will
maintain control of your job search.

ORGANIZING AND TIMING THE CAMPAIGN

An effective job search campaign is more than just developing and
implementing a variety of career planning activities. Above all, it requires an understanding of how to organize as well as how to relate the
activities within alternative time frameworks. Lacking this understanding, the job search can become confusing, frustrating, and ineffective.

You can easily begin your job search from your office, filing ca-
binet, desk drawer, or closet. The only investments and supports you
need are paper, pens, a typewriter, envelopes, stamps, a telephone,
notebooks, index cards, file folders, a nearby library, access to a copy
machine, and this book. If necessary, read a book on "time management"
in order to better organize and utilize your time. For example, you
may need to follow several of these time management practices:

* evaluate how you normally utilize your time each
  day with particular attention given to identifying
  time wasters; keep a "time log" to monitor your
  time patterns.

* set objectives and priorities.
* plan daily activities by listing and priori-
  tizing things "to do."
* create some flexibility in your daily schedule;
  do not over-schedule.
* organize 2-3 hour blocks of time for concen-
  trated work.
* avoid interruptions.
* organize your workspace.
* process your paperwork faster by responding to
  it immediately and according to priorities.
* learn to say "no" and to shut your door.
* do one thing at a time.
* improve your ability and speed to remember,
  comprehend, and read.
* continually evaluate how you are best utilizing
  your time (Lakein; MacKenzie; Riley).

You should begin with a clear understanding of what you are doing.
Your goal--defined as a measurable outcome--is to get a job outside
education that *is right for you*. This requires organizing a campaign
of specific activities within a definite time period. Since the activities are interrelated, they must be internally organized in reference
to your final goal. We suggest that you treat your job search campaign
as if you were conducting a $500,000 research project. After all, your
campaign could well result in a $500,000 or more increase in income over
the next 20 years.

As you organize your campaign, your major job search activities
will include the following:

1. identifying abilities and skills
2. setting objectives
3. writing a resume
4. conducting research on individuals, organizations,
   and communities
5. prospecting, networking, and conducting informational interviews
6. interviewing for a specific position
7. negotiating the job offer

These activities can be conducted on a full-time or part-time basis,
depending on your goals and your time schedule. However, there are certain activities you should engage in on a full-time basis. These involve questioning, listening, evaluating, critiquing, adjusting, and
thinking about what you are doing and where you are going. Many people
tend to become too involved in their work and thus neglect to occasionally stand back and *think* about what is happening around them. This
tendency toward tunnel-vision needs to be corrected with a broader and
more integrated level of thinking. Do reflective and meditative thinking by occasionally sitting down for an hour or two to evaluate your
situation.

Depending on your personal situation, you may wish to initiate a
one, three, six, or twelve-month job search campaign. Obviously, the
shorter your campaign period, the more hours you must devote to each

job search activity. In Figure 7 we present a hypothetical job search
campaign conducted over a six-month period. Remember, this is hypothetical and not necessarily the way you may wish to organize your time. If
you choose such a plan, your monthly activities could be further divided
into weekly and daily targets as well as related to specific source materials and time periods. We strongly suggest that you plan job search
activities in advance and set aside time each week, preferably each day,
to accomplish them. Again, these are ideal models which merely suggest
possible alternative ways of organizing a job search campaign.

We caution you not to become a victim of *too much* planning by following such a detailed calendar. Planning is fine, but flexibility and
receptivity to the unexpected experience of serendipity is even better.
The most important goal of such planning is to reserve specific time
periods each day or week for activities related to your job search. You
designate your job search as a top priority activity in your daily life.
The tendency--especially when you see no immediate results, such as a
job interview and offer next week--is to procrastinate by saying you can
do this work tomorrow or next week. The job search should become routinized as a top priority activity in your daily schedule. As such,
it should play a central role in your overall time management scheme.

RELATING ACTIVITIES AND GOALS

Each of the major job search activities are closely interrelated.
They are based upon our generalized career development model in Chapter I. Hence, there is a logical ordering and sequencing of activities
that should be followed. If you neglect the sequence, your job search
may result in the self-fulfilling prophecy that "you can't do this on
your own--you need someone's professional help."

The most important overall relationship is the historical observation that your past is related to your future. Irish best redefines
this relationship as "the past is never past (Faulkner), and that the
future is now (George Allen)" (Irish: 41). Your past becomes your present and future when you engage in the key job search activity of identifying your abilities and skills. Without knowing these, you cannot
develop a realistic objective which, in turn, is closely related to your
resume, research, informational interviews, and job interview and negotiation activities. Setting your objective must come prior to writing
your resume, and the resume must come before conducting informational
interviews as well as before interviewing for job openings. Your research and informational interviews (developing contacts and referrals)
will feed back into your objective and resume as you adjust your job
search campaign to the realities of new information and experiences.
Therefore, you must learn about and organize your past in order to direct your present and future. Figure 8 relates these temporal concepts
and activities within the framework of your job search campaign.

You identify your present inventory of abilities and skills by
analyzing your past accomplishments, which are based upon diverse experiences. These experiences include your hobbies, education, volunteer
work, leisure activities as well as past jobs. Your career and job objective becomes a function of your ideals, fantasies, or dreams and

FIGURE 7

ORGANIZATION OF JOB SEARCH ACTIVITIES

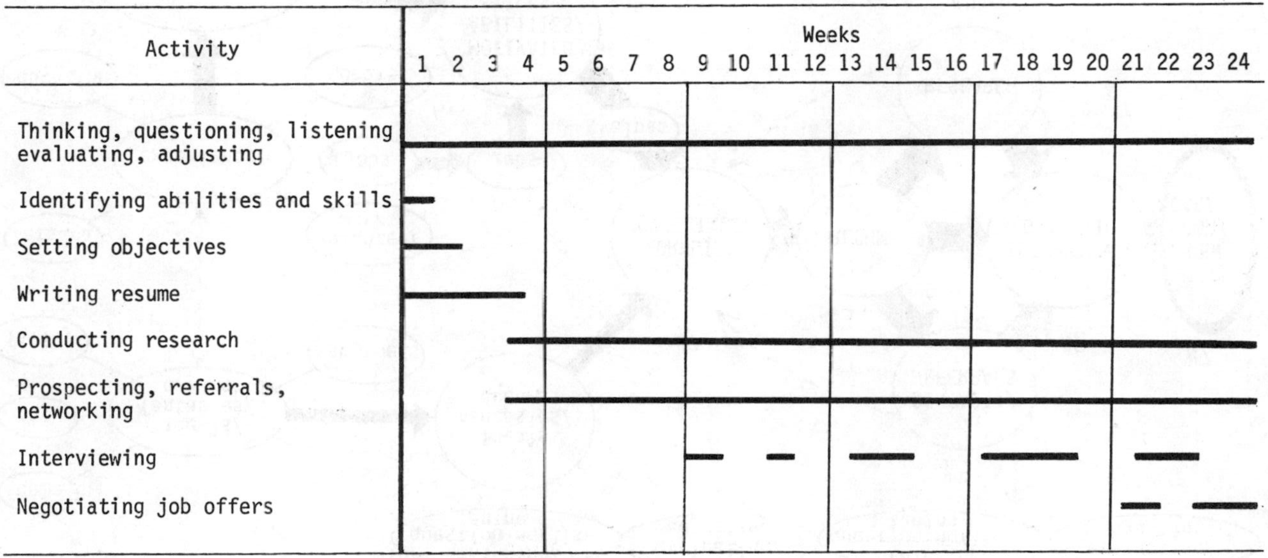

FIGURE 8

RELATIONSHIPS OF ACTIVITIES IN JOB SEARCH CAMPAIGN

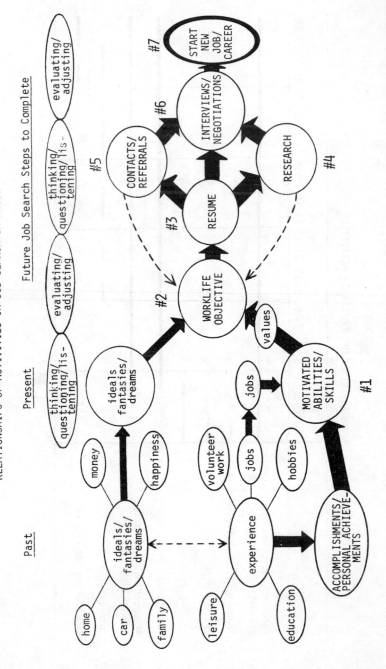

motivated abilities and skills. While you possess many motivated abilities and skills--perhaps you can tear down an automobile transmission--
your values filter which abilities and skills you prefer relating to
your worklife objective--such as your leadership abilities for becoming
an executive with a leading advertising agency. These concepts are
further examined and related in the next two chapters.

CONTINGENCIES AND REDUNDANCIES

One final note is necessary before we begin examining the individual job search steps. Contingencies and redundancies can be virtues
in attempting to organize and penetrate the inherently disorganized job
market. Do contingency planning by anticipating Murphy's Law: "If anything can go wrong, it will." Be prepared to discard well thought-out
plans which do not work well in reality. Be willing to start over, head
into new directions, and follow your intuition and common sense. At the
same time, try to incorporate redundancy into your planning. Don't
worry if one activity overlaps with another; indeed, plan for such overlap. For example, if you are interested in a particular organization,
make contacts within the organization at more than one level or with
more than one individual at the same level. The single source of information or single contact may need to be checked with other sources
of information or with other contacts. The same is true when identifying your skills and objectives. You have several alternative approaches to choose from. We recommend using several approaches in
order to check one with another. Make contingencies and redundancies
work in your favor.

These preliminary considerations should prepare you for a productive start on your job search campaign. As you begin scheduling and
routinizing your job search activities, you will begin seeing a new
world outside education take shape and direction for you. You will be
prepared to engage in the more systematic, rigorous, and high-payoff
activities outlined in subsequent chapters.

CHAPTER V

ASSESSING ABILITIES, SKILLS, AND QUALIFICATIONS

Why should I hire you? Few people are prepared to answer this
question in a positive, intelligible, in-depth, and effective manner.
Most job seekers don't know what they _want_ to do because they lack a
clear understanding of what they _can_ do. Many go from one job to another in the hope that each job will bring renewed satisfaction. As a
consequence of failing to articulate their abilities and goals, many
job seekers lack self-confidence, direction, purpose, and realism; they
both oversell and undersell their abilities on resumes and in interviews;
and they find the job search process to be difficult and depressing.
Such a job search approach is perhaps one major reason for the high degree of underemployment and job unhappiness in society.

Your job search campaign must first begin with a clear understanding of your abilities, skills, and qualifications. All other job search
steps are dependent upon effectively completing this one. Specifying
your worklife objective--your second job search step--must be grounded
on a thorough understanding of _who you are_ in terms of your strengths,
abilities, talents, and skills. Without knowing these, your job search
campaign will be ineffective.

Identifying your abilities, skills, and qualifications is not an
easy process. Indeed, the field of career planning offers job seekers
numerous alternatives to completing this job search step. These range
from the simple and increasingly popular self-directed "skills" exercises (Holland; Bolles; Crystal and Bolles) to batteries of costly psychological tests. Each of these techniques has advantages and disadvantages as well as strengths and weaknesses. Some essentially are
historical exercises, i.e., give you a snapshot of your past capabili-
ties, while others have greater prescriptive and predictive value.

In this chapter we examine these alternatives from a critical perspective. Our purpose is to best help you make informed choices among
competing alternatives. While all of the alternatives are better than
doing nothing, some are more useful than others. In addition to presenting and evaluating the alternatives, we present what we consider to
be the _most useful_ and powerful technique for identifying your motivated
abilities: SIMA. We base our preference for SIMA on several years of
successful experience.

MANAGING CAREERS FROM STRENGTH

Several years ago Peter Drucker stressed the importance of making
strength productive (Drucker: 71-99). Effective executives, according

to Drucker, make decisions to *maximize strength* rather than minimize weakness. Leading from strength, these executives staff for *excellence* by hiring individuals who perform exceedingly well in specific areas. Furthermore, they focus upon *opportunities* rather than problems.

Drucker's leadership principles are relevant to managing careers. Ask employers what they look for in prospective employees; they want employees with abilities to get things done. Your career will not advance if you focus upon your weaknesses. Therefore, you must recognize, understand, and manage your strengths. For the key to effective career management lies in making productive use of your abilities by focusing upon your positives, leading from strength, and recognizing and seizing opportunities which utilize your strongest talents.

While this positive and common sense concept of career management is not new, the vast majority of individuals we continue to counsel stress their weaknesses, negatives, and problems. As bona fide experts on what's *wrong* with them, they remain functional illiterates on what's *right* with them. They articulate in rich detail their shortcomings and fears, but they stumble and hesitate when asked: What's right with you? What are your strengths? What can you offer an employer? We rarely encounter an individual who can describe his or her strongest assets with precision and ease. However, this is what you must do in order to be effective in finding a highly satisfying job.

TAKING CONTROL

An individualistic, ethical philosophy underlies our concept of career management. We are responsible for our own career decisions, and thus no one should decide our futures. This perspective does not deny the role of luck, risk, or social environment in influencing our career development. Rather, it stresses the importance of taking initiative in shaping your future and being responsible for your own fate.

Individuals often blame their employers, supervisors, parents, spouses, schools, co-workers, and others for their career dilemmas. We meet them all the time. These "victimized" people believe others always control their lives. Such an attitude tends to create a self-fulfilling prophecy of acquiescing to the control and direction of others. While there are indeed forces beyond your control affecting your situation-- as we noted in Chapter II when we examined the macroscopic forces impacting on education--you must not re-live your past and acquiesce to others. The main issue is how you will proceed from here: What are you planning to do about your situation, and how will you follow-through in achieving your goals? There is neither comfort nor progress in managing your career by shifting responsibility for your fate onto others.

Individuals need to assume full responsibility for their career development. Avoid the failures of others. For example, many job searchers begin by looking for "*the* test which will tell me what I should do" or by assuming that a career counselor can "fix" their problems. Another common approach is to look for job vacancies with the underlying assumption that "I'll fit into what's available out there." This approach implies that the vagaries of the labor market control the individual's job search and career direction. If you practice these approaches, you need to reassess your operating assumptions in relationship to the realities of the job market.

The issue of self-responsibility regularly surfaces. For example, when talking with us on a one-to-one basis, a student, workshop participant, or client may feel that something is wrong, out of kilter, or off center. Work is neither satisfying nor fulfilling. Sometimes the individual feels that something must be wrong with him or her since others appear to be productive and happy in their work. Actually, few people openly talk with others about their feelings and dissatisfactions, thus contributing to the general impression of normalcy and job satisfaction. Since others appear "normal," the career disturbed individual begins feeling "abnormal." However, after discussing these concerns and hesitations, these individuals tend to be relieved and more willing to confront their career situation. This process is not easy. Some people want to rush through it in order to avoid the discomfort of uncertainty, new awareness, and hard decisions. Such an approach can be dangerous. It leads to premature decisions based upon superficial information. More importantly, it may actually worsen one's career problem over the long run.

The preferred approach is to directly face the dissonance and uncertainty in anticipation of encountering new information, understanding, and career direction. When people do this, some experience a sense of anger or disappointment in not having dealt with their career situation earlier. Some feel a sense of loss or tragedy from having "wasted" so much precious time. Many feel a sense of guilt for misusing time, failing to maximize their potential, and not utilizing their talents in a conscious, deliberate manner. While it is difficult to admit such losses and guilts, doing so has a positive and energizing influence on the entire career planning and job search process.

If these issues relate to you, feel comforted by the fact that you share the company of many strong, healthy, and talented persons who are grappling with the same problems. Thousands of professionals go through major career upheavals each year, and they do so successfully. Career change is unsettling for the strongest of us. While it may involve hard decisions and significant costs, it can be handled effectively.

The first step in the career planning process can be approached in many ways. We begin with what we consider to be the most useful concept and technique for initiating other career planning steps--identifying your motivated abilities through SIMA. We subsequently discuss alternative approaches popularized in the traditional career planning literature.

IDENTIFYING MOTIVATED ABILITIES

Our preferred approach is not new. Its roots date to the late 1940s and the work of Bernard Haldane, one of the pioneers in the career and job search counseling profession. Similar, although less sophisticated, approaches appeared in career counseling circles during the early and mid-1970s. Nonetheless, this approach is neither widely known nor practiced. We believe it represents a major breakthrough in understanding human motivation and is the most promising approach for enhancing the occupational mobility of displaced educators.

In 1958, Arthur F. Miller, a personnel executive with a major U.S. corporation, chaired a week-long seminar on personal development for the American Management Association. There he was exposed to Bernard Haldane's "success factor analysis" which was a system for identifying individuals' skills based upon an analysis of their achievements. Miller and his associates subsequently developed a systematic and effective method for describing a person's strengths and attendant motivations. The method is called SIMA--System for Identifying Motivated Abilities. It is described in the book *The Truth About You* (Miller and Mattson), which we recommend as a companion piece to this section of our book.

Working with nearly 5,000 clients over the past twenty years, Miller and his associates observed that each person has a highly individualistic, unique, and dynamic pattern of behavior which is expressed in a consistent, voluntary manner throughout life. Each individual has a characteristic manner of behaving, a preferential style of operating, or a way of superimposing his or her "personality" onto situations. This style or *motivated pattern of behavior* is most clearly revealed when a person gives a detailed description of his or her most significant and enjoyable personal achievements.

While at first appearing to be a determinist theory of human behavior, it is also a probabilistic theory; it views present and future behavior following the patterns of past behavior. In this sense there is nothing new and profound about the approach. Indeed, Miller does not claim to have developed a new theory and approach to human behavior. He simply reports his and other's observations (and we concur) of patterns and recurring themes which emerge when people discuss their achievements. In counseling and clinical settings, the careful observation of patterns and recurring themes has led in other cases to the development and testing of theories about human behavior (Holland).

SIMA is based upon a detailed elaboration and study of an individual's achievements. An achievement is defined as a specific experience which an individual enjoyed, believed he or she did well, and felt a sense of satisfaction and pride in doing. The individual is the central actor and is instrumental in making the achievement occur; it is not something that simply happens to a person. The person is the only judge of the significance and importance of the achievement; others' opinions, evaluations, and interpretations are not relevant. The individual defines the parameters of the achievement.

You are viewed performing at your best and enjoying your experiences when you analyze your achievements. This information reveals your motivations since it deals entirely with your voluntary behavior. In addition, it identifies what is right with you by focusing on your positives and strengths. In contrast to the typical "shotgun" approach to career assessment, such as writing a full work autobiography, SIMA "rifles" in on your most positive experiences and thereby constructs a useful data base for strengthening your career planning process.

Each individual has a recurring pattern of behavior which can be identified through a careful analysis of achievements. Components of this behavior fall into five categories:

1. *Abilities* you are motivated to use.
2. *Subject matter* or content you are motivated to work with and use.
3. *Circumstances* you are motivated to work within and around.
4. *Relationships* you are motivated to seek and establish with others.
5. *Primary motivational result* you are motivated to seek and accomplish.

Taken together, these categories and corresponding components comprise a Motivated Abilities Pattern or MAP. The average MAP has about eighteen recurring components. Examples of these may include:

1. *Abilities*: administer, schedule, design, experiment, persuade, assemble, organize, analyze, conceive ideas, write, research, execute, interview, counsel, teach, promote.
2. *Subject matter*: budgets, details, graphics, concepts, methods, human behavior, money, problems, people, relationships, systems, words, symbols, policies, living things.
3. *Circumstances*: competition, deadlines, projects, trouble, novel situations, stress, group activities.
4. *Operating relationships*: individualist, team member, coach, director, manager, coordinator, facilitator.
5. *Primary motivational result*: serve others, acquire money and material things, gain recognition, improve or enhance, overcome and prevail, achieve potential, master/perfect, build/develop.

The relationship of the MAP to the individual is depicted in Figure 9.

An analysis of an individual's MAP can vary from two to 40 pages depending on the degree of details desired. The following is an example of the shorter pattern report:

Primary Motivational Result

Demonstrate Competence--Achieve Potential: Show adaptability to new situations. Develop knowledge and technique to the point of demonstrable competence, then seek new avenues for learning and demonstration. You like to stimulate others to move beyond limited ways of thinking and pioneering as well. You learn "how to" in many fields.

Motivated Abilities

Learning: by studying, reading, listening, expressing, doing, trying out
Investigating: by interviewing, inquiring
Evaluating: by appraising worth, assessing value

FIGURE 9

COMPONENTS IN INDIVIDUALS MOTIVATIONAL ABILITIES PATTERN (MAP)

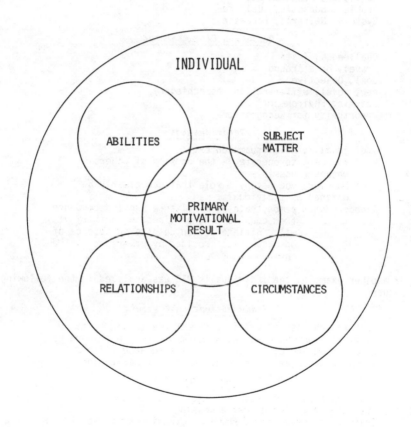

Conceptualizing: by hypothesizing, theorizing
Planning: by setting goals, arranging details,
           scheduling, practicing, getting ready
Developing: by adapting, modifying, improvising
Teaching: by stimulating, eliciting response

Recurring Subject Matter

Ideas, Theories, Philosophy
Principles, Concepts
Knowledge, Information
Logistics, Arrangements
People: Societies, Cultures
Systems, Networks, Processes

Recurring Circumstances

Challenges, Tests
Travel, Move Around
Goal, Objective
New, Novel, Different (to the achiever)
Learning Environment
Opportunity for Recognition

Relationships

Individualist Role (team context):
  * You want to operate in the company of others
    whenever possible.
  * However, you occupy a role that can clearly be
    defined as individual.
Independent: demonstrate self-reliance and independence
             from constraining or directing authority;
             will initiate action despite an absence of
             opportunities provided by others or by the
             environment.

In another example, the individual's MAP was analyzed in the following
manner:

Primary Motivational Result

Meet the challenge/pull it off/meet the test: Meets
difficult deadlines, solves problems, comes up shining
under demanding circumstances, wants to accomplish
specific tasks and pass tests which are challenging.

Motivated Abilities

Learn by observing, researching, and studying.
Evaluate by analyzing and assessing.
Train by demonstrating, showing...causing response.
Plan by scheduling, making arrangements, getting ready,
    preparing.
Oversee by coordinating and controlling.
Implement by executing, doing, maintaining, and following
    up.
Influence by convincing, promoting, persuading, negotiating.

Organize by manualize, routinize, categorize, gather,
    and integrate.
Communicate, explain.

Recurring Subject Matter

Relationships (difficult people, animals)
Projects/Programs
Efficiency/Productivity
Data/Details
Equipment/Machines

Recurring Circumstances

Problems/Needs
Challenges/Difficulties/Tests
Parameters/Deadlines
New/Novel/Different (to the achiever)
Tangible/Visible
Angles/Techniques/Tips/Schemes

Relationships

Coordinator: coordinates the activities of others
                in a participative fashion; _prefers_
                not to confront or use hire-fire or
                administrative authority; often causes
                others to take action who are not under
                her immediate jurisdiction.
Key Contributor: enjoys filling a key role whose input
                is critical to success of overall
                effort; likes to step in with her
                advice or expertise; need not be
                involved in actual administration or
                implementation as long as others adopt
                and/or realize her advice or contribution.
Independent of Authority: demonstrates self-reliance and
                           independence from constraining
                           authority.

Identifying the components of a client's MAP may take hours of
analyzing both written and oral data. The analyst must identify, as
in the above examples, each component related to the client's achievements and carefully document all conclusions. After completing this
procedure the client reviews the results and usually sees the MAP operating in his or her life across a broad variety of situations. Although
a client may dislike certain aspects of the MAP because they challenge
previous myths and self-perceptions, this information is important for
realistically assessing strengths for the career planning process. The
method examines _what_ the person achieved--not _why_ the person achieved
it. The individual data is neither interpreted nor compared with other
individuals, groups, or norms. SIMA makes no attempt to explain the
reasons for, or the causes behind, the MAP, or to deal with the underlying psychological make-up of the client.

After working with thousands of clients during the past twenty
years, Miller observes that motivational patterns have the following

dynamics:

Enduring: The MAP emerges early and remains consistent throughout your life. It does not appear to change regardless of environment, education, parents, values, or attempts by you to alter it.

Irresistible: The MAP is dynamic and "self-serving"; it will express itself somewhere in your life, regardless of environment or circumstances. If your job is not congruent with your MAP, you will use your "gifts" on non-job related activities. Or, you will attempt to bend the job around your pattern, regardless of job descriptions and requirements.

Controlling: Although you may be unaware of your MAP, it influences how you approach situations. For example, you will attempt to adapt your job to your pattern. In a sense, the pattern leads you. Consequently, it is best to select a job which will both accommodate and fully utilize your pattern.

Explanatory: A precise understanding of your pattern will enable you to diagnose your job satisfactions and dissatisfactions.

Predictive: Because of the enduring nature of the motivational pattern, it can be used to estimate and predict future performance in different settings.

These are rather bold claims! In our early work with SIMA, we were skeptical. SIMA did not fit into prevailing theories of human behavior and it challenged our assumptions about "human potential" and "self-actualization" (Maslow). But recent empirical studies of individual success have further challenged previous theories of human behavior (Jencks, 1979). At the same time, SIMA fit accurately with our understanding of *our* experiences and behaviors vis-a-vis the five components of our MAP. The inherent validity of our own patterns held up over time. They were clearly evident in high school and visible in elementary school. Moreover, our patterns were obvious in new achievements.

We had further doubts. Perhaps the knowledge of our patterns was biasing the way we interpreted our experiences. We talked with many others who had gone through SIMA and found remarkable similarities. Our families "validated" our patterns through very specific childhood experiences and under the microscope of daily living. Then, as we began cautiously using SIMA, clients confirmed its value.

One of the critical turning points for us occurred when several social scientists, career counselors, and industrial psychologists confirmed the accuracy and validity of SIMA for themselves. Although they had gone through therapy and other personal assessments as part of their training, they found that SIMA complemented these other techniques.

The proof for you, of course, is in the pudding. If you choose to use SIMA, it is available at several levels of sophistication and detail. While SIMA requires professional assistance to get the best results, you can proceed on your own by following the instructions in Miller's and Mattson's book, *The Truth About You*. If you seek professional assistance, contact the developer at the address given in the Preface of this book.

Available SIMA options include:

1. *Full Pattern Report:* 30-40 page detailed report which documents conclusions and includes a full transcript of your achievements.
2. *Summary Pattern Report:* 12-15 page report with substantial documentation.
3. *Basic Pattern Report:* 2-4 page pattern approximation developed in a group workshop.
4. *Self-reports:* Uses several methods outlined in *The Truth About You:*
   a. *Free recollection:* identify the recurring threads running through your achievements, preferrably with the help of others.
   b. *Checklist:* identify 4-6 abilities, 2-3 subject matters, 2-3 types of circumstances, one way of relating to others, and one motivational thrust.
   c. *Pattern approximation:* After identifying your top eight achievements, elaborate on each one by talking into a tape recorder. Type the transcript and study it carefully. Identify all *verbs* that describe your achievements and group them into *ability* categories. List all *nouns* which describe the *subject matter* and *circumstances* in your achievements. Identify your *relationships* by determining the active *roles* you played with others. Study the phrases which describe the relationships. Match this information with the relationship definitions in the book. Define the *one motivational thrust* evident in *each* achievement. Match your understanding against the definitions provided in the book.
   d. *Detailed report:* Have someone conduct a two-hour taped interview in which you describe your major achievements. Interviewing instructions are outlined in the book. Transcribe the taped interview, leaving wide margins on the pages. Note in the margins the specific components of your MAP.

You may feel that the SIMA process is too involved, complex, or difficult. People rarely achieve satisfactory results on their own. Therefore, we suggest strongly that you find two other kindred spirits who need clearer self understanding and career direction and go through the SIMA process together. A trio of diverse abilities will enhance the precision, quality, and pleasure of the assessment process and you will have more confidence in the outcome.

We believe that SIMA provides the *foundational understanding* you need to chart your career course and to evaluate job offers. Understanding your MAP is central to effectively managing your career. But SIMA takes time and effort whereas most people want quick, easy, and simple answers to complex questions. If SIMA seems too complex, time consuming, or difficult, you have other options which also can be useful.

TRANSFERABLE SKILLS

Your major alternatives to SIMA are several self-directed "skills identification" exercises which provide you with an inventory of transferable skills. Essentially historical exercises lacking the focus and depth of SIMA, they are useful approaches nonetheless. They especially help uninitiated job seekers better _understand_ the career planning process as well as _articulate_ a rich job search language.

Transferable skills are skills which can be utilized in different job settings. Several studies have verified that each individual possesses hundreds of these skills (Ashley; Sjogren; Stump; Wiant). The major transferable skills are outlined in Appendix A. However, most people cannot describe many of their skills. Educators are a case in point. While they possess expertise in particular subject matters and can transfer this expertise from one educational institution to another with ease, it is more difficult to transfer this expertise to non-educational settings. What do you do with a historian specialized in ancient Greek history? At best, this historian will look for non-academic employment with a museum specializing in ancient Greek artifacts or a library with a unique Greek collection.

The example of the Greek historian represents traditional thinking about the qualifications, experience, and expertise of educators. Such thinking stereotypes educators as lacking experience and qualifications for jobs outside education. Furthermore, it results in self-fulfilling prophesies, generates low self-esteem, and contributes to the general lack of self-confidence among educators seeking opportunities outside education. Representing a major obstacle to career advancement, this thinking is widely shared among educators and others.

While educators tend to view their qualifications as the mastery of specific disciplines and subject matters, they also possess functional skills which are transferable to jobs and careers in business, industry, and government. These skills first developed in childhood and subsequently expanded through other life experiences, such as schools, universities, community organizations, and educational positions.

While little systematic information is available on the transferable skills of educators, a recent study of career perspectives of Ph.D.s in the humanities is one of the most revealing for our purposes. When former graduate students in English, foreign languages, philosophy, and history where asked which were the most important transferable skills they acquired in graduate training, they identified the following in order of importance:

1. critical thinking
2. research techniques
3. perseverance
4. self-discipline
5. insight
6. writing
7. general knowledge
8. cultural perspective

9. teaching ability
10. self-confidence
11. imagination

12. leadership ability
(Solomon, Ochsner,
Hurwicz: 70-76)

At the same time, these graduates found a high degree of congruency between the most important skills acquired in graduate school and those utilized in their present jobs outside education. Not surprisingly, leadership ability was viewed as the weakest skill acquired in graduate school. We suspect this finding is generally true for graduates in other disciplines. After all, graduate students are followers of mentors; they have few opportunities to acquire leadership roles and skills.

Most graduate students know that success in graduate school does not depend on exceptional intelligence. Successful graduate students have two critical skills and qualities: _analytical thinking and perseverance_. Analytical thinking--the ability to organize large amounts of data into new and coherent schemes, as well as the ability to think critically, utilize imagination, and gain insights--is one of the most sought-after judgment job skills outside education. Other highly valued transferable skills are perseverance and self-discipline. The fact that leadership ability and self-confidence rank low on the transferable skills totem-pole does not speak well for graduate training in the humanities nor does such training appear to assist graduates in seeking responsible management positions outside education. This finding also points to one problem some readers may need to address in conducting their job search campaign: develop greater self-confidence, self-esteem, and leadership abilities.

Educators possess many of these graduate school skills as well as many additional transferable skills acquired while performing the role of educator. Teaching, for example, involves several skills other than instructing:

organizing	problem solving	coordinating
making decisions	public speaking	managing
counseling	advising	reporting
motivating	coaching	administering
leading	evaluating	persuading
selling	training	encouraging
assessing	supervising	improving

Research and publication activities of academicians involve many additional transferable skills:

initiating	interpreting	analyzing
updating	planning	designing
communication	estimating	implementing
performing	achieving	reviewing
attaining	negotiating	maintaining
		responsibility

Interacting with students, faculty, administrators, and staff requires using several skill-related personality qualities:

dynamic	unique	challenging
imaginative	versatile	sophisticated

innovative	responsible	diplomatic
perceptive	concerned	discrete
outstanding	successful	creative
tactful	easy-going	effective
reliable	humanistic	adept
vigorous	competent	efficient
sensitive	objective	honest
accurate	warm	aware
trained	broad	self-starter
expert	outgoing	strong
astute	experienced	talented
calm	democratic	empathic

In addition, Crystal and Bolles (209-213) note that individuals are capable of working with different types of objects and publics:

data	reports	designs
recommendations	systems	unusual conditions
inefficiencies	programs	research projects
facts	conclusions	communication systems
feelings	groups	statistical analyses
procedures	art	approaches
techniques	methods	presentations
project planning	objectives	problems
relations	individuals	goals
events	information	theories
processes	records	journals
statistics	handbooks	human resources
equipment	inputs	costs
living things	investigations	duties
tools	outputs	plants
training programs	charts	surveys
points of view	strategy	energy
prima donnas	growth	senior executives

The rich vocabulary generated from this skills approach is conceptually similar to the components in the SIMA Motivational Abilities Pattern. When applied to educators, we discover they utilize an incredible number of skills which go beyond simply teaching and conducting research in highly specialized and esoteric subjects. While many educators are unaware of the multiplicity and variety of their transferable skills, employers outside education are similarly ignorant. Consequently, educators must first educate themselves concerning their 500 to 800 transferable skills, and then communicate their skills to employers outside education. Thus, the skills identification approach enhances the important communication function between job seekers and employers.

METHODS FOR REDISCOVERING YOUR PAST

Identifying your transferable skills may be simple or complex, depending on how much time and effort you wish to invest. Career counselors have developed numerous inductive approaches--mostly self-directed exercises--for helping you identify your skills. While we prefer the SIMA technique, "skills identification" exercises are none-theless useful. Since you may want options, we identify the various alternative "skills" approaches, point out their strengths and weak-nesses, and emphasize the importance of incorporating redundancy in your assessments. We advise you to try several approaches and assess which ones give you the most useful information.

Intensive Skills Identification

This technique is similar to SIMA but doesn't go into as much depth. While you can utilize this technique on your own, you will get more accurate results if you work with others, such as a friend or your spouse.

This technique is widely used by career counselors but originated with Bernard Haldane. First known as "Success Factor Analysis" (Germann and Arnold: 44-58), it is also called the "System to Identify Motivated Skills" (Haldane). Since you will need six to eight hours to properly complete this exercise, divide your time into two or three work sessions. The exercise consists of six steps:

1. Identify 15-20 *achievements* (anything *you* enjoyed doing, believe you did well, and felt a sense of satisfaction, pride, or accomplishment in doing) in your lifetime, beginning with your childhood. Your achievements should relate to specific ex-periences--not general ones--and may be drawn from work, leisure, education, military, or home life. Select achievements important to you; what others may think is irrelevant. Put each achievement at the top of a sheet of paper. For example your achievements might appear as follows:

   "When I was 10 years old, I started a small paper route and built it up to the largest in my district."

   "I started playing chess in ninth grade and earned the right to play first board on my high school chess team in my junior year."

   "Learned to play the piano and often played for church services while in high school."

   "Designed and constructed a dress for a 4-H demonstration project."

   "Although I was small compared to the other guys, I made the first string on my high school football team."

   "I graduated from high school with honors even though I was very active in school clubs and had to work part-time."

   "I was the first in my family to go to college and one of the few from my high

school. Worked part-time and summers. A real
struggle, but I made it."

"Earned an 'A' grade on my senior psychology
project from a real tough professor."

"Finished my master's degree while teaching
full-time and attending to my family responsibilities."

"Got an 'A' in student teaching."

"Proposed a chefs' course for junior high boys.
Got it approved. Developed it into a very
popular elective."

"Developed a career education project for my
students which involved their parents and some
local businesses. Had media coverage and lots
of recognition."

"Writing and finishing my dissertation."

"Designed the plans for our house and had it
constructed within budget."

"Have developed a reputation as a good teacher.
I especially enjoy working with the so-called
apathetic students and getting them involved
and interested in the subject matter."

"Designed three new courses for my department
and had them approved."

"Chaired a special committee which investigated
the school's recruiting and selection procedures
and wrote the final report."

2. Study your achievements and prioritize the seven most
    significant ones.
3. Write a full page on each achievement by describing:
    a. how you became involved initially.
    b. the details of _what you did_ and _how you did it_.
    c. what was especially enjoyable or satisfying to
        you.
4. Elaborate on your achievements by having one or two
    other people interview you. For each achievement have
    them note on a separate sheet of paper any terms used
    to reveal your skills, abilities, and personal qualities.
    To elaborate details, the interviewer(s) may ask

    "What was involved in the achievement?"
    "What was your part?"
    "What did you actually do?"
    "How did you go about that?"

    Clarification of any vague areas should be probed by
    asking:

    "Would you elaborate on one example of what
    you mean?"

"Could you give me an illustration?"
"What were you good at doing?"

This interview should clarify the details of your activities by asking only "what" and "how" questions. The interview may take 45 to 90 minutes.

5. Following the interview, examine the interviewer's notes. Together identify the recurring skills, abilities, and personal qualities _demonstrated_ in your achievements. Search for patterns.

6. Your motivated skills pattern should be clear at this point and you should feel comfortable with it. If you have questions, review the data. If you disagree with a conclusion, disregard it. The results must accurately and honestly reflect how you operate.

Next, synthesize the information by clustering similar skills into categories. For example, your skills might cluster as follows:

Investigate/Survey/Read
Inquire/Probe/Question

Learn/Memorize/Practice
Evaluate/Appraise/Assess/Compare

Influence/Involve/Get participation
Publicize/Promote

Teach/Train/Drill
Perform/Show/Demonstrate

Construct/Assemble/Put together

Organize/Structure/Provide definition
Plan/Chart course/Strategize
Coordinate

Create/Design
Adapt/Modify

After completing this exercise, you will have a relatively comprehensive inventory of your motivated skills related to your achievements. With this information, you will be better able to use a "skills vocabulary" when identifying your objective, writing your resume, and interviewing. Moreover, your self-confidence and self-esteem should increase.

Checklist Method

One of the most popular approaches to skills identification is Richard Bolles' "Quick Job Hunting Map." It is found in Appendix A of his book, _What Color Is Your Parachute?_, or it can be purchased as a separate workbook in both beginning and advanced versions (Ten Speed Press, Berkeley, California 94707, $1.25). Use the advanced version. We recommend this resource if you cannot use the more comprehensive and intensive SIMA and skills identification techniques or if you need a quick approximation of your skills. The "Map" contains the most comprehensive skills checklist and helps build your skills vocabulary. In using the "Map," you simply identify your seven most satisfying accomplishments, jobs, or roles in life and relate these to a checklist of 222 skills. Depending on how thorough and detailed you treat each experience, this exercise may take six hours to complete.

The "Map" is easy to use and it yields an enormous amount of interrelated information. However, the "Map" is also deceptively simple. There is nothing magical about the categories, interrelationships, and results. The exercise gives you a fairly comprehensive snapshot of your past skills and patterns within specific "skill" categories. It does not give you a picture of your future. For some people, this can be a disappointing experience. For example, someone hoping to work in human services may discover through the "Map" that most past accomplishments, jobs, or roles required only physical and clerical skills. While this individual may dislike using these skills, the "Map" implies that these past skills should be stressed in the future. Since the "Map" gives no guidance on how to overcome one's past, people who believe in "thinking big" and setting goals for improving their careers may become frustrated by this exercise.

Other Alternatives

Several other techniques are available to identify transferable skills. Most of these alternatives consist of inductive self-directed exercises which generate similar sets of skills based upon past experiences. Most have the advantages and disadvantages of Bolles' "Map." Any of the following exercises can be used interchangeably to inventory your skills. Refer to the appropriate references for further details on how to complete each exercise:

1. Acquire a list of Bolles' 100 skills; check off which skills you possess and arrange them into clusters and priorities (Bolles, 1978b: 169-175).
2. Develop a "Career Analysis Worksheet" which involves identifying your general, strongest, and specific functional abilities along with an assessment of your personal relationships, pay goals, and ideal job, work environment, and fields of work (Lathrop,1977: 52-69).
3. Write your autobiography with special emphasis on your pleasures and accomplishments. This may run from 30 to 200 pages or more. Analyze this document by identifying those things you most enjoyed doing and wish to continue doing in the future. Identify which skills cluster with your favorite experiences (Bolles, 1980: 83-83; Irish: 40-41; Crystal and Bolles: 207-221).
4. List all your hobbies and analyze what you do in each, which ones you like the most, what skills you use, and your accomplishments (Bolles, 1980: 84-85).
5. Take John Holland's "The Self-directed Search." It is found in his book, _Making Vocational Choices: A Theory of Careers_; professionals can purchase it

for around one dollar by writing to: Consulting Psychologists Press, 577 College Avenue, Palo Alto, California 94306.

6. Conduct a job analysis by writing about your past jobs and identifying which skills you used in each job. Cluster the skills into related categories and prioritize them according to your preferences.

INCREASING VALIDITY THROUGH REDUNDANCY

All of these self-directed "skills" exercises generate similar information. They help you identify transferable skills you already possess. Furthermore, they assist you in developing a rich skills vocabulary for stating your objective, constructing your resume, and conducting informational and job interviews. As such, these exercises present you with a picture of your present skills. While aptitude and achievement tests may yield similar information, the self-directed exercises have three major advantages over the standardized tests: less expensive, self-monitored and evaluated, and measure motivation _and_ ability (Irish: 41; Germann and Arnold: 54).

Completing each exercise demands a different amount of time. Writing your life history and completing SIMA, Haldane's "Success Factor Analysis," and Bolles' "Map" are the most time consuming. On the other hand, Holland's self-directed search can be completed in a few minutes-- if you are in a hurry! But the more time you invest with each technique, the more useful information you will generate. We recommend creating redundancy by using two or three different techniques. This will help reinforce and confirm the validity of your observations and interpretations. If you are making a mid-career change and/or have a considerable amount of experience, we recommend using the more thorough exercises. Remember, the more you put into this stage of the job search, the more you will benefit from this and all subsequent stages.

QUALIFYING AND COMMUNICATING

Many people want to know about their futures. If you expect our techniques to spell out your future, you will be disappointed. Fortune tellers, horoscopes, and various forms of mysticism may be what you need. We have no magic, and we are not competing with soothsayers.

Our recommended techniques are historical devices which integrate past achievements, abilities, and motivations for projecting future performance. They clarify past strengths and recurring motivations for targeting future jobs. Abilities and motivations are the _qualifications_ employers expect for particular jobs. Qualifications consist of your past experience _and_ motivated abilities.

The assessment techniques provide a bridge between your past and future. As such, they treat your future preferences and performance as functions of your past experiences and demonstrated abilities. This common sense notion is shared among employers: past performance is the best predictor of future performance.

Yet, employers hire a person's _future_ rather than their past. And herein lies an important problem you can help employers overcome. Getting the job that is right for you entails communicating to prospective employers that you have the necessary qualifications. Indeed, employers will look for signs of your future productivity _for them_. You are an unknown and risky quantity. Therefore, you must communicate evidence of your past productivity. This evidence is revealed clearly in your past achievements which you outlined by using our assessment techniques.

The overall value of using these assessment techniques is that they should enhance your occupational mobility over the long-run. The major thrust of all these techniques is to identify abilities and skills which are _transferable_ to different work environments. This is particularly important for educators who are looking for career alternatives outside education but who tend to think about their abilities, skills, and qualifications in traditional terms. Employers may view you initially as another "burned out" educator looking for another job and more money. You must overcome employers' negative expectations and objections toward educators by clearly communicating your transferable abilities and skills in the most positive terms possible. Our assessment techniques are designed to do precisely that.

CHAPTER VI

SETTING REALISTIC OBJECTIVES

Once you have identified your motivated abilities and skills, developing your objective becomes a much easier task. However, one major problem remains: how do you identify objectives that are not mere reflections of your history? Or are we victims of our past? We assume you want to advance your career rather than mimic your past accomplishments. Therefore, we have developed methods for helping you deal with this problem of historical determinism.

USING OBJECTIVES

Most job hunters lack clear objectives. Many engage in a random, and somewhat mindless, search for jobs by trying to first identify available job opportunities and then adjusting their skills and objectives to "fit" specific job openings. While you will get a job using this approach, you probably will be misplaced and unhappy with what you find. You will fit into a job rather than find a job that is fit for you.

Knowing what you want to do can have numerous benefits for you and your future. First, you define the job market rather than let it define you. As you begin systematically organizing job opportunities around your specific skills and objectives, you will discover that the inherent fragmentation and chaos of the job market are advantageous for you. Second, since your resume will focus on an objective (Chapter VII), you will appear very professional and comprehendible to prospective employers. Employers will have a more precise indication of your interests, qualifications, and purposes. This places you on a more equal and professional plane with employers and ahead of most other applicants. Third, being purposeful means being able to communicate to employers what you want to do. Employers are not interested in hiring indecisive and confused individuals. They want to know what it is you can do for them. With a clear objective, based upon a thorough understanding of your motivated abilities, skills, and interests, you can take control of the situation, generate self-confidence, and demonstrate your value to employers. Moreover, few employers really know what they want in a candidate. Like most job seekers, employers lack clear employment objectives and knowledge about how the job market operates. Thus, if you know what you want and can help the employer define his or her "needs" as your objective, you will have achieved a tremendously advantageous position in the job market.

DEFINITIONS AND REALISM

Objectives can be defined from several perspectives. In its simplist and most traditional form, an objective is a statement of what you would like to do. Some writers equate the use of particular job-related skills as your objective, i.e., repeat what you are strong in doing. Others view an objective as a statement of what you will do for an employer. Still others see an objective as a measurable outcome as well as try to distinguish an objective from goals and targets. We have no problems with these different definitions; each is useful for various purposes. However, we prefer having you develop an objective which communicates what you can do for employers. If you think in terms of measurable outcomes and results, your objective will communicate clearly that you are a purposeful individual. This perspective makes considerable sense once you specify your job objective on the resume.

Objectives can be stated over different time periods as well as at various levels of abstraction and specificity. You can identify short, intermediate, and long-range objectives and very general to very specific objectives. Whatever the case, it is best to know your prospective audience before deciding on the type of objective. Your objective should address not only what _you_ are intrinsically interested in pursuing. Since your objective must be accomplished through other individuals, include _their_ needs into your thinking.

Another important dimension of an objective is its realism. You may want to become President of the United States or solve all the world's problems. However, these objectives are probably unrealistic. While these may represent your ideals and fantasies, you need to be more realistic in terms of what you can personally accomplish in the immediate future. What is it that you are prepared to deliver to prospective employers over the next few months? While it is good to set challenging objectives, you can overdo it. Refine your objective by thinking about the next major step or two you would like to make in your career advancement--not some grandiose leap outside reality!

PROJECTING INTO THE FUTURE

Specifying an objective can be the most difficult and tedious step in the job search process. This simple one-sentence, 25-word statement can take days or weeks to formulate and clearly define. Yet, it must be specified prior to engaging in other job search steps. An objective gives meaning and direction to all other activities.

Your objective should be viewed as a function of several influences. Since you want to build upon your strengths and you want to be realistic, your abilities and skills will play a central role in formulating your work objective. At the same time, you do not want your objective to become a function solely of your past accomplishments and skills. You may be very skilled in certain areas, but you may not prefer utilizing these skills in the future. As a result, your values and interests filter which skills you will or will not incorporate into your work objective.

Overcoming the problem of your future merely reflecting your past requires incorporating several additional components into defining your objective. One of the most important is your ideals, fantasies, or dreams. Everyone engages in these, and sometimes they come true. Your ideals, fantasies, or dreams may include making $1,000,000 by the age of 45; owning a Mercedes-Benz and a Porshe; taking trips to Rio, Hong Kong, and Rome; owning your own business; developing financial independence; writing a best-selling novel; solving major social problems; or winning the Nobel Peace Prize. Most of your fantasies will require more money than you are now making. Consequently, you will need to incorporate monetary considerations into your work objective. For example, if you have these fantasies, but your sense of realism tells you that your objective is to move from a $16,000 a year education position to an $18,000 a year position outside education, you will be going nowhere, unless you can fast-track in your new position. Therefore, you will need to set a higher objective to satisfy your fantasies.

There are many ways to develop realistic objectives. We don't claim to have a new or magical formula, only one which has worked for many individuals. Some of our suggestions may be more helpful to you than others; therefore, we have incorporated redundancy in order to give you options as well as enable you to evaluate one data source with another. We assume you are capable of making intelligent career decisions if given sufficient data. This approach is designed to provide you with sufficient corroborating data from several sources and perspectives so that you can make preliminary decisions. If you follow our steps in setting a realistic objective, you should be able to develop a clear direction in your job search. If you encounter difficulties, discuss your concerns with a friend or a career counselor.

OBJECTIVE SETTING PROCESS

In Figure 10 we outline the four major steps involved in developing a work objective. Each step can be implemented in a variety of ways.

Step 1

Develop or obtain the foundational data on your Motivated Abilities Pattern or your functional/transferable skills. You should have this data based upon your work in Chapter V.

Step 2

Acquire corroborating data about yourself from others, tests, and yourself. Several resources are available for this purpose:

1. *From others*: Obtain "Support Statements" from three to five individuals who know you well enough to answer these three questions:
   a. What are your significant vocational strengths?
   b. What weak areas may you need to improve?
   c. What do you need to make you happy in your work?

FIGURE 10

OBJECTIVE SETTING STEPS

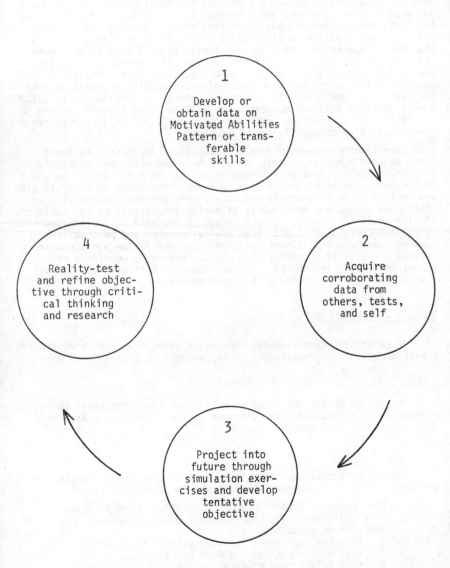

1
Develop or obtain data on Motivated Abilities Pattern or transferable skills

2
Acquire corroborating data from others, tests, and self

3
Project into future through simulation exercises and develop tentative objective

4
Reality-test and refine objective through critical thinking and research

Explain to these people that you are reassessing your career direction; you believe their candid appraisal will help you gain a better understanding of your strengths and weaknesses from the perspectives of others (Germann and Arnold: 53).

2. *From Vocational Tests*: Although we prefer self-generated data, vocationally-oriented tests can help clarify, confirm, and translate your understanding of yourself into occupational directions. If you decide to use vocational tests, contact a professional career counselor who can administer and interpret the tests. We recommend several of the following tests:

    * *Strong-Campbell Interest Inventory*
    * *Career Assessment Inventory*
    * *The Self-Directed Search*
    * *Temperament and Values Inventory*
    * *Sixteen Personality Factor Questionnaire*
    * *Edwards Personal Preference Schedule*
    * *Myers-Briggs Type Indicators*
    * *Self-Description Inventory*

3. *From Yourself*: Numerous alternatives are available for you to practice redundancy:

    a. Develop a comprehensive list of your past and present *Job Frustrations and Dissatisfactions* to help you identify negative factors which should be avoided in future jobs.
    b. Identify what you don't want in a job by describing the *working conditions* you would find *distasteful* (Crystal and Bolles: 22).
    c. Brainstorm a list of *Twenty Things I Love to Do*; classify each item in reference to:
        * work, learning, or leisure;
        * data, people, or things.
    Also, indicate when you last engaged in each activity (Simon, Howard, and Kirschenbaum).
    d. List 10-15 *Things That Mean the Most To Me* in your work.
    e. List 10-15 *Conditions That Mean the Most to Me* in your work.
    f. Take 10 sheets of paper and write *"Who Am I?"* at the top of each. Write one answer to the question on each sheet. Then review each answer and write below it what is satisfying about your answer. Next, review each sheet and arrange them in order of priority for you. Finally, examine each answer and identify the recurring elements of each which satisfies you (Bolles, 1980: 91-93).
    g. Visualize a *Board of Directors* comprised of individuals, or "significant others", in your

life, living or dead, who are having positive
and/or negative effects on your career decision-
making. You are "Chairperson" of the "Board"
and your task is to identify each of the "Board
Members". Use the following illustration for
this purpose:

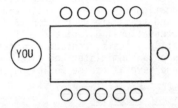

Next, ask yourself:
   * Who sits on my board?
   * Why is each person on my board?
   * What is the nature of each person's
     influence upon me?
   * How extensive is that influence?
   * How do I feel about that influence?
   * Are there any changes I would like to
     make in my Board? (Kirshenbaum)
h. Work environments are _people environments_.
    Some people add to your energy, productivity,
    and self-esteem; others add to your work
    hassles. Identify the types of men and
    women you _like_ and _dislike_. In so doing,
    think about specific individuals you have
    known. Compare and contrast the lists and
    try to analyze the reasons behind your feelings
    (Crystal and Bolles: 45-46).
i. Develop a list of _work satisfiers_ which add to
    your work pleasures and productivity. These
    may include: distant supervision; outdoor work;
    work as a member of a team; work alone; struc-
    tured environment; small organization; flex-
    time; and a certain type of boss.

Step 3

   Project into the future by completing simulation and creative
thinking exercises which focus your values and preferences for developing a tentative objective:

1. _Ten Million Dollar Exercise_: First, assume that you
   are given a $10,000,000 gift; now you don't have to
   work. Since the gift is restricted to your use only,
   you cannot give any part of it away. _What will you_
   do with your time? At first? Later on? Second,
   assume that you are given another $10,000,000, but

this time, you are required to give it all away.
What kinds of causes, organizations, charities,
etc., would you support? (Crystal)

2. _Obituary Exercise_: Make a list of the most
important things you want to do or accomplish
before you die. Be as specific as possible.
Alternatively, write an article on "Before I
die, I want to...." (Bolles, 1980: 95).

3. _What Needs Doing in the World_? This is a practical exercise in creative future-thinking. Take a
few minutes to think about the world's problems
and those things you would like to change for the
better. Write a brief description of several
things you would like to see improved. Pick any
topic which interests you; feel free to tackle
problems which have stumped "the experts" for
years. In each case, outline how you would al-
leviate the problem and how you would like to
participate in making improvements (Crystal and
Bolles: 88-90).

4. _Ideal Work Week_: Starting with Monday, place each
day of the week on the headings of seven sheets of
paper. Develop a daily calendar with 30-minute
intervals, beginning at 7 a.m. and ending at mid-
night. Your calendar should consist of a 119-hour
week. Next, beginning at 7 a.m. on Monday (sheet
one), identify the _ideal activities_ you would
enjoy doing, prefer doing, or need to do for each
30-minute segment during the day. Assume you are
capable of doing anything; you have no constraints
except those you impose on yourself. Furthermore,
assume that your work schedule consists of 40 hours
per week. How will you fill your time? Be
specific.

5. _Ideal Job Specifications_: Develop a list of _all_
your ideal and desired future job specifications.
Be sure you include:
   a. specific interests you want to build
      into your job
   b. work responsibilities
   c. working conditions
   d. earnings and benefits
   e. interpersonal environment
   f. working circumstances, opportunities,
      and goals (Crystal and Bolles: 52).
Based upon a synthesis of these job specifications,
write a detailed paragraph which describes the kind
of job you would be most productive and happy doing.

Step 4

Test your objective against reality. Evaluate and refine it by
conducting market research, a force field analysis, library research,

and informational interviews:

1. _Market Research_: Four steps are involved in conducting market research:
   a. _Products or services_: Based upon all other assessment activities, make a list of what you _do_ or _make_.
   b. _Market_: Identify _who_ needs, wants, or buys what you do or make. Be specific. Include individuals, groups, and organizations. Then, identify _what_ specific _needs_ your products or services fill. Next, assess the _results_ you achieve with your products or services.
   c. _New markets_: Brainstorm a list of who _else_ needs your products or services. Think about ways of expanding your market. Next, list any _new_ needs your current or new market has which you might be able to fill.
   d. _New products and/or services_: List any new products or services you can offer and any of the new needs you can satisfy (Kirn: 9.1).
2. _Force Field Analysis_: Once you have developed a tentative or firm objective, force field analysis can help you understand the various internal and external forces affecting the achievement of your objective. Force field analysis follows a specific sequence of activities:
   a. Clearly state your objective or course of action.
   b. List the positive and negative forces affecting your objective. Specify the internal and external forces working _for_ and _against_ you in terms of who, what, where, when, and how much. Estimate the impact of each force upon your objective.
   c. Analyze the forces. Assess the importance of each force upon your objective and its probable affect upon you. Some forces may be irrelevant to your goal. You may need additional information to make a thorough analysis.
   d. Maximize positive forces and minimize negative ones. Identify actions you can take to strengthen positive forces and to neutralize, overcome, or reverse negative forces. Focus on the key forces which are real, important, and probable.
   e. Assess the feasibility of attaining your objective and, if necessary, modifying it in light of new information (Kirn: 24.1-7).
3. Conduct library research to strengthen and clarify your objective as outlined in Chapter VIII.
4. Conduct informational interviews as outlined in

Chapter IX. This may prove to be the most
useful way of clarifying and refining your
objective.

After completing these steps, your thinking for formulating an objective should be relatively comprehensive. You have identified what it
is you _can_ do (abilities and skills), enlarged your thinking to include
what it is you would _like_ to do (fantasies), and probed the realities
of implementing your objective. Thus, setting a realistic work objective
is a function of the diverse considerations represented in Figure 11.

Your work objective is a function of both subjective and objective
information as well as idealism and realism. We believe the strongest
emphasis should be placed on your motivated abilities and should include
a broad data-base. Your work objective is realistic in that it is tempered by your past experiences, accomplishments, skills, and current
research. An objective formulated in this manner permits you to think
beyond your past experiences.

STATING A FUNCTIONAL OBJECTIVE

One of the best ways to state a work objective is to follow Bernard
Haldane Associate's advice (Germann and Arnold: 54-55). For them, a
functional job objective consists of functions, activities, or duties
you prefer in a job. The functions are the skills or Key Success
Factors (Haldane) identified in Chapter V. Your functional job objective will be stated at two different levels: a general objective and a
specific one for your resume.

In stating the general objective, begin with the statement: "I
would like a job where I can use my ability to _____ which will
result in _____." This statement views the objective as both a
skill and an _outcome_. For example, you might state: "I would like a
job where my experience in program development, supported by innovative
decision-making and systems engineering abilities, will result in an
expanded clientele and a more profitable organization." At a second
level, you may wish to re-write this objective to target it at various
consulting firms. For example, it might appear on your resume as
follows: "An increasingly responsible research position in consulting,
where proven decision-making and system engineering abilities will be
utilized for improving organizational productivity."

If you have completed your Motivated Abilities Pattern in Chapter
V, your objective can reflect key elements in your MAP. For example,
your statement of objective may include:

* "A job working with..." (insert your _subject matter_--
     people, ideas, numbers, structural things)
* "Where the conditions of the work..." (insert your
     circumstances--are project oriented, require
     operating under stress, allow some freedom of
     movement, etc.)
* "And where I can operate..." (insert your _way of_

108

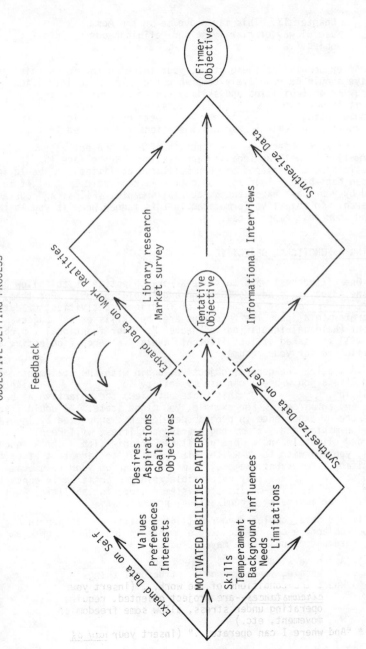

FIGURE 11

OBJECTIVE SETTING PROCESS

Firmer Objective

Synthesize Data

Library research
Market survey

Informational Interviews

Expand Data on Work Realities

Tentative Objective

Feedback

Desires
Aspirations
Goals
Objectives

Synthesize Data on Self

Values
Preferences
Interests

MOTIVATED ABILITIES PATTERN

Skills
Temperament
Background influences
Needs
Limitations

Expand Data on Self

    operating with others--member of a team, or
    in a defined role, or in a leadership capacity,
    etc.)
  * "Using my motivated abilities to..." (insert your
    motivated abilities--investigate for the facts,
    analyze their significance, improve a solution,
    organize others involved, oversee the implemen-
    tation, etc.)
  * "And which leads to..." (insert your *one motivational*
    thrust--a finished product, chance for advance-
    ment, greater responsibility, recognition for
    my contribution, etc.) (People Management: 7)

It is important to think of your job objective more in terms of what you can contribute rather than solely what you want. When you get to the stage of writing your resume, you will have to relate your objective to a well-defined audience. Your audience is more concerned with what you can do for them than with what they can do for you. You should practice writing functional job objectives by using this format as well as by orienting yourself more to your potential audience. Remember, *your objective should be work-centered, not self-centered*.

CHAPTER VII

CREATING A RESUME FOR EMPLOYMENT
OUTSIDE EDUCATION

Writing a resume for jobs outside education is a new and unfamiliar task for many educators. Elementary and secondary educators complete lengthy application forms for school boards in lieu of writing a resume. College and university educators write something approximating the normal resume. Known as vita, curriculum vita, or academic resumes, these documents tend to be lengthy, self-serving, and archaic obituaries which are incomprehensible to individuals outside education. Given the nature of these documents, it is surprising how colleges and universities can make informed staffing decisions!

The academic resume is unique and confined mainly to the halls of academe. Taken outside education, it is both pretentious and ineffective; it is one reason why non-educators have difficulty understanding what educators are capable of doing outside education. Academic resumes list teaching fields, publications, professional papers, positions, and a helter-skelter collection of other oddities which are supposed to "impress" as well as communicate something relevant to fellow educators. Indicative of the non-performance rank and status thinking of many educators, these resumes are bad habits that should be broken. As you look outside education for a job, hide your curriculum vita! Nobody wants it other than fellow educators. Instead, keep a clear and open mind, and begin by building upon your skills and job objective by writing an effective non-educational resume which will get you interviews. This chapter is designed to help you do precisely this.

ADVERTISING YOURSELF

A great deal of mysticism and confusion still surround resumes. Some people believe a resume will get one a job. Others believe it is a personal statement of belief in one's greatness. Still others believe a resume is an inventory of professional experience and personal information. In a strict definitional sense, a resume is a summary of your past history. However, in terms of its _purpose_, a resume should be a factual summary of your qualifications and organized around a particular job objective. Confusion arises over (1) what should be included in the resume, and (2) how information should be presented.

A resume is your personal advertisement. Since you are selling a valuable product--yourself, your resume should reflect the value of the product. It is your chief marketing tool or calling card for opening doors of employers. It will not--except in very unusual circumstances--

get you a job. The purpose of resumes is to get interviews. Only interviews result in job offers. Therefore, when writing your resume, always
remember that you are *advertising yourself* for an *interview*. Your resume should neither answer questions nor raise negative questions in the
mind of the reader. An effective resume should result in a positive
response from a prospective employer: "Very interesting qualifications,
seems very professional. I want to know more about this person. Let's
get on with a formal interview." Above all, your resume should factual-
ly communicate who you are and what abilities, skills, and qualifications
you can offer an employer. It should be impeccably honest, positive,
concise, and easy to read.

FUNCTIONS, STYLES, AND PITFALLS

Resumes are important for several reasons. Employers obviously
expect to receive resumes in order to initially screen applicants. If
they like what they see on your resume, they may invite you to an interview.

Although your ultimate goal is to get interviews and job offers,
an effective resume has other important uses for both you and prospective employers:

* reviews your experience and communicates your
  potential value to employers.
* provides information as part of your file in
  any placement service you use.
* accompanies your application letters in response
  to vacancy announcements.
* is an integral part of the informational interview process.
* focuses and communicates your job objective and
  qualifications.
* serves as supplemental information to employment
  applications and letters of inquiry about possible
  job openings.
* informs your personal contacts--friends, relatives,
  colleagues, alumni, former employers, etc.--and
  those writing letters of recommendation and providing reference information for you about your
  job objective and qualifications.

Since resumes are multi-functional, there is no single best resume
format or style. Resumes are more or less effective, depending on your
goals, style, and audience. The most effective resumes focus upon your
unique qualities and experiences and are highly personalized and results-
oriented. Ideally, then, your resume should:

* focus on the employer's needs.
* communicate your job-related abilities rather
  than your past or present job duties.
* stress your productivity and extent of contributions.
* indicate where you want to go rather than where

          you have been.
        * create an immediate favorable impression.
        * be appealing to the eye, easy to read, and
          dignified in appearance.
        * be concise.
        * communicate that you are a responsible and pur-
          poseful person who gets things done (Lathrop,
          1977; Germann and Arnold).

    Employers receive and quickly dispense with hundreds of resumes.
Most resumes do not catch the reader's interest. Therefore, the challenge is to make your resume stand out from the rest. At the very least,
you should avoid these common resume pitfalls frequently identified by
employers and placement specialists:

        * too long
        * poor layout
        * misspellings
        * poorly typed and printed
        * lengthy phrases, sentences, and paragraphs
        * poor punctuation and grammar
        * irrelevant information
        * too much technical jargon
        * hard to understand
        * unexplained time gaps
        * does not convey accomplishments
        * text does not support objective
        * unclear objective (Jackson, 1981: 15).

Lathrop (1977: 115-121) provides a handy checklist of 96 appropriate and
inappropriate characteristics by which to evaluate your completed resume.
Similar to the list of common resume writing mistakes, this checklist
would be useful to review _prior to_ writing your resume. Thus, while
there is no perfect resume, there are many ineffective resumes which fail
to avoid the common pitfalls.

PREPARATION AND WRITING

    Producing a resume is a two-stage process: preparation and writing.
The preparation stage involves developing a solid data-base from which
to initiate the writing stage. However, most people fail to devote sufficient time to this stage. A thorough preparation means conducting a
comprehensive self-inventory based upon a complete review of your work,
education, and related experiences as well as a clear understanding of
your accomplishments and skills. The comprehensive data-base you generated in Chapter V on your abilities, skills, and qualifications will
directly assist you in completing this preparatory stage.

    We recommend that you write your own resume. This is a time con-
suming process, but the final product will reflect _your_ goals, abilities,
and style. For a minimum of $50.00, commercial resume writing services
will quickly produce a resume for you. However, they tend to follow a
standard format which does not incorporate your unique qualities and
abilities. Save money and retain quality control by doing it yourself.

CHOOSING FORMATS

Many excellent books and guides are available on how to write an effective resume. You may wish to consult several of these for examples of different types of resumes and corresponding formats. But do so with a critical eye. Since we do not wish to duplicate these efforts, we present some basic concepts and outline a useful strategy for developing your own resume and for evaluating others' resumes.

We do not suggest, as do many books and guides, one best way of writing a resume. Depending on your goals, style, and audience, there are many alternative routes to writing an effective resume. Most important of all, you should analyze your audience and develop your resume in reference to your audience. Remember, you are not writing the resume to your mother, spouse, or yourself. Using your common sense will be far more effective than following the rigid advice and homilies of others on how to write a good resume. Audiences differ and so should resumes in communicating to diverse audiences.

Resume writers ordinarily choose one of four types of resumes:

* chronological resume
* functional resume
* combination resume
* resume letter

Examples of these are presented in Appendix B. Each resume has advantages and disadvantages, although our preference leans toward the combination resume.

The _chronological resume_ seems to be everyone's favorite; it is the standard resume, characteristic of probably 80 percent of all resumes written today. Academic curriculum vitae usually are written in this format. Chronological resumes also are known in some quarters as "obituary resumes." In other words, if you died today and we looked at your chronological resume, we could write a standard three-inch column obituary about what you did in the past. Furthermore, some people feel that this resume "kills" your chances of changing careers because it locks you into your past. This resume often lacks a job objective. Work experience usually is listed in reverse chronological order with no attempt to communicate your abilities and skills. Dates appear first, followed by the names and locations of former employers and your positions. It may also include a brief statement of your formal duties and and responsibilities. While this is the easiest resume to write, as traditionally written it is the least exciting and effective type of resume for someone making a major career change. It forces the reader to interpret your background and qualifications in relationship to his or her needs and biases. You play a game of chance with this resume, a chance your esoteric and helter-skelter background will interest someone enough to interview you.

If you insist on using the chronological resume format, you should at least improve on its past weaknesses. For example, de-emphasize your employment dates by listing them at the end of each position. Eliminate some of the extraneous information which usually clutters this type of resume, such as height, weight, hobbies, and references.

Chronological resumes have several advantages and disadvantages. While they are much maligned by "expert" resume writers today, they do have one major advantage. Since most employers still think in chronological terms and are familiar with this type of resume, they expect to encounter it. Indeed, if you wrote a functional or combination resume and sent it in response to an academic vacancy, it would probably be rejected because of its uniqueness as well as its violation of the traditional norm of chronology. An audience that thinks in traditional terms will not necessarily appreciate a non-chronological resume. After all, one of the major advantages of a chronological resume for employers is that they can interpret your experience and qualifications in relationship to *their* needs; they use *their* "judgment" to discriminate one candidate from another. On the other hand, functional and combination resumes enable you to structure the thinking of your audience around your functional categories; this places you in a stronger position with a prospective employer. In fact, you may both exceed and raise his or her expectations!

Chronological resumes have other advantages too. They are relatively easy to write. You can highlight simply and effectively stable employment history. Employers find these resumes useful outlines for discussing your past employment record during the interview.

The disadvantages of the chronological format are particularly evident for individuals changing or entering careers. Employment gaps stand out sharply. The format may emphasize too many unrelated job experiences. Your strongest competencies are not emphasized to your advantage. Overall, this format does not provide the best presentation of your background and abilities if you are trying to enter a new occupation.

Since the majority of job applicants use this format, you can make your chronological resume stand out from the rest if it is well written and tastefully designed. You can do this by (1) including a functional work objective and (2) writing functional descriptions of your work experience immediately following your previous position titles and places of employment.

The *functional resume* tends to be the logical opposite of the chronological resume. It de-emphasizes dates, positions, and responsibilities and emphasizes qualifications, skills, and related accomplishments. Beginning with a functional job objective, it organizes skills into functional categories. The functional resume is internally coherent because all elements focus on an objective and an audience. This resume essentially outlines abilities and transferable skills and tells employers what you will most likely do for them.

Functional resumes are especially useful for individuals lacking work experience or for those trying to enter a new occupation where they lack direct job-related experience. While this is one of the most difficult resumes to compose, it is much easier once you have developed the data-base on your objective, skills, and accomplishments in Chapters V and VI.

Lathrop (1977: 61-112) prefers calling functional resumes "qualification briefs." We believe they are fine for inexperienced individuals.

However, functional resumes can communicate "fluff" if not expertly structured around concrete experience and a clear objective. Lacking content, they may raise more questions than you want to answer. Nonetheless, a well-structured functional resume can be an outstanding document for presenting your skills.

Like chronological resumes, functional resumes have both advantages and disadvantages. The major advantages include (1) stressing skills which are of interest to the employer or are readily marketable, (2) covering employment gaps with ease, (3) informing employers that skills are transferable to different work environments, and (4) enabling applicants to include non-paid experiences as part of their "work" history. Furthermore, since this type of resume is not used by most applicants, it is likely to attract more attention than resumes in the other formats. Disadvantages include (1) having to provide evidence of additional work history to curious employers, (2) not allowing previous employment to be highlighted, and (3) encountering difficulty in writing this type of resume--if you do not thoroughly study your skills and accomplishments. Overall, audiences will differ in terms of their degree of acceptance or rejection of functional resumes.

The _combination resume_ combines the best elements of the chronological and functional formats. Although similar to the functional resume in describing and explaining experience, this format includes a brief employment history section.

Combination resumes stress skills and competencies yet include names and dates. These resumes enable you to stress your qualifications in both chronological and functional terms as well as handle employment history easily. As such, this is a unique and complete resume.

These resumes have one major problem: they are usually difficult to write. In addition, their functional and chronological sections may overlap and create annoying redundancy. Since they take longer to read, they should be concise, very well written, and attractively laid out.

The _resume letter_ should be used when your resume is not available or if you determine the situation is not appropriate for sending a resume. This letter is addressed to a person in an organization that interests you. Your goal is to communicate your specific skills and qualifications and to show how they relate to the employer's needs. The letter also provides an opportunity to make a direct, personal presentation to the employer based upon your organizational and individual research (Chapter VIII). The resume letter should follow the same rules for writing a good resume: be concise, use action verbs, identify the needs of the employer, and show how your abilities and skills can meet the employer's needs.

The format you choose should reflect your own personal situation. Consider your qualifications, your objective, your work history, and the kind of employer you want before you select a style. The functional and combination resumes are conceptually superior to chronological resumes, especially if your audience understands the superior quality of such resumes and knows what type of person they want to hire. These resumes are also the most effective ones in getting interviews which result in job offers (Lathrop, 1977; Germann and Arnold). Functional and combination resumes communicate what it is you _want to do_, what it is you _have done_, what it is you _can do_, and what it is you _will most likely do_ for prospective employers. But there is no inherent superiority to any of these resumes--only audiences with different expectations, likes, and dislikes. We recommend writing a combination resume which emphasizes functional categories more than chronological ones, because it is important to communicate your transferable skills when making a career change out of education. Furthermore, this resume best bridges the gap between traditional and functional thinking. It should satisfy all audiences without alienating any particular ones. But remember, _we_ are not your audience, _we_ will not be interviewing you, and _we_ will not be offering you a job. Therefore, use _your_ own judgement based upon _your_ information on _your_ audience. If you are uncertain about which format to use, experiment with the chronological, functional, and combination styles to see which one has the most advantages for you.

After choosing your format, you will be ready to organize pertinent information for producing an effective resume. Organization and production should follow four distinct steps:

* Step 1: Creating a Data-Base
* Step 2: Producing a First Draft
* Step 3: Critiquing and Evaluating
* Step 4: Production and Distribution

CREATING A DATA-BASE

It is essential that you organize a sufficient data-base from which to develop each section of the resume. The data-base is developed by taking an inventory of your experience and motivated abilities and skills. Begin by taking several separate sheets of paper on which you list as many of the ten items outlined below which are relevant to you. Next, write all facts pertinent to each item. Be as thorough and detailed as possible. Go for volume; you can always condense the information later.

1. _Contact Information_:
   * _full name_
   * _address_: include both office and home
   * _telephone number_: list all contact numbers
2. _Career or Job Objective_: Refer to Chapter VI for defining your work objective. When transferring this information to your resume, the objective should appear at the top immediately following your name, address, and telephone number. While some people consider this to be an unnecessary, pretentious, and optional item, we see it as necessary, professional, and thoughtful. You have one of two options in this matter: place an objective on the resume; or leave it off, but include it in your accompanying cover letter. If you put it in your cover letter, you won't have to re-type your resume every time you want to focus

your objective more specifically on a particular position. This is especially true if you have gone through the expense of having your resume professionally printed. Use your own judgment. We still prefer the objective at the top of the resume, because it should be the central focal point from which all other elements in the resume emanate and are interrelated. If you know what you want to do and can state your objective in general terms, it can be used repeatedly for different positions, assuming you know your audience. The relative impact of these different strategies may be the old proverbial "Six one way, half a dozen another." It may not make much difference in the end. But be sure you communicate, in some manner, your career direction. Otherwise, you might as well forget everything we have said thus far, and take your chances by conducting a traditionally disorganized job search using a weak chronological resume.

3. *Education*: List information for the following categories on your master data sheets:
   * *degree(s)*: major(s) and minor(s); date(s). Place highest degree first.
   * *school(s)*: location(s)
   * *highlights*: extracurricular activities; honors; awards; research; publications; significant projects.
   * *special training/courses*: separate from your degrees but relevant to your work objective.

4. *Work Experience*: Include all paid and non-paid experiences--full-time, part-time, and summer employment; internships; and significant volunteer work. For each experience item, list the information in the following manner:

   Job title, Organization, Location. Functional description of work performed. Significant contributions/achievements. Demonstrated skills and abilities. Dates of service.

   Stress items which point toward your effectiveness-- raises, promotions, expansion of duties, etc. Refer to Chapter V and Appendix A for identifying and stating your work-related motivated abilities, skills, and qualifications.

5. *Military Experience*:
   * *rank, service*.
   * *assignments, dates*.
   * *significant contributions/achievements*.
   * *demonstrated skills and abilities*.
   * *reserve status*.

6. *Community/Civic Involvement*: Include offices held,

organizations, dates; significant contributions, projects; demonstrated skills and abilities.
7. *Professional Affiliations and/or Status*:
   * *memberships, organizations.*
   * *offices held, projects.*
   * *certification, licenses.*
8. *Special Skills*: Foreign languages--read, write, speak. Others.
9. *Interests and Activities*: Avocations, hobbies, etc. Can you think of anything that supports your objective?
10. *Miscellaneous*:
    a. Salary requirements: Amount expected? Bare minimum needed?
    b. Extent of job-related travel acceptable.
    c. Are you willing to relocate? To where?
    d. When can you be available to start work?
    e. References: May present employer be contacted for a reference? How you identified individuals who can attest to your past or present performance?
    f. Anything else you think is important.

After completing this step, you will have the essential data for writing the various sections of your resume.

PRODUCING A FIRST DRAFT

Your next step is to condense the information on your master data sheets, merge it with your abilities/skills information, and write an initial draft of your resume. As you do this, you should consider the following *general guidelines* for producing an effective resume:

1. *Format and Organization*: The internal organization of your resume can include several items. The following are *highly recommended* for all resumes:
   a. contact information: name, address, telephone number
   b. objective
   c. qualifications or a series of functional experience categories
   d. educational background
   You should consider including some of the following *optional* elements:
   a. work history or professional experience
   b. publications and presentations
   c. memberships and affiliations
   d. personal data
   e. references
   f. miscellaneous information: hobbies, licenses, special skills, personal summary statement
   One of the most effective resumes would combine several highly recommended and optional elements within a one or two-page format. The format should

be enticing to the reader's eyes. Avoid cluttering; provide ample spacing and margins so the reader can breathe. Knowing that our eyes tend to focus on the middle and move from left to right, we suggest using the following format:

a. Center your name, address, and telephone number at the top of the paper. Capitalize your name.

b. Capitalize all headings and run them along the left side of the paper.

c. Place all descriptive material to the right of the headings.

You should examine other formats. However, we believe this one is the kindest to yourself and your audience, because it is easy to follow and read.

2. *Length*: We agree with most resume advisors on the appropriateness of the one or two-page resume. The one-page resume is preferred, because it is concise and easy to read; it does not lose the reader's attention as he or she turns pages. This is a definite asset when you realize that many employers must read 500 resumes or more in a few hours. At first the notion of a one-page resume may pose problems for you, especially if you already possess an "impressive" 10 to 20-page chronological academic resume. But don't worry. Many executives with 25-years of experience, who are making $100,000 or more a year, manage to get all their major qualifications onto a one-page resume. If they can do it, so can you.

3. *Sequencing*: The sequence of elements will vary depending on the type of resume you decide to use. The *chronological resume* should have the following order of elements:

a. contact information

b. objective

c. work experience (or education, depending on your objective and audience)

d. education

e. optional personal statement

We recommend the following order of elements for a *functional resume*:

a. contact information

b. objective

c. presentation of transferable skills supported by achievements ("areas of effectiveness")

d. education

e. optional personal statement

A *combination resume* should include the following sequence of elements:

a. contact information

b. objective

    c. presentation of transferable skills supported
       by achievements
    d. brief outline of work history
    e. education
    f. optional personal statement

In all three types of resumes, always place the _most important information_ first on your resume. If your work experience is most relevant to your objective, place it immediately following the objective.

4. _Details and Balance_: Lengthy, detailed descriptions often fail to secure an audience and can be a liability rather than an asset. Get to the point. Emphasize specific areas of expertise beneficial to the employer. Keep it neat, organized, and balanced.

5. _Abbreviations_: Do not use abbreviations. Use full descriptions and spellings.

6. _Documentation_: The text of your resume should support your objective with specific documentation, much like you would support comments in a research paper with references to relevant literature.

7. _Consistency_: Format should remain consistent, i.e., tense of verbs, order of information, layout, etc.

8. _Language_: Use crisp, succinct, and pithy language. For example, avoid stating an objective as follows:

> "I would like to work with a consulting firm where I can develop new programs and utilize my decision-making and system engineering experience. I hope to improve your organization's business profits."

Instead, re-word the objective so it reads like this:

> "An increasingly responsible research and development position, where proven decision-making and system engineering abilities will be utilized for improving organizational productivity."

Use the first person, but do not refer to yourself as "I" or "the author." Active verbs and parallel sentence structure are important. Avoid introductory and wind-up phrases like "My duties included...," or, "My responsibilities were to...," or "Position description reads as follows..." Do not use jargon unless it is appropriate to the situation: "can program in Fortran and COBAL."

9. _Appearance_: The communication of important aspects of your resume can be emphasized through various visual techniques--spacing, marginal descriptions, centered headlines, underlining, all caps treatment. Be sure to develop an attractive, uncrowded format.

Individual elements within the resume should follow these major guidelines:

1. _Contact Information_: This information should always appear at the top of the resume and include:
   a. _full name_: State your full professional name and avoid the coldness of abbreviations, such as "I. T. Snell." Don't appear pompous and distant by using titles such as "Dr., Ph.D., Mr., Mrs., Ms."
   b. _address_: Use your home mailing address. If you are at a temporary address, include both permanent and temporary addresses. Don't forget to include your zip code.
   c. _telephone number_: List telephone numbers you can be reached at during most periods of the day and night. If you are highly mobile, enlist a telephone answering service or buy a relatively inexpensive telephone recorder/ answering device; many sell for under $100.

2. _Statement of Objective_: Your objective should be a concise statement of what you want to do and what you have to offer The position you seek is "what you want to do" and your qualifications are "what you have to offer." Your objective should be stated in terms of your strongest qualifications which are likely to be identical to an employer's needs. It should communicate what you have to offer an employer without emphasizing what you expect the employer to do for you. In other words, your objective should be work-centered, not self-centered; it should not contain trite terms which emphasize what you want: opportunity for advancement; position working with people; a challenging position; a progressive company; a creative position; etc. Such terms are viewed as "canned" resume language which say little of value about you.

   Objectives may be stated in various styles and at different levels of sophistication. At the most basic level, an objective may be stated as an occupational designation: "Mechanical Engineer" or "Elementary Education Teacher" or "Accountant." An objective also may be stated as an occupational designation with a specialty area: "Electrical Engineer--Research and Design" or "Special Education Teacher--Learning Disabilities" or "Public Accountant--Taxes."

   The following are examples of weak and strong objective statements. Various styles are also presented:

Weak Objectives

   "Management position which will utilize business education degree and will provide opportunities for rapid advancement."

"A position in social services which will allow me to work with people in a helping capacity."

"A position in Personnel Administration with a progressive firm."

"Sales Representative with opportunity for advancement."

Stronger Objectives

"To work in _computer software development_ involving scientific and graphic applications and operating systems."

"A public relations position which will maximize opportunities to develop and implement programs, to organize people and events, and to communicate positive ideas and images. Effective in public speaking and in managing a publicity/promotional campaign."

"A position as a General Sales Representative for a pharmaceutical house which will use chemistry background and ability to work on a self-directed basis."

"A position in data analysis combining skills in mathematics, computer programming, and deductive reasoning."

"Retail Management position which will utilize sales/customer service experience and creative abilities for product display and merchandising. Long term goal: Progression to merchandise manager with corporate-wide responsibilities for product lines. Willing to travel and relocate."

"Responsible position in investment research and analysis. Interests include securities analysis, financial planning, and portfolio management. Long range goal: to become a Chartered Financial Analyst. Willing to travel and relocate."

Another way of stating an objective is to utilize information generated entirely from an individual's Motivated Abilities Pattern (Chapters V and VI). For example, you might begin with a lengthy MAP objective:

"A position as a _manager_ or _team leader_ working with ideas, concepts, methods, techniques, systems, structures, relationships, projects, and people; using _abilities_ in researching, investigating, organizing, synthesizing, planning, strategizing, evaluating, promoting, communicating, implementing, and executing; where the _conditions of work_ include groups, organizations, enterprise, feedback, visibility, some structure, and opportunity for development; which results in establishing respect and rapport while _developing programs and organizational units_."

The objective should be condensed into a crisp three to five line statement and placed at the top of the resume.

3. _Description of Experience_: Do not list formal duties and responsibilities. Describe your experience in functional terms as outlined in Chapter V. Stress your accomplishments. Use _action verbs_ (Chapter V and Appendix A) in outlining your experiences and qualifications: managed, created, supervised, coordinated, planned, analyzed, and initiated. Be sure everything you state here is related to your objective.

4. _Education_: Make this simple, particularly if you have a Ph.D. Don't look over-educated or under-educated. In general, this item should appear after your objective, qualifications, and experience. Educators should especially de-emphasize their educational training, unless it enhances their marketability outside education. Do not unnecessarily draw attention to your educational background and thus reinforce the negative stereotypes many employers already have of educators by going into great detail about your wonderful educational achievements. Your degrees may threaten many prospective employers. You can always deal with the educational question during an interview.

5. _Personal Information_: You may want to disregard this section altogether. If you include it, keep it brief and to the point. Avoid extraneous information, such as your height, weight, hair color, state of health, and other personal characteristics, unless they are essential to your job objective. In some cases this information merely raises negative questions. If you are single, divorced, or separated, so what? Your sex and marital life are not your employer's business, unless you make it so. If you are single, and you are applying for a job requiring considerable travel, identifying your marital status can be a plus in your favor. On the other hand, if a job requires stability, and you are married and have children, include your marital status--but don't include the names of your children, even though you are proud of them! As for age, if it will help, put it down. Specify your age in years ("35") rather than following the traditional "Date of Birth," "Born," or "Birthdate" categories. We know you weren't "hatched," and a number implies your age. Leave your "age" off altogether if it serves no useful purpose, particularly if you are middle-aged or over. You may wish to include some other personal information for strengthening your objective. For example, your personal data could

include the following:

"35 . . . in excellent health . . . married . . .
two children . . . enjoy challenges . . . interested
in productivity"

Alternatively, you could write a personal statement about
yourself so that the reader might remember you in particular. However, avoid trite statements. See Lathrop
(1977: 81-112) for examples of the personal statements.

6. _References_: Never list your references on your resume.
Always control these yourself. Be sure to inform your
references of your job search activities. Give them a
copy of your resume so they understand your objective and
qualifications. Your choices are two-fold: leave this
section off altogether since it is an empty category
without names, or use the following statement:

"References: Available upon request."

We see no useful purpose served by stating this. It
merely takes up valuable space that can be allocated to
a more thorough discussion of your qualifications. If
you drop this category completely, any half-way intelligent reader should know it implies you do have references,
but you will make them available upon request. Employers
will ask you for references when the time is right--which
is usually during the interview. Sometimes they never ask
for references nor contact the individuals on your list.
However, it is good practice to list the names of your
professional references on a separate sheet of paper and
to carry the list with you to interviews. The list
should be typed and should contain the full name, title,
business address, and telephone number of each person.

7. _Miscellaneous Information_: Other possible information
to include on your resume includes special skills, professional memberships and affiliations, and hobbies.
If you have special licenses or special training and
skills (can program a computer, invented the lazer gun)
relevant to your job objective, include this information
on your resume. However, most people understand the
nature of professional memberships and affiliations:
you do little other than send an organization your yearly
dues; it is another empty category which takes up valuable
space on resumes. Hobbies are like your height and
weight; few enhance your objective, and most distract by
raising unnecessary questions about your sanity or
"normality." Nonetheless, you may engage in some hobbies or activities that will strengthen your professional
and personal marketability, such as writing books, articles, and speeches-- or composing music. Such hobbies
stress your organizational, communication, and creative
abilities. Other hobbies may leave a lasting positive
impression on the reader and thus he or she will remember
you in particular. But swimming, collecting stamps, and

playing cards may communicate the wrong things--you're
a jock, withdrawn, or a gambler. Never, never, never,
put your salary expectations on your resume! Salary
is the last thing you discuss in a job interview, and
it is negotiable (Chapter X).

In writing this first draft of your resume, remember these major
points:

1. Your resume is your personal *advertisement*.
2. The purpose of the resume is to get you an *interview*.
3. Take the offensive by developing a resume that *structures the reader's thinking* in your favor.
4. The resume should *generate positive thinking*, rather than raise negative questions or confuse readers.
5. The resume should be focused on your *audience* and should communicate clearly what it is you can do.
6. Always be *honest* without being stupid. Stress your positives; do not confess your negatives.

CRITIQUING AND EVALUATING

After completing the first draft, ask several individuals who are
familiar with your abilities, skills, and objective to evaluate your
resume. Be prepared for all kinds of feedback. Some comments will be
valid; others should be taken, politely, with caution. Incorporate any
advice you consider to be relevant to your situation. In assessing the
overall reactions to your resume, address the following considerations:

1. *Overall Appearance*: Do you want to read it? Is it easy to read? Does it look professional? Does it create an immediate favorable impression?
2. *Contact Information*: Is it clearly presented on the top of the first page? Are both permanent and temporary addresses provided? Do you provide both day and evening telephone numbers where you can be reached or where a message can be left? If you have a two-page resume, does your name appear at the top of the second page?
3. *Objective*: Is it clear? Is it stated in terms of your strongest qualifications which are likely to match the employer's needs? Is it reasonably short? Does it convey your career purpose?
4. *Organization*: Are your strongest qualifications presented immediately under your objective? Do your strong points stand out? Is layout consistent?
5. *Content*: Do the contents support and substantiate your objective? Do you stress skills, accomplishments, and results, rather than duties? Do phrases begin with action verbs? Do you use short, action-oriented phrases instead of full sentences? Has extraneous material been eliminated?
6. *Length*: Is it brief (one page, not more than two)?

For one of the most systematic and comprehensive self-evaluations of your resume, consult Lathrop's checklist of 96 appropriate and inappropriate resume characteristics. The checklist evaluates all possible elements in your resume under six general categories: appearance and format, organization, objective, content, writing style, and overview (Lathrop, 1977: 115-121).

PRODUCTION AND DISTRIBUTION

After completing the revisions, you will need to decide how best to produce and distribute the resume. Every resume advisor gives different advice on these points. The importance of knowing your audience is still the best single piece of advice we can give you.

If you are competing for a position with 500 other applicants, you will need to vary your production strategy so it results in getting your resume noticed among the others. However, you will probably not be competing for such highly competitive jobs because you will be seeking jobs with less competition in the hidden job market (Chapter IX). The highly competitive jobs are listed in the newspapers, and in general you want to avoid them. If you decide to shoot for such competitive positions, make your resume stand out.

Let's assume you will be seeking the higher-level positions where there is less competition and larger stakes. In this case, your resume should befit the type of position you are seeking and it should look professional. Such a resume can be produced in the following manners:

1. *Home production*: Home produce your resume on an IBM Selectric typewriter by using interchangeable typing elements and a carbon ribbon. You can achieve a professional looking resume which also communicates your own personal style. In addition, you maintain the flexibility to make any internal alterations without incurring the expenses of a typesetter.

2. *Typesetting*: Have a printer typeset and print a master copy of the resume. Typesetting may cost you $30 per page and up. While you will achieve a very professional looking resume, typesetting has its negatives: (1) costly, (2) you lose control and the flexibility to change elements in the resume, and (3) it may appear *too* professional or too slick and thereby give the impression to employers that you may have been too lazy to write your own resume, even though you did do it yourself! Use your own judgment on typesetting the resume. Again, know your audience. Some audiences prefer the extreme professional look whereas others like the home-grown professional look.

3. *Paper*: Use a high quality paper. A conservative off-white, ivory, light tan, or light gray paper is preferable to other colors. Bond paper will cost anywhere from 2¢ to 6¢ per sheet, and it can be

purchased through major stationary stores and printers. Other colors are less desirable, test poorly, and appear less professional. However, if you are competing with hundreds of other applicants for one of those low stakes positions, take your chances with a different colored paper so you will stand out amidst the crowd--for better or for worse!

4. _Reproduction_: Reproduce your resume by using an off-set process or a high quality copying machine that gives you as good as, if not better than, original quality reproduction. The off-set process is relatively inexpensive, ranging from 2¢ to 5¢ per copy, and the quality is usually very good. Make sure your original has dark, clear type, and no errors. Your master should not be on erasable bond or onion skin paper since it is very difficult to reproduce resumes on this type of paper.

Producing your resume in these manners will be relatively inexpensive, yet it will look very professional. Whatever you do, please do not get cheap at this stage by (1) making copies of your resume on a chintzy copy machine, or (2) substitute 1¢ a sheet mimeograph paper for 3¢ a sheet high quality, off-white bond paper. At best you will probably save $5.00 on 100 copies. This is not the place to cut corners since your resume is your calling card for getting interviews. Pay the extra pennies, nickels, and dimes required to produce a professional looking resume.

Since a resume is your advertisement to get an interview, we recommend that you carry extra copies with you. You never know when your resume will come in handy. You meet new people constantly, and many people may be interested in looking at your resume or passing it on to others. Indeed, as we note in Chapter IX, the resume plays an important role in prospecting, networking, and conducting informational interviews.

Other distribution networks involve sending your resume in response to job listings in the newspapers and trade journals. You may also choose to conduct mass mailing by "shot-gunning" a few hundred organizations with resumes or engage in direct application by sending several letters requesting informational interviews. Such contacts usually require the use of cover letters, resumes, and telephone calls. We discuss the relative merits of doing this in Chapter IX.

Given these different distribution networks, you should be prepared to copy and distribute numerous resumes. At times you will be playing the odds against 300 to 500 other players with your resume. At other times, your resume will be the only game in town. Be prepared to play the different games with different odds. Your resume is your calling card for moving outside of education. It must be a first-class professional document. Treat it like a loving member of your family-- with great concern, attention, and care.

FURTHER GUIDANCE

While we have presented the basics for developing an effective resume and included examples in Appendix B, there are numerous other sources you can consult for further guidance. However, be careful with several of the mass market resume writing books. Many teach you bad habits, such as how to write poor versions of the traditional helter-skelter chronological resume. The best resume guides address objectives, skills, and audiences in relationship to the internal structure of the resume.

Several resume guides are consistent with our perspective. If you need further guidance, we recommend the following books, in order of importance:

Richard Lathrop, _Who's Hiring Who_ (Berkeley, Calif.: Ten Speed Press, 1977).

Tom Jackson, _The Perfect Resume_ (Garden City, N.J.: Anchor Books, 1981).

John McLaughlin and Stephen Merman, _Writing a Job-Winning Resume_ (Englewood Cliffs, N.J.: Prentice-Hall, 1980).

Harold Dickhut, _Professional Resume/Job Search Guide_ (Chicago, Ill.: Management Counselors, Inc., 1978).

Robert Jameson, _The Professional Job Changing System_ (Parsippany, N.J.: Performance Dynamics, 1978).

Always remember to write your own resume. Never copy or edit someone else's. Your resume should reflect _your_ goals, abilities, skills, and style.

CHAPTER VIII

RESEARCHING ORGANIZATIONS, INDIVIDUALS, AND COMMUNITIES

Research is a discovery process involving investigative strategies for uncovering information. Within the context of your job search, research integrates the individual job search activities and provides feedback for adapting strategies to the realities of the job market. Although we present this as a separate step, research is a continuous process which should be conducted in all stages of your job search campaign. While your resume is designed to get you interviews, your research largely will determine where to target your resume. Research assists in identifying skills, formulating a lifework objective, writing the resume, and conducting informational and job interviews. Without an active research campaign, your job search will lack content and direction for accomplishing your goals.

RESEARCH EXPECTATIONS

Most people are reluctant to initiate a research campaign which involves using libraries and telephoning and meeting new people (Figler: 133-159). Such reluctance is due in part to the lack of knowledge on how to conduct research and where to find resources, and in part to a certain cultural shyness which inhibits individuals from initiating contacts with strangers. However, research is not a difficult process. After all, most people conduct research daily as they read and converse with others about problems. This daily research process needs to be specified and focused on your job search campaign. As an educator, we believe you are particularly adept at conducting the research necessary for an effective job campaign.

Research serves several purposes when adapted to your job search campaign. First, knowing the "who, what, when, and where" of organizations and individuals is essential for targeting your resume and conducting informational and job interviews. Second, the research component should broaden your perspective on the job market in relationship to your motivated abilities, objectives, and interests. Since there are over 20,000 different job titles as well as several million job markets, even a full-time research campaign will uncover only a small segment of the job market relevant to your interests.

A third purpose of research is to better understand how to relate your motivated abilities to specific jobs and work environments. The real value of SIMA becomes evident in this phase of your job search. Once you research and understand the critical requirements of a given job in a specific work environment, you can assess the appropriateness of that job for you vis-a-vis your motivated abilities pattern.

Fourth, researching organizations and individuals should result in systematically constructing a set of contacts for developing your job search network. One of your major research goals should be to compile names, addresses, and telephone numbers of individuals who may become important resources in your new network of job contacts.

A fifth purpose of research is to learn the _languages_ of alternative jobs and careers. While educators' disciplines have specialized languages, jargon, and vocabularies, so do disciplines, jobs, and careers outside education. You can learn to better converse in these languages by reading trade journals, annual reports, pamphlets, and other organizational literature as well as talking with people in various occupational fields. Knowing these languages--especially asking and answering intelligent questions in the language of the employer--is important for conducting successful referral and job interviews.

Finally, research should result in bringing some degree of structure, coherence, and understanding to the inherently decentralized, fragmented, and chaotic job market. Without research, you place yourself at the mercy of chance and luck; thus, you become a subject of your environment. Research best enables you to take control of your situation. In the job search, _information is power_.

TARGETING PEOPLE AND PLACES

Four major job search targets need to be researched: occupational alternatives, organizations, individuals, and communities. Your initial research should help familiarize you with _job and career alternatives_ to education. For example, the United States Department of Labor identifies approximately 20,000 job titles. Most individuals are occupationally illiterate and unaware of the vast array of available jobs and careers. Therefore, it is essential to investigate occupational alternatives in order to broaden your perspective on the job market.

Organizations are your second research target. After completing research on occupational alternatives, identify specific organizations which you are interested in learning more about. Next, compile lists of names, addresses, and telephone numbers of important individuals in each organization. Also, write and telephone the organizations for information, such as an annual report and recruiting literature. The most important information you should be gathering concerns the organizations' _goals, structures, functions, problems, and projected future opportunities and development_. Since you invest part of your life in such organizations, treat them as you would a stock market investment. Compare and evaluate different organizations. You may encounter some dying organizations. Other organizations are young, growing, and vibrant. Avoid the dying ones, unless you are a specialist in organizational retrenchment!

Information on organizations is available through numerous sources. Reference librarians can be extremely valuable sources of information. They are more than just "keepers of the books." Tell them what you are doing, and ask them for assistance. It is best to ask specific questions since librarians often have a wealth of specialized knowledge. Most will get you started on your research by pointing you to the major directories on organizations and specialized libraries:

* *Directory of Professional and Trade Organizations*
* *Dun and Bradstreet's Million Dollar Directory*
* *Standard and Poor's Industrial Index*
* *Subject Collections: A Guide to Special Book Collections in Libraries*

Many librarians also know a great deal about specific communities. They should know where to locate regional, state, metropolitan, and city directories and magazines. Within their own community, they may be helpful in giving you other types of information, such as who is influential in the community or who might know who is influential. Always treat librarians with courtesy and kindness.

The librarian in charge of documents should be helpful in identifying information on government and quasi-governmental organizations as well as annual reports on selected businesses. In addition, you usually can get copies of annual reports, pamphlets, newsletters, and related materials by telephoning or writing an organization directly, or, if it is listed on the stock exchange, by contacting a stock broker. Additional sources of organizational information include trade publications, newspapers, professional associations, Chambers of Commerce, and state manufacturing associations.

Your third research target should be *individuals* who can help build your job search network; we provide a detailed discussion of this subject in the next chapter. From reading trade journals and magazines you will identify leaders in various specialized fields. Several reference books will further assist you in identifying these people:

* *American Men and Women in Science*
* *Standard and Poor's Corporation Records: Register of Corporations, Directors, and Executives*
* *Who's Who in America*
* *Who's Who in Commerce and Industry*
* *Who's Who in Finance and Industry*
* *Who's Who in the East*
* *Who's Who in the West*
* Directories of any professional association

As you focus on specific organizations, the key people will be well placed in organizations and most will have the power to hire (Bolles, 1980: 42-43). Seldom, if ever, will these people work in personnel offices. Finding who has the power to hire is not difficult once you realize it isn't someone in the personnel office. Formal organizational charts usually identify the key individuals as the heads of various operating units. As you research organizations, identify these key people and keep a list of their names, addresses, and telephone numbers for future reference. These people will most likely become the basic building blocks for developing your network of job contacts.

Your fourth research target is central to all other research targets and it may occur at any stage in your research. *Identifying the geographical area where you would like to work* will be one of your most

132

important decisions. Once you make this decision, other job search decisions and activities become easier. For example, if you live in a
small college town, you will probably need to move in order to change
careers. If you are a member of a two-career family, opportunities for
both you and your spouse will be greater in a growing metropolitan area.
If you decide to move to another community, you will need to develop a
long-distance job search campaign which has different characteristics
from a local campaign. As we outline in Chapter XII, a long-distance
campaign entails writing letters, making long-distance phone calls, and
visiting a community for strategic one to two-week periods during your
vacations.

Deciding where you want to live involves researching various
communities and comparing advantages and disadvantages of each. The
major writers on career planning give similar advice on how to approach
new communities. For example, Bolles outlines six principles to follow
when surveying communities from a distance:

1. Identify the different kinds of information you
   will need:
   a. Skills you demonstrate and enjoy.
   b. Specialties for using your skills.
   c. Organizations that you like, can use your
      skills, and are in your preferred geographical
      area.
   d. Names of organizations in your preferred cities.
   e. Problems of these organizations.
   f. Influential person(s) with the power to hire
      at your job level.
2. Categorize which information you can gather at
   your present location versus information you
   must get from your preferred cities.
3. Specify your time frame for finding a job.
4. Schedule a visit to your preferred city or cities.
5. Prior to your on-site visit, do as much research
   as possible on your communities by using
   a. newspapers
   b. Chambers of Commerce and City Halls
   c. local libraries and reference librarians
   d. personal contacts
   e. state and local government agencies and
      other groups
6. Practice your job search activities in your
   present community in order to get experience which
   can be transferred to other communities (Bolles,
   1980: 128-133).

Bernard Haldane Associates similarly identify four major steps in
conducting a long-distance job search campaign:

1. Decide where you want to live and work.
2. Conduct a limited Referral campaign where you
   now live.
3. Conduct a research program, designed to identify
   people and organizations that play a key role in
   the community in which you plan to live. Write

letters to key individuals to set up Referral
interviews.
4. Schedule a trip to your target area--spend two
weeks in the community developing networks
through Referral interviews (Germann and Arnold:
168-171).

Our advice on community-based research is similar to Bolles' and
Bernard Haldane Associates'. However, we also believe your research
should include non-job related information. After all, you will live
in the community, buy or rent a residence, perhaps send children to
school, and participate in community organizations or events. Often
these environmental factors are just as important to your happiness and
well-being as the particular job you accept. For example, you may be
leaving a $20,000 a year academic job for a position in your favorite
community--San Diego, California. But you may quickly find you are
worse off with your new $40,000 a year job, because you must pay
$250,000 for a home in San Diego which is nearly identical to your
$60,000 home in your college-town community. Consequently, it would be
foolish for you to take a new job without first researching several
facets of the community in addition to job opportunities.

Research on different communities can be initiated from your local
library. While most of this research will be historical in nature,
several resources will provide you with a current profile of various
communities. Statistical overviews and comparisons of states and cities
are found in the U.S. Census Data, The Book of the States, and the
Municipal Yearbook. Many libraries have a reference section of telephone books on various cities. If this section is weak or absent in
your local library, contact your local telephone company. They may
have a relatively comprehensive library of telephone books. In addition to giving you names, addresses, and telephone numbers, the Yellow
Pages are invaluable sources of information on the specialized structures of the public and private sectors of individual communities. The
library may also have state and community directories as well as sub-
scriptions to some state and community magazines and city newspapers.
Research magazine, journal, and newspaper articles on different communities by consulting references in the Reader's Guide to Periodical
Literature, the Social Science and Humanities Index, the New York Times
Index, and the Wall Street Journal Index.

After narrowing down the number of communities that interest you,
further research them in depth. Ask your relatives, friends, and acquaintances for contacts in the particular community; they may know
people whom you can write or telephone for information and referrals.
Once you have decided to focus on one community, visit it in order to
establish personal contacts with key reference points, such as the
local Chamber of Commerce, real estate firms, schools, libraries,
churches, Forty-Plus Club (if appropriate), government agencies, and
business firms and associations. Begin developing personal networks
based upon our research and referral strategies in the next chapter.
Subscribe to the local newspaper and to any community magazines which
help profile the community. Follow the help-wanted, society, financial,
and real estate sections of the newspaper--especially the Sunday edition.
Keep a list of names of individuals who appear to be in influential

community positions; you may want to contact these people for referrals. Write letters to set up informational interviews with key people; give yourself two months of lead time to complete your letter writing campaign (Germann and Arnold: 171). Your overall community research should focus on developing personal contacts which may assist you in both your job search and your personal move to the community.

UNCOVERING INFORMATION

Your most important research and information sources will be individuals you meet in conducting informational interviews. While published materials are important, they should be viewed as information sources for developing personal contacts which, in turn, will yield more information, referrals, and job leads.

Most published sources of information can be found in libraries or accessed by directly writing to individuals and organizations. Numerous directories, books, and articles are available which survey job opportunities in individual occupational fields, such as advertising, arts, communication, consulting, education, electronics, finance, health, international business, leisure, manufacturing, publishing, public administration, retail trades, and social services. Many of these sources provide useful lists of names, addresses, and telephone numbers. Most libraries will have some of these directories and books. If many cannot be found in your library, you may want to consult _Books in Print_ (Subject Index) and order the ones which appear to be most useful in your occupational and career area.

Reference sections of libraries have a wealth of primary sources from which you can conduct your initial research. Your major information categories and sources will include:

Career and Job Alternatives:	* _Dictionary of Occupational Titles_ * _Encyclopedia of Careers and Vocational Guidance_, William E. Hopke (ed.) * _Guide for Occupational Exploration_ * _Occupational Outlook Handbook_ * _Occupational Outlook Quarterly_
Industrial Directories:	* _Bernard Klein's Guide to American Directories_ * _Dun and Bradstreet's Middle Market Directory_ * _Dun and Bradstreet's Million Dollar Directory_ * _Encyclopedia of Business Information Sources_ * _Geographical Index_ * _Poor's Register of Corporations, Directors, and Executives_ * _Standard Directory of Advertisers_ * _The Standard Periodical Directory_ * _Standard and Poor's Industrial Index_ * _Standard Rate and Data Business_

	Publications Directory
	* *Thomas' Register of American Manufacturers*
Associations:	* *Directory of Professional and Trade Organizations*
	* *Encyclopedia of Associations*
Government Sources:	* *The Book of the States*
	* *Congressional Directory*
	* *Congressional Staff Directory*
	* *Congressional Yellow Book*
	* *Federal Directory*
	* *Federal Yellow Book*
	* *Municipal Yearbook*
	* *Taylor's Encyclopedia of Government Officials*
	* *United Nations Yearbook*
	* *United States Government Manual*
	* *Washington Information Directory*
Newspapers:	* *The Wall Street Journal*
	* Major city newspapers
	* Trade newspapers
	* Any city newspaper--especially the Sunday edition
Business Publications:	*Barron's, Business Week, Business World, Forbes, Fortune, Harvard Business Review, Money, Newsweek, Time, U.S. News and World Report*

Other Sources:
* Trade journals (refer to the *Directory of Special Libraries and Information Centers* and *Subject Collections: A Guide to Special Book Collections in Libraries* for information on specialized libraries of businesses, governments, and associations)
* Chambers of Commerce
* State Manufacturing Associations
* Federal, state, and local government agencies
* Telephone books--the Yellow Pages
* Civic and volunteer organizations
* Stock brokers
* Better Business Bureaus
* Richard Bolles, *What Color is Your Parachute*, Appendix B
* Eric Kocher, *International Jobs: Where They Are, How to Get Them*
* Trade books on "How to get a job"
* Any organization--write for annual report and any other literature outlining the goals, structure, functions, and problems of the organization

KNOWING WHAT'S IMPORTANT

Reviewing these published sources can be extremely time consuming if taken to the extreme. While you should examine several of them, do not spend an inordinate amount of your time reading and taking notes. Your time will be best spent in gathering information through meetings and conversations with key people. Remember, "the most important information, leading to the best jobs and the most fulfilling careers, comes through word of mouth, through contacts. Contacts lead to interviews, interviews lead to jobs, and jobs lead to careers" (Germann and Arnold: 69). Your primary goals in conducting research should be identifying people to contact, setting appointments, and asking the right questions which lead to more information and contacts. If you engage in these activities, you will know what is important when conducting research.

CHAPTER IX

PROSPECTING, NETWORKING, AND INFORMATIONAL INTERVIEWS

Approaches to getting a job vary. Some are best suited for finding low-level jobs; others are most effective for high-level positions. Since your career should advance to the higher levels, we present one approach which has proven to be very effective for many professionals.

Our approach is variously referred to as networking, conducting informational and referral interviews, using the "old boy" network, prospecting, capitalizing on informal relations, working your "contacts" and "connections," calling in your debts, playing the patron-client game, and being "ascriptive" and "particularistic." Another version of this approach is known as using your "pull." According to Stanat, it's okay to use people-resources when looking for a job:

Use pull. It gets big parts for marginal movie stars. It gets laws through Congress. It helps put multi-million dollar business deals across. And it can help you get a job. Pull is any force you can exert on the hiring process from inside the organization....There are six kinds of pull:
* Pull based on blood relationship.
* Pull based on business obligation.
* Pull based on friendship.
* Pull based on professional respect.
* Pull based on common bond.
* The pull of casual acquaintance.
CAUTION: When you use pull, be absolutely certain that you can do the job. And if you get the job, you must work extra hard to produce. The professional credibility of a friend or other connection is riding on your performance. So you must deliver (Stanat: 94-98).

Pull, then, means calling in your personal debts as well as becoming indebted to others when looking for a job. Stanat's word of caution places this approach in proper perspective. Using pull is an important way of _communicating_ to prospective employers that you are _qualified_ for a position; it does not mean that you should be hired because you know someone.

The approach we outline is a three-step process: (1) prospecting, (2) networking, and (3) conducting informational interviews. The purpose of this approach is to find jobs in the hidden job market which will lead to formal job interviews as well as job offers.

BEING PERSONAL AND PROFESSIONAL

Many myths exist about how society and the job market operate. One of the biggest myths is that people get jobs and advance their careers according to merit, qualifications, and "achievement" and "universalistic" criteria. This simply is not true, and it is one reason why so many people remain illiterate about how to function in the job market. Furthermore, this myth contributes to the hiring problems of employers.

Employers want to hire the best qualified individuals. However, it is difficult to determine who is best qualified because of the unstructured nature of the job market and because of a narrow and incomplete concept of "qualifications." Employers dread facing the uncertainty, risk, and costs of finding new employees. Communication within the job market is often disorganized, erratic, incomplete, and inaccurate. Employers who are able to attract applicants are often overwhelmed by the volume of responses. For example, we know of one Fortune 500 high technology firm which receives over 400,000 resumes and applications each year. A major aircraft manufacturing firm averages 45,000 resumes and applications each year. Faced with such numbers, how do employers manage to hire the best qualified individuals?

Given these organizational and communication problems, employers recruit and hire with incomplete information on candidates. They seek shortcuts which will minimize risks and costs yet maximize information on the quality of candidates. The shortcuts are found in the informal and personal system of network relationships which involve candidates, employers, friends, and professional acquaintances.

A major dilemma is evident in the hiring process. Employers want to hire people who have _both_ personal and professional qualifications. Hiring someone solely on the basis of their professional qualifications is bad hiring, because it neglects other equally important considerations. Nonetheless, many individuals still believe people are hired on the bases of merit and qualifications.

In fact, employers identify communicating, problem solving, analyzing, assessing, and planning as the most important transferable skills they desire in candidates (Stump: 95). These are the major on-the-job problems employers encounter with employees, problems which they desire to resolve by hiring better "qualified" individuals. Technical expertise usually ranks third or fourth in importance. At the same time, and with all due respect for affirmative action and equal opportunity principles, employers want to hire people they _like_. While assessing the technical qualifications of an individual does take time, knowing how well the individual will "fit into" an organization is much more difficult to assess. Employers do not talk about this problem in public--especially during interviews--because it is not considered "professional" to discuss "personal" or "particularistic" matters which do not directly relate to the formal job qualifications. Indeed, it is now illegal for employers to inquire about certain traditional personal considerations, such as sex, age, and marital status.

Assuming a person is professionally qualified, employers want to know if the person can communicate well. Will the person be loyal and trustworthy? Will the person work with us or against us? Employees that do not work out on the job usually are ones who encounter "personal" and "political" difficulties with their superiors and co-workers rather than professional problems relating to their qualifications to perform the job. As we noted earlier, personal and political conflicts are the major reasons for personnel turnovers relating to firings and forced resignations--not incompetence (Kennedy, 1980a; Irish: 181; Eisen: 26; Dubrin).

How, then, do employers manage to hire people they hope will meet both personal and professional requirements? Perhaps the best answer to this question is: with great difficulty and through several indirect methods of communication! Since employers want to hire productive people, they look for "signals" to indicate how productive an individual might be on the job (Granovetter, 1979: 86-87). Productivity signals may include educational level, specialized training, certification, previous work experience, personality characteristics, and demonstrated skills. While employers search for productivity signals through formal methods, such as screening, testing, and reference checks, most employers prefer to use informal methods such as personal contacts. As Granovetter notes,

> This preference can best be understood in the context
> of the costs and benefits of information: a) informa-
> tion gotten through personal contacts is less costly
> to obtain than by other means, in terms of both time
> and effort, and b) such information is also of better
> quality than that received from formal sources (1979:
> 87).

Since many people look productive on paper, screening hundreds or thousands of applications and resumes is potentially cost prohibitive and the results may be unreliable for employers. An informal screening process, based upon personal contacts, is more cost effective and trustworthy; it narrows the applicant pool to a manageable number and improves the reliability and quality of information on candidates. Furthermore, when high quality, intensive information is available on a specific candidate, the employer is less likely to view the individual in a preconceived or stereotypic manner (Granovetter, 1979: 89). This observation has important implications when dealing with employers who may have biases or prejudices against hiring educators (Chapter III). Using this informal system, educators can communicate more clearly to employers their ability to be productive.

Employers also gather information on candidates' personal qualities as signs of productivity. They look through letters of reference for clues concerning the trustworthy, dependable, loyal, friendly, cooperative, personable, and sociable nature of the individual. They call references and ask broad and leading questions: "What type of person is this candidate?" They interview the candidate and take notes on how the candidate "handled" him or herself in the interview: dress, physical appearance, eye contact, humor, personality, enthusiasm, logic, attitude, and poise. During interviews employers may ask very little about candidates' ability to handle the job in terms of their technical knowledge and skills. After finishing interviews, candidates often know no more about the content of the job than when they started. The reason is simple: employers assume you already have or can learn the technical qualifications--otherwise they would not have invited you to an interview. At this stage, in addition to confirming your ability to do the job, they want to know about your "body warmth"--will they _like_ you and will you "fit into" their organization.

You can assist employers in overcoming their fears and obstacles by developing a personal strategy for communicating your qualifications and signaling your productivity. Our strategy of prospecting, networking, and conducting informational interviews is realistic in recognizing that employers want to hire individuals who are both competent and likable.

Several standard methods of conducting a job search are alternatives to direct personal contacts. Djeddah identifies and evaluates 10 of these methods:

1. Go from door to door: almost worthless approach.
2. Sell some ideas and yourself: few can do this.
3. Buy a business: only 4 percent survive.
4. Place an ad about yourself in the newspaper: ludicrous and fruitless.
5. Apply for a government job: covers a small percentage of the market.
6. Hire your own employment agency to find you a job: expensive way to employ someone else.
7. Contact an executive recruiter: these flesh peddlers only cover 2 percent of the job market.
8. Find management consultants in the hope they will know about jobs with their client firms: covers 2 percent of the job market.
9. Answer want ads in the newspaper: high expectations and competition for low level jobs which only cover 7-8 percent of the job market.
10. Write letters directly to employers: the best of all these methods (Djeddah: 44-65).

Most of these methods are ineffective because they are based upon faulty assumptions about the structure of the job market as well as the structure of human relationships. Your single best strategy will be a highly personalized one of prospecting, networking, and conducting informational interviews. This strategy recognizes the realities of _both_ the job market and human behavior. It is effective in penetrating the hidden job market and uncovering high-level positions and opportunities related to your motivations, abilities, and skills. This strategy should occupy a majority of your job search time. It should result in formal job interviews and a job that is right for you.

The first thing you should do is re-examine your own myths and preconceptions about the role of merit and qualifications in the hiring process. Most employers do not--and seldom have--hired the best qualified individuals. The job market is not capable of yielding complete information on who are the best qualified candidates at any given time. Employers have no objective indicators for determining who has the best personal and technical qualifications. Instead, employers tend to hire individuals who know how to get hired, i.e., have the best strategy for convincing employers that they--rather than others--possess the best combination of personal and technical skills. Understanding this reality is important for being successful in the job market.

USING ROLE-SETS AND NETWORKS

What we have outlined thus far is nothing new. Behavioral scientists long ago recognized the importance of interpersonal networks, or role-sets, in shaping individual behavior (Merton, 1957). Empirical sociological analyses have consistently pointed to the importance of informal relationships and networks (Blau; Crozier; Dalton; Gross, Mason, McEachern; Leinhardt; Selznick; Travers and Milgram). Political scientists and anthropologists have similarly found networks important to explaining political and administrative phenomena (Barnes; Foster; Heclo; Krannich; Lande; Nelson; Peters; Powell; Scott; Wolf).

The interpersonal nature of the job search is well documented. Since the 1930s several studies of blue collar, white collar, managerial, technical, and professional workers indicate that "formal mechanisms of job allocation rarely accounted for more than 20 percent of placements. By contrast, 60-90 percent of jobs were found informally, principally through friends and relatives but also by direct application" (Granovetter, 1974: 5). The U.S. Department of Labor found that 63.4 percent of all workers used informal methods. Bernard Haldane Associate's analysis of 4,800 clients found that 72 percent used informal methods (Germann and Arnold: 65). Even with the highly structured government recruiting procedures, informal mechanisms of job placement play an important role. For example, in a study of over 2,500 Canadian government workers, approximately 43 percent found jobs through personal contacts, despite the government's formalized recruitment practices (Granovetter, 1980). These findings are equally valid for acquiring government employment in the United States. Indeed, as we later note in Chapter XI, the recent decentralization of the personnel function in federal agencies will encourage the use of personal contacts (Hawkins; Irish: 203-216; Waelde). Similar findings are reported for educators. Brown (1965; 1967) found a surprising 84 percent of college professors used informal job application methods, with 65 percent using the ubiquitous old boy network of personal "contacts." This finding reinforces other findings that individuals place greater reliance on informal job search methods for acquiring higher level jobs.

Studies consistently find that impersonal communication is the least effective means of getting a job: advertisements, public and private employment agencies, and job listings provided by universities and professional associations. The most widely used and effective methods are informal and personal: personal contacts and direct application (Granovetter, 1974: 10-11). The personal contact is the major job-finding method, utilized by over 60 percent of all job seekers (Germann and Arnold: 65). These research findings should finally lay to rest the widespread myth about formal "ascriptive" and "universalistic" procedures for getting jobs (Granovetter, 1974: 100-103). Since informal job placement approaches predominate in practice, educators should understand and deliberately utilize these approaches for enhancing their occupational mobility.

The research of Granovetter and others indicates that both employers and employees prefer the informal and personal methods for several reasons. Personal contacts are thought to result in more accurate and up-to-date *information*. Individuals who use personal contacts are more *satisfied* with their jobs; those who find jobs using formal methods tend to have a greater degree of job dissatisfaction. Those using informal methods tend to have *higher incomes*, and their jobs are in the highest income brackets. Overall, "Better jobs are found through contacts, and the best jobs, the ones with the highest pay and prestige and affording the greatest satisfaction to those in them, are most apt to be filled in this way" (Granovetter, 1974: 22).

These research findings are not surprising to people who work in highly interpersonal environments outside education. Insurance, real estate, and other direct-sales businesses have perfected several face-to-face sales techniques such as networking strategies, pyramiding, and client referral systems. Several career planning writers, using the nomenclature of "networking" and "referral interviews," adapted these techniques to the job search process. The goals and situations are analogous. First, your goal is to sell an important high quality product--yourself--by shopping around for a good buyer. Second, the buyer wants to be assured, based upon previous performance and current demonstration, that he or she is investing in a high quality and reliable product. Third, face-to-face communication, rather than impersonal advertising, remains the best way of making buying/selling decisions. Finally, since interaction between buyer and seller results in better information on each other, the new relationship will probably be mutually supportive, beneficial, and satisfying.

The techniques for building networks, pyramids, and referrals are relatively easy to learn and utilize. However, one must first understand the nature of networks, pyramids, and referral systems. A network is basically a role-set (Merton, 1957) involving yourself and the people you know, who are important to you, and whom you interact with most frequently. For example, if you are a college or university educator, your role-set will be a network of individuals you normally interact with on a day-to-day basis. Many of these people influence your behavior. Other individuals may also influence your behavior, but you interact with them less frequently. As illustrated in Figure 12, this role-set may consist of family, friends, assisters, professional colleagues, students, faculty, staff, department chairperson, and dean. Your network of relationships involves *people*--not data or things, such as your knowledge of a particular subject matter--and your transferable skills are directly related to how you manage your role-set relationships. For example, on a day-to-day basis, you manage both your role-set relationships and subject matter by using transferable skills:

FIGURE 12

ROLE-SET OF AN EDUCATOR

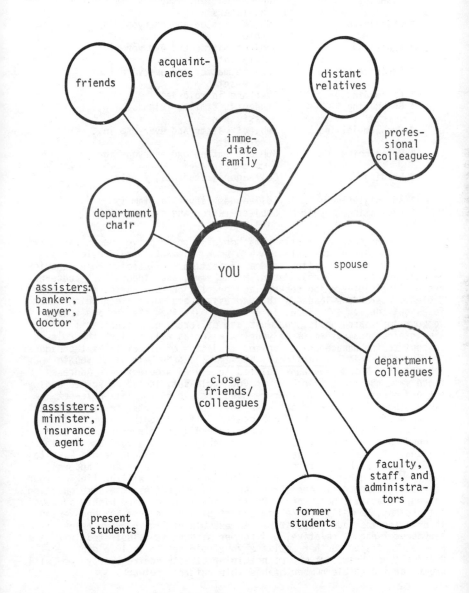

Transferable Skill	Object
* Communicating	Everyone in role-set
* Supervising	Students, family, some assisters
* Planning	Subject matter, students, family, assisters
* Organizing	Subject matter and everyone in role-set
* Analyzing	Subject matter and everyone in role-set
* Decision-making	Subject matter and everyone in role-set
* Persuading	Everyone in role-set
* Delegating	Students, family, friends, assisters
* Problem-solving	Subject matter and everyone in role-set
* Researching	Subject matter and everyone in role-set
* Leading	Colleagues, students, family, friends
* Administering	Colleagues, students, family
* Evaluating	Subject matter and everyone in role-set

While we can analyze role-sets, develop descriptive and explanatory theories concerning the relationship among elements within role-sets, and specify the expectations and anticipations influencing role behavior (Biddle and Thomas; Gross, Mason, McEachern), such theoretical concerns are of little use to job seekers and practitioners. Furthermore, these "role" concerns are loaded with unnecessary academic jargon which confuses outsiders. Therefore, in order to make the role-set applicable to your job search goals, you must ask different questions pertinent to the interpersonal dynamics of your role-set as well as link the role-set concept to the nonacademic, applied tradition of direct-sales techniques. For example, which _professional colleagues_ can be helpful to you in your job search? Whom do you know related to your job objective? Address these same questions to others in your role-set, including former employers and others who are further removed from your immediate role-set. Since others in your role-set have their own role-sets, their "contacts" may be useful to you in your job search. If you contact a professional colleague and ask him or her for advice and referrals concerning your planned career change, this person probably will give you names of individuals to contact in his or her role-set. Since most people like to give advice (perhaps everyone has a secret desire to be Ann Landers!) and they know other people who can do the same, you will be linking your role-set to your colleague's role-set. If you address the same question to your relative (Uncle Joe in Dallas) and a former, and highly successful student, you will create new opportunity structures for uncovering information for your job search. An example of linking your role-set to your colleague, relative, and former student is illustrated in Figure 13. If you further activate your role-set to include other individuals you know, but who do not interact with you regularly, you will create an incredible number of possible referral networks.

145

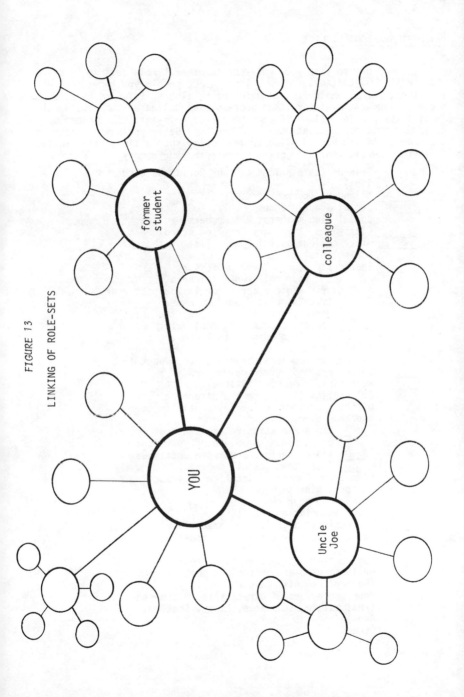

FIGURE 13

LINKING OF ROLE-SETS

DEVELOPING A CONTACT LIST

A good way to link your role-set to others' role-sets is to develop a list of contacts. Make a list of 200 people you know; include relatives, former employers, acquaintances, alumni, friends, bankers, doctors, lawyers, ministers, and professional colleagues. Perhaps only 15 of these people will be in your immediate role-set. The others may be former friends, acquaintances, or your Aunt Betsy you haven't seen in ten years. If you have difficulty developing such a list, refer to the following checklist of categories to refresh your memory:

_____ Friends (take a look at your Christmas card list)
_____ Neighbors (current and past)
_____ Social acquaintances: golf, swim, tennis, social club members, PTA members
_____ Classmates: from any level of school.
_____ Other college alumni (get a list of those living locally)
_____ Teachers: your college professors
                         your children's teachers
_____ Anybody you wrote a check for in the past year
        _____ tradespeople, drugstore owner
        _____ doctor, dentist, optician, therapist
        _____ lawyer, accountant, real estate agent
        _____ insurance agent, stock broker, travel agent
_____ Manager of the local branch of your bank
_____ Co-workers and former co-workers
_____ Relatives, even your in-laws
_____ Politicians (local leaders often are businessmen/women or professionals in town and know everybody)
        _____ the administrative assistant of your Congressman/woman and of your Senator
        _____ state senators and representatives
        _____ local town council members
_____ Chamber of Commerce executive in town
_____ Pastors, ministers
_____ Members of your church
_____ Trade association executives
_____ Professional organization executives
_____ Other members of your professional societies
_____ People you met at conventions
_____ Speakers at meetings you've attended
_____ Business club executives and members (Rotary, Kiwanis, Jaycees, etc.)
_____ Representatives of direct-sales businesses (real estate, insurance, Amway, Shaklee, Avon)
_____ Others

After developing your comprehensive list of contacts, classify the names
into different categories: individuals most likely to refer you to
others; individuals with job leads; individuals with long-distance contacts; and individuals in influential positions. Select at least 25
individuals from your list of 200 names for initiating your first round
of contacts. You are now ready to begin an active prospecting and networking campaign which should lead to informational interviews, formal
job interviews, and job offers.

PROSPECTING AND NETWORKING

Contacting people in your network as well as building new networks
involves prospecting for information and new job leads. Many people in
direct-sales quit at this point because they lack the prerequisites for
success. Prospecting techniques require you to:

1. develop enthusiastic one-on-one appointments and
   informational interview presentations.
2. be consistent and persistent in how you present
   your case.
3. give prospecting a high priority in your overall
   daily routine.
4. believe you will be successful given your persistence with these techniques; prospecting is
   a probability game involving both successes and
   failures

Above all, prospecting and networking requires persistence. For example,
it takes about 20 minutes to initiate a contact by telephone--longer by
letter. If you contact at least one person in your immediate network
each day, your prospecting should yield 15 new contacts each week for a
total investment of less than two hours. Each of these new contacts
could possibly yield three additional contacts or 45 new referrals.
However, some contacts will yield more than three and others may yield
none. If you develop contacts in this manner, you will create a series
of small pyramids of networks, as illustrated in Figure 14. If you expand your prospecting from one to three new contacts each day, you could
generate 135 new contacts and referrals in a single week. If you continue this same level of activity over a two-month period, it is possible to create over 1,000 new contacts and referrals! At this pace, your
odds of uncovering job opportunities, being invited to formal job interviews, and receiving job offers will increase dramatically.

The linkages and pyramids in Figure 14 constitute your _job search
network_. While each individual is involved in a one-on-one situation
with you, taken together all of these individuals should be viewed as
critical elements in your network. Always remember to nurture and manage your network so that it performs well in generating information and
job leads. As you follow-through on making new contacts, expect over
half of the contacts to result in referrals. However, a few of your
contacts will actively work in your job campaign by continuing to give
you referrals beyond an initial three. Consequently, you need to continually prospect for new contacts and build new networks. As you

148

FIGURE 14

DEVELOPING NETWORKS THROUGH DAILY PROSPECTING

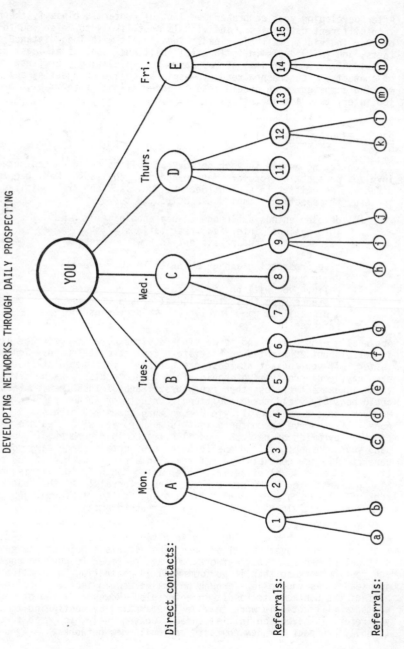

conduct informational interviews, ask your contacts to keep you in mind if they hear of anyone who might be interested in your qualifications.

Bernard Haldane Associates refer to this system of prospecting and networking as the R & R (Research and Referral) Interview System. While this is an excellent way to create contacts, it also helps you develop a realistic objective, interviewing skills, and self-confidence. In utilizing this system, you will seldom be turned down for an informational interview and you should uncover jobs on the hidden job market as well as place yourself in a positive position to take advantage of such job opportunities.

APPROACH LETTERS

So far we have outlined a one-on-one prospecting technique which involves contacting individuals in your role-set as well as people referred to you. Another prospecting technique is direct mail or direct application for gaining access to individuals without prior contacts. This is an effective, yet controversial approach, which does not immediately result in building pyramids or creating depth in your job search network. Some career counselors evaluate it as "absolutely terrible and worthless" whereas others consider it to be "outstanding." Others see it as a "shotgun technique" that wastes time and money. Your success in using this technique will largely depend on how you use it and how your target audience receives it. For example, Richard Irish finds this to be an effective technique, if you target your "shotgun" in a particular manner. He suggests doing an indiscriminate mass mailing of hundreds of functional resumes to specific names within your "field." At the top of each resume, write a note that you will be calling on a certain day to make an appointment. Follow-up this mailing with the telephone calls (Irish: 101). This approach should result in many appointments, interviews, referrals, and the further building of new networks. Irish believes your results will also impress direct-mail experts. The telephone call is the key to making this an effective prospecting and network building method. However, Irish does not mention the possible financial obligations you may incur with your telephone company if most of your calls are long-distance!

While Irish claims impressive results with his version of a shotgun method, we do not endorse it with enthusiasm. Employers are being flooded with hundreds and thousands of such resumes and phone calls these days. As reported in *The Wall Street Journal*, the "shotgun approach to job hunting is on the rise, especially among middle management. Some fear that the trend can undermine efforts to hire the most capable managers" (Ricklefs). The entry of copy machines and word processors into the job search market has led to a tremendous increase in such mass mailings over the past five years. As employers become increasingly inundated with slick resumes and cover letters--many from the mailings of professional job search firms--this approach will lose whatever positive effects it once had in the pre-word processing days.

Another technique which has proven successful for many people consists of writing letters to prospective employers or to individuals who might provide you with useful job search information and referrals. Normally you should not include your resume with this letter. Instead, take your resume to the informational interview and discuss it near the end of the interview. When using this approach, tailor the contents of the letter to your audience. However, certain common elements should appear in most of these letters:

1. Open the letter with a warm, personal statement which connects you to the reader. If you lack a referral to this person, you might open with:

> "I am writing to you because of your position as...," or "Because of your experience in...," or "We have a common interest in...," or "Since we are both alumni of X school I thought..."

If you have a referral, you might start with: "Mr., Ms., Dr., Professor X suggested that I contact you..."

2. Get to the point and take the pressure off the reader. Explain that you do not expect the reader to know of any current job openings, but you would like his or her help, advice, suggestions, guidance, etc. Stress the purpose for requesting an interview: to get his or her reaction to your career plans or to obtain information related to the reader's occupation. Explain your current situation and your concerns. If you enclose a resume, make reference to the enclosed information on your background, objective, work experience, skills, etc.

3. Close your letter by requesting an appointment. Mention that you recognize the value of his or her time and that you will call in a few days to see if a brief meeting can be arranged at a mutually convenient time.

The letter should follow these additional rules:

1. Be clear. Have a specific purpose in mind before writing this letter.
2. Always address the letter to a name, never to a position or title.
3. Make your letter brief, unless there are special reasons for going into detail.
4. Make your letters warm and personal. Avoid officious, stereotyped, or jargonistic language.
5. Carefully proofread for grammatical, spelling, or typing errors.
6. Neatly type your letter, unless the situation indicates otherwise. Leave wide margins and use a new typewriter ribbon.
7. Use plain, good quality stationery. Do not use erasable bond, ditto, or colored paper.

8. Keep copies of all correspondence in an
efficient filing system for follow-up purposes.

Remember, each person's situation, personality, and manner of expression is unique. While you will find numerous examples of these letters in resume writing books (Chapter VII) and other career planning literature, never copy or edit one of these letters for your own use. Follow our general rules, target yourspecific audience, and convey your message in your own way.

Never directly ask for a job while prospecting, networking, and conducting informational interviews. Asking for a job is tacky and it is the quickest way to be politely shown to the door. The basic principle behind networking is: *the best way to get a job is never ask for a job; always ask for information, advice, and referrals*. By doing this, you will be interviewed and eventually offered a job through one or more of your contacts (Germann and Arnold: 79-80).

Our prospecting system is similar to the networking techniques used in the direct-sales businesses. These proven, low-keyed sales techniques require hard work, persistence, a personable approach to people, and the ability to share a product and offer an opportunity to prospective clients. This low stress approach does not threaten individuals by asking them to buy something, or, in your case, give you a job. Some of the most successful businesses in the world have been built on this simple one-on-one networking and referral strategy. When adapted to the career planning process, the same strategies have resulted in extremely successful job search campaigns. Most important of all, these strategies are based upon a realistic understanding of both the job market and human motivation and behavior.

CONDUCTING INFORMATIONAL INTERVIEWS

At least 50 percent of your prospecting and networking should result in informational interviews. An informational interview is a low stress, face-to-face meeting with a contact or potential employer for the purpose of getting (1) *information* on job opportunities in your interest and skill areas, (2) *advice* on your job search campaign, and (3) *referrals* to other people who might be able to give you more information, advice, and referrals which, in turn, will lead to job interviews and offers.

Informational interviews have five major purposes:

1. Establish rapport with your contact.
2. Get your contact's reaction to your presentation and resume, as well as advice on how to improve, expand, and sharpen each of your job search steps, especially your job objective.
3. Gather current information on the job market on developments in your specific professional area.
4. Obtain one or more referrals to others who can further assist you in building your network

and adding to your knowledge of the job market.
5. Be remembered for future reference (Germann and
    Arnold: 74-84).

While the definition and purpose of these interviews are relatively
clear, there is less agreement on where and how to target informational
interviews. Bolles suggests targeting one major audience: the person who has the power to hire you (Bolles, 1980: 158-179). Haldane
Associates concur and further advise you to focus on busy people: "The
best kind of interviewer is a very busy person. Busy people are active,
involved, and usually knowledgeable. You can get more information from
such a person than from a dozen others" (Germann and Arnold: 118). Lin,
Dayton, and Greenwald agree and they talk about a "prestige principle"
to point you to the top. Simply put, this principle advises you to
contact individuals at the top of an organizational hierarchy because
people at the top are supposed to have greater access and control over
resources. Gaining access to influential persons and their resources
should facilitate finding a job (Lin, Dayton, Greenwald: 3-7).

We suggest conducting informational interviews with two audiences:
individuals with useful job search information and contacts and potential employers. At the same time, you should not confine your contacts
to a single level in an organizational hierarchy or assume that people
at the top are the most influential. We don't always know who can be
the most helpful in giving information, advice, and referrals. Sometimes your Aunt Betsy or Uncle Joe can be more helpful than a top executive in a multi-million dollar corporation. While it is desirable to
make contacts with top executives, gaining access to these people is another matter. After all, more and more job seekers are bothering top
executives with their job search campaigns, and more and more executives
are keeping their doors shut because they understand what these people
are doing. Don't forget individuals at other levels. They, too, can be
helpful. Indeed, many middle-level managers know more about their organization and are more willing to talk with you than the influentials
at the top. Furthermore, the top is not always where the influence lies.
Frequently top-level executives are removed from the day-to-day operating realities of their organizations. Furthermore, some organizations
may decentralize the hiring power to lower levels in the organization.
You must research organizations to identify where to best target your
campaign internally (Chapter VIII). Therefore, don't neglect nor limit
yourself to the top. Above all, _know thy organization_ and probe it
according to our principle of redundancy in Chapter IV.

Why should influential people want to talk with you? Executives
may find one or more of the following reasons to agree to meet with you
in the format of an informational interview:

1. window-shopping for new talent.
2. professional courtesy.
3. superstition and fatalism.
4. acquire information from you.
5. relaxation.
6. curiosity.
7. recruiting for a friend.
8. sounding-board: test out his or her ideas on you.

9. ego need to live up to your expectations.
10. desire to "play God", and help those who help themselves.
11. internal politics: spread word on the grapevine that he or she is looking around for new talent.
12. need to save time and money.
13. your persistance overcomes his or her resistance.
14. unconscious fear: "there but for the grace of God go I."
15. pay back the world; he or she was once helped by others.
16. reciprocity: he or she may need you some day.
17. compulsion to solve human relations problems.
18. discover genius or hidden talent.
19. enjoys opportunity to criticize.
20. coincidence of timing: he or she is actively looking.

At the same time, be prepared to encounter individuals who may have another 20 reasons for not seeing you. In that case, you must be persistent or reassess your approach.

The procedure for conducting an informational interview can vary depending on your audience. Irish believes "cold-turkey" interviews with important *strangers* in key positions are very effective (Irish: 109). Haldane Associates outline four distinct steps that should be followed:

1. *Send an approach letter:* Follow the advice on writing this type of letter.
2. *Make an appointment by telephone:* This follows your letter and should result in setting a specific time and date. Avoid conducting a telephone interview.
3. *The interview:* Seek information, advice, and referrals, and ask to be remembered.
4. *Send a thank-you letter:* Be sure it is warm and sincere (Germann and Arnold: 84-85).

The structure of a one-on-one informational interview should remain fairly consistent. Develop a script that is low-keyed, yet assertive enough to clearly communicate your objective and enthusiasm. Prior to the actual interview, role play with a friend. Approach your interview with these purposes in mind: (1) make a favorable impression, (2) get information, (3) get referred, and (4) be remembered for future referrals. The best script to develop is one which promotes a low stress situation and has a futuristic orientation. Most people do not want to be put on the spot and be responsible for your employment fate. However, most people like to give advice. Indeed, many people are flattered when you ask them for advice; indirectly you are telling this person that you value their opinions and knowledge and they are influential. Such compliments will most likely result in willing cooperation and useful information and job leads. Many interviewers will feel obliged to see you achieve your goals. While you should de-emphasize the fact that you are looking for a job and stress that your primary purpose is to gather information about future job possibilities, you should not hide the fact that you are looking for a job--if indeed you are. For example, you might say to your interviewer: "While I don't expect you to have a job vacancy now, I would like to talk to you about future opportunities." Bluntly asking for a job will likely make the person feel uncomfortable, and you are likely to prematurely end your relationship. Even with friends, such questions smack of exploitation; never exploit friends and acquaintances.

Therefore, you should ask for information and advice about career opportunities and your job objective. You need such information and advice in order to make sound decisions about your future. Also, ask the person to critique your resume, and ask for advice on how to proceed toward achieving your objective. Such a line of questioning should result in capturing the empathy of your interviewer. Many people will be able to relate to your job search campaign in a sympathetic and positive manner. After all, everyone has gone through the process of job hunting; many have made career changes and will have to do so in the future. Most people will volunteer the names of three or four other individuals you can contact for further information, advice, and referrals.

In conducting an informational interview, your approach and line of questioning might approximate the following:

"Mr. Roberts, hello. It's a pleasure to meet you, and I really appreciate your taking some time to see me."

"As I said in my letter to you, I am in the process of reassessing my career direction and I'm actively researching several options. Your type of work interests me very much and I'd like to learn more about the details and daily activity of working in (technical writing, accounting, sales, personnel administration, etc.). I want to reiterate that I don't expect you to have or even know of a job vacancy."

"If it's okay with you, I'd like to ask you some questions about your type of work:
  * What's involved in doing your job in terms of regular tasks and activities?
  * What skills and abilities are required to do a good job?
  * What kind of relationships with others are expected in performing your job?
  * What is the work environment like in terms of pressure, deadlines, routines, new activities, etc.?"
(discussion of work requirements normally should take 15-20 minutes)

"This has been very helpful to me. You've given me information that I've not read nor even considered before."

"I'd like to shift the focus a bit and ask your
opinion about the employment outlook in _____
(advertising, banking, various research fields):
   * Are job prospects good, stable, or very
     competitive?
   * What's the best way to apply for jobs in
     _____?"
(discussion of employment outlook, job hunting,
and application procedures should take approximately 10 minutes)

"If you don't mind, could you look over my resume
and give me your opinion on its clarity and any
other suggestions you have for improving it?"

"How would someone with my background get started
in _____? What kinds of positions could I
qualify for?" (discussion of occupational opportunities)

"You've been most generous with your time, and the
information you've given me has been very useful.
It's clarified and reinforced a number of points
for me. I don't want to take up any more of your
time; however, I'm wondering if you would be willing
to do two more things for me? The jobs you thought
might be appropriate for someone with my skills
sound interesting and I'd like to find out more
about those possibilities. If you know individuals
in those kinds of jobs, would you be willing to
provide me with their names so I could talk with
them much like we've talked?" (about half will
provide you with multiple referrals)

"Finally, would you be willing to keep my resume
for the next 3 or 4 months and keep me in mind if
you hear of a vacancy which would be appropriate
for someone with my skills?"

"Thanks again for taking the time to see me.
You've been very helpful and I appreciate it."

BEING THOUGHTFUL AND REPEATING

Upon completion of the informational interview, be sure to express
your gratitude for the person's time and assistance. Make sure the
person has your resume. Keep this interview to about 30-45 minutes.
However, don't be surprised if it runs longer than anticipated; many
interviewers enjoy discussing your topic and giving you advice. Try
not to let this interview go beyond one hour. Within five days, write
a thank-you letter in which you again express your gratitude for his or
her assistance and emphasize once again that you would appreciate
being kept in mind if he or she hears of any opportunities for someone
with your qualifications. Some career planners advise you to hand

write this note; others tell you to type it since typing looks more professional than handwriting. We think this is another one of those proverbial "six one way, half a dozen another" situations. Do what best fits your style and your understanding of your audience. But be *sure* you send a thank-you letter. This could be the most effective aspect of your whole job search. The thank-you letter communicates an important personal element: you are a considerate and thoughtful person. Employers want to hire such people. Just think, when was the last time you received a thank-you note from someone you assisted?

Continue repeating the prospecting, networking, and informational interviews. While your short-term goal is to get a job, always keep your long-term goals in mind. Do not use people or forget them once you achieve your objective. You owe a debt to the people who helped you. Keep them in mind. When you finally get a job, write these people a letter informing them of your success and thanking them once again for their assistance. They may later contact you for assistance, or you may want to contact them again during your next career change. In many cases, you will develop new and lasting relationships based upon your prospecting, networking, and informational interview activities. This dimension of the job search process may well become one of your most personally rewarding experiences. Much of getting ahead involves maintaining and building your personal networks. Your most important resource will be the people you keep in your network.

EXPECTED RESULTS

This approach is based upon years of successful experience with thousands of clients. Most major professional career counseling groups teach this method to their clients and they report excellent results. We experience similar results with our clients. You, too, will be successful in getting job interviews and offers if you continue prospecting networking, and conducting informational interviews. The odds are in your favor as long as you constantly repeat these activities. In general, your odds are about 50 percent that employers will meet with you based upon your approach letter. At the end of informational interviews, expect another 50 percent to refer you to three or four others. Consequently, if you feel you need more contacts, informational interviews, and referrals, just increase the level of your prospecting and networking activities. Over the long-run the odds are in your favor for achieving success.

It is difficult to give precise estimates on when you can expect your first formal job interview and offer based upon this approach. Some people get lucky and follow-through on their first referral with an informational interview which yields a job offer. Others repeat these activities for four to six months before receiving a job offer. A realistic prospecting plan is to initiate six new contacts each week or one each day. Within the first month, you will have developed your major contacts and completed your first round of informational interviews. During the second month, the number of informational interviews should increase considerably. Within two and a half to three months,

firm job offers should be forthcoming. Again, job offers can occur at
any time, from your first informational interview to your 100th interview six months later. But if you initiate six new contacts each week
and increase the pace of your informational interviews during the second
month, you should begin receiving job offers within two and a half to
three months.

CHAPTER X

INTERVIEWING AND NEGOTIATING THE JOB

This is _the_ critical step in the job search process. All previous steps lead to this one. Put simply, no interview, no job offer; no job offer, no negotiations, no salary, and no job.

Your previous job search activities have assisted you in getting this far, but the interview itself will determine whether you will be invited to a second interview and offered a position. How you approach the interview will make a difference in the outcome of the interview. Therefore, you need to know what best to do and not to do in order to make a good impression on your prospective employer.

INTERVIEWING STRESS

Interviewing stress occurs among both interviewees and interviewers. Both are stressful roles. For example, employers need to fill vacancies due to personnel problems. Employees may be incompetent and lazy; many don't "fit into" the organization or get along with their superiors and co-workers. Consequently, some people must be terminated. Others leave for greener pastures. In other cases, organizations are growing and need to fill new positions.

Contrary to popular myths, employers are not in the driver's seat. As we noted in Chapter IX, recruiting new personnel can be costly and risky. Employers lack information on the number and quality of candidates available at any given time. The employment process often involves sorting through 300 resumes, interviewing 10 candidates, negotiating, training, and then discovering the wrong person was hired. To further compound the problem, many employers are uncertain about the type of person they need, and thus they let the market largely control the process. Knowing this, you can help define employers' needs by communicating to them that it is _you_ they should want. You do this by establishing open communication with the employer and presenting your strengths as _their_ needs.

PLAYING ROLES AND BEING YOURSELF

A great deal of literature is written on how to interview for a job. You will find just about every conceivable approach and gimmick on how to conduct an effective interview. Much of this advice is contradictory, naive, and faddish; it is based on a combination of speculation, folk tales, role theory, assertiveness training, sales strategies, and common sense. Every writer is convinced his or her approach is the most effective. Consequently, you will receive advice on everything, from the color of your shoes to the twinkle in your eye.

The art of interviewing is usually approached from two perspectives: play a role or be yourself. The _role perspective_ is the predominant approach. Based upon a theatrical analogy, this perspective takes the position that you (the actor) must adjust your behavior to the expectations of others (your audience) in order to have an effective relationship (Biddle and Thomas: 3-19). Thus, a good actor is one who pleases both the director and the audience. Applied to the interview situation, the actor is you, the director is the "how to" advice, and the audience is your prospective employer. What you need to do is learn your script so you can please your audience.

The role perspective results in all kinds of advice on how to talk, dress, sit, eat, drink, laugh, shake hands, and listen. Based upon both verbal and nonverbal communication and role theories, Komar identifies a secret formula for success in interviewing. His key concept is _presence_:

PRESENCE = GROOMING + CLOTHING + NONVERBAL
           COMMUNICATION (Komar: 40)

Lathrop tells you to consider the following if you plan to conduct a successful interview:

1. proper attire
2. good grooming
3. firm handshake
4. appearance of control and confidence
5. smile and display appropriate humor
6. show interest in the employer and listen attentively
7. be positive about past performance
8. empathize with the employer and appear willing to help him or her
9. communicate solid ideas
10. take control if the employer has difficulty interviewing (Lathrop, 1977: 181)

Neglecting any one of these considerations can lead to failure, according to Lathrop.

Lathrop further advises you to prepare ahead of time. He provides a checklist of items you should attend to, perhaps do a "dry run" with your spouse or friend, before you go to the interview:

_____ Research the organization and the interviewer ahead of time.
_____ Think about what it is you want to contribute to the interviewer and his or her organization, such as increase quality and productivity. Be prepared to communicate this information in the interview.
_____ Learn to ask intelligent questions about job duties and personal qualities desired in employees. Be prepared to demonstrate how you meet or exceed the employer's expectations. Avoid questions about pay, vacations, and other benefits until later.

_____ Be prepared to ask questions and discuss problems
facing the interviewer's employees in order to
stress your qualifications in relationship to the
problems.

_____ Be well groomed. Wear attire appropriate to the
job you will be interviewing for. Avoid faddish
clothing and hair styles as well as heavy perfumes.

_____ Take to the interview extra copies of your resume,
a list of references, and a sample of your work,
if design or writing skills are required.

_____ Confirm your appointment time and arrive five
minutes early.

_____ Communicate energy, self-confidence, sincerity,
and friendliness. Smile, have a firm hand shake,
be relaxed, and maintain eye contact (Lathrop,
1977: 182).

Bolles concurs with this advice, especially the need for you to know
the problems of the employer and suggest possible solutions as a way to
impress the employer (Bolles, 1978: 121-150; 156). Stanat sees dangers
in such an approach. Self-proclaimed saviors are somewhat presumptuous
and may step on someone's favorite creation (Stanat: 159-162).

Everyone has a checklist of "Do's" and "Don'ts" for the interviewee.
For example, you should _do_ the following:

_____ _Do_ have attractive hands--clean and nails
trimmed.

_____ _Do_ comb your hair and wear it in a conservative
style.

_____ _Do_ use a _moderate_ amount of perfume or cologne.

_____ _Do_ use the restroom before the interview.

_____ _Do_ get a good night's sleep.

_____ _Do_ maintain eye contact since interviewers
place a great deal of emphasis on it.

_____ _Do_ appear enthusiastic. Use gestures but make them
smooth.

_____ _Do_ smile.

_____ _Do_ learn the name of the interviewer and use it
occasionally during the interview.

_____ _Do_ take enough money with you, just in case you
have an emergency of some kind.

_____ _Do_ research the organization ahead of time. Observe
the dress modes and working environment.

_____ _Do_ take notes during the interview since the interviewer will be doing the same. Jot down some of
your questions before the interview.

_____ _Do_ defer to the interviewer in setting the interview pace.

_____ _Do_ let the interviewer close the interview.

_____ _Do_ inquire about when you might expect to hear
from the interviewer next (Stanat: 105-107).

And, then, there are several things you should _not do_:

_____ _Don't_ be late to the interview.

_____ *Don't* wear an overcoat, topcoat, or rubber boots into an interview--you look anxious to leave.

_____ *Don't* sit down or dash to your chair until the interviewer gives some indication to be seated; otherwise, you look forward.

_____ *Don't* have a mouthful of anything except your teeth.

_____ *Don't* lean on the interviewer's desk. Sit erect in your chair.

_____ *Don't* wear dark glasses.

_____ *Don't* carry a large handbag.

_____ *Don't* have extremely long fingernails

_____ *Don't* demonstrate your nervousness by tapping your fingers, swinging your leg, or playing with your hands.

_____ *Don't* fidget with your clothes.

_____ *Don't* play with your hair.

_____ *Don't* compare this interviewer with others.

_____ *Don't* pick up items on the interviewer's desk unless invited to do so.

_____ *Don't* appear to eavesdrop on any phone calls the interviewer receives in your presence.

_____ *Don't* stand if someone enters the office during the interview.

_____ *Don't* read materials on the interviewer's desk.

_____ *Don't* refer to the interviewer as "sir" or "ma'am".

_____ *Don't* use the interviewer's name too much.

_____ *Don't* over-extend your jokes and humor.

_____ *Don't* answer questions with one- and two-word remarks.

_____ *Don't* dominate the conversation. Answer the questions without lingering.

_____ *Don't* interrupt the interviewer.

_____ *Don't* swear, even though the interviewer may.

_____ *Don't* use slang.

_____ *Don't* gush or be syrupy.

_____ *Don't* punctuate your conversation with "you know".

_____ *Don't* use the interviewer's first name.

_____ *Don't* be preachy.

_____ *Don't* mumble.

_____ *Don't* interpret your resume unless asked to.

_____ *Don't* try to impress the interviewer by bragging.

_____ *Don't* lie.

_____ *Don't* criticize your employer.

_____ *Don't* get angry or irritated during the interview.

_____ *Don't* answer questions you consider too personal-- but explain your reason for doing so.

_____ *Don't* glance at your watch.

_____ *Don't* ask if you can have the job. Instead, indicate your interest in the job.

_____ _Don't_ mention salary in the initial interview
(Stanat: 102-105).

Irish adds a few more "Do's" and Don'ts" for the curious interviewee:

_____ Women should take the initiative in extending the
handshake when meeting the interviewer.
_____ Don't smoke, chew gum, tobacco, or your fingernails.
_____ Maintain eye contact, but don't stare at the interviewer. Occasionally glance off into another
direction.
_____ If the interviewer seems to run out of questions,
ask him or her if you are giving them the information they want.
_____ If a question sounds irrelevant, unprincipled, or
unimportant, ask why the interviewer feels its important.
_____ Don't be "cool" and laid-back in the interview,
unless you want to let the interviewer know you
are a con-artist (Irish: 134-125)

Dress is an important theme in the "how to" interview literature.
John Molloy tells men and women to "dress for success" (1975; 1977).
For upper-level positions, men should wear clothing that is "conservative, traditional and conventional. All items should be elegant and
costly and perfectly coordinated" (Molloy, 1975: 225). A dark blue or
gray suit and a good quality standard white or pale blue solid shirt
will be best for the interview. Women should wear a dark blue or gray
suit (avoid green), light make-up, and a minimum of jewelry (no one is
hiring gypsies this season!).

Interview questions are another important consideration. Lathrop
prepares you for these questions by listing the most frequently asked
questions and suggesting that you learn to give positive answers to
each _before_ you engage in the interview. Try several of these questions:

* Why do you want to join our organization?
* Why do you think you are qualified for this position?
* Tell me about yourself?
* What salary do you expect?
* Why are you looking for another job?
* Why do you want to make a career change?
* What ideally would you like to do?
* Describe your educational background?
* Why should we want to hire you?
* How would you improve our operations?
* What are your three major positives and negatives
for this job?
* What are your major achievements?
* Have you ever been terminated?
* Why did you change jobs before?
* What are your major weaknesses?
* What is the lowest pay you will take?
* Why do you think we should pay you $____?
* What do you want to be making in the next five years?
* Will you tell me about your divorce?

* Were you ever arrested?
* Do you own a home or car?
* How much insurance do you have?
* How heavily in debt are you?
* Will you be willing to work overtime or
  travel extensively?
* Who are your references? (Lathrop: 183-185)

Some of these questions are obviously illegal--marital situation, con-
victions, personal finances--but you may be asked them nonetheless.
Learn to handle them firmly but without getting angry. Irish identifies
what he considers to be "the real hummer of a question, the one absolutely guaranteed to bring you to your knees and confess your incompetence:
'What do you really _want_?'" (Irish: 127).

   Going one step further than just _answering_ the interviewer's questions, you should be prepared to take the initiative in _asking_ several
questions:

* Could you describe the duties of this job?
* Where does this position fit into the organization?
* What type of people do you prefer for this job?
* Is this position new?
* What experience is ideally suited for this job?
* Was the last person promoted?
* Who would I be reporting to? Can you tell me a
  little about these people?
* Are you happy with them?
* What have been some of the best results you have
  received from these people?
* Who are the primary people I would be working with?
* What seem to be their strengths and weaknesses?
* What are your expectations for me?
* May I talk with present and previous employees
  about this job?
* What are some of the problems I might expect to
  encounter on this job, i.e., efficiency, quality
  control, declining profits, evaluation?
* What has been done recently in regards to ...?
* How is this program going?
* Can I tell you anything more about my qualifications?
* What is the normal pay _range_ for this job?
* If you don't mind, can I let you know by (date)?
  (Lathrop: 186-187)

At the same time, you should be aware of several areas you should _not_
probe directly in the initial interview: salary, vacations, and other
benefits, overtime, morale within the organization, promotions, and
raises (Fox: 150-153). Keep these for the negotiation session.

   Taking all this advice together, the role perspective provides a
useful checklist of items you should consider when preparing yourself
for the interview situation. However, there are limitations you should
also be aware of before you redesign your wardrobe and personality.
Taken to an extreme, the role perspective can result in making you look
like a well-groomed mannequin and talk like a smoothy or con-artist.

Furthermore, your interviewer may have read the same books, and he or she may not like actors--however good they may be. Common sense, moderation, and sensitivity may be lacking when using the role perspective.

Unfortunately, the role perspective assumes you can know the expectations of your audience. On the contrary, interviewers differ in their likes, dislikes, prejudices, and preferences. Some employers can't stand "dress for success" types. Others like thoroughly conventional types or "good old boys." Many employers, however, have a "hidden agenda" of biases. Irish, for example, frankly acknowledges his "hidden agenda"; he discriminates against hiring divorced men (can't manage their own home life), men with paunches and pates, Black Power rhetoricians, White Liberals with cheek tics, and bearded men (Irish: 113). The role perspective often neglects some important facts of life: audiences differ in their expectations; audiences often like to have their expectations _raised_ rather than met; and it is extremely difficult to know someone else's expectations without psycho-analyzing them--and that's difficult to do with an interviewer!

Although we find the role perspective useful in many respects, we also believe it can be too extreme in its application to the interview situation. Most of all, it tends to be deceptive, manipulative, and exploitive--behaviors you should avoid communicating in your job search, especially at this crucial interview stage.

The second perspective may be best termed _just being yourself_. This approach is difficult to describe and explain because it is tautological. It tends to reject role playing advice and instead stresses the importance of being honest, forthright, and nice. This is an appealing and valid approach for many people. However, this approach is somewhat naive. Just being yourself may mean you will communicate some of your bad habits to a prospective employer, such as the fact that you are an academic slob who goes to work everyday in a T-shirt, blue jeans, and cowboy boots. Unless you are interviewing for the rodeo, don't "just be yourself" in an interview for a $40,000 a year public relations job. Honesty and forthrightness can also translate into a lengthy confessional about your problems with previous employers and your weaknesses. Such honesty and forthrightness mean you have a bad case of stupidity. As Bolles notes, "Never lie; but do select your truths carefully. Don't volunteer something negative" (1980: 154). You can be honest and forthright while also being positive and intelligent. Always remember that an employer is hiring you to play in his or her sandbox--not yours. It is naive to think you can do whatever you feel like doing as long as it doesn't hurt others. Such individuality is a commentary on why we should take Victorian sex laws out of the bedroom--not why you should be hired on someone else's expense account. Expect to accommodate your behavior to others' expectations, especially when _they_ pay the bills.

Our approach to interviewing is a combination of the role and "just be yourself" perspectives. We view these as extreme positions on a continuum. What both approaches lack is a good dose of common sense and a clear understanding of the employment process. Yes, be yourself, but don't be stupid by neglecting conventions which make positive impressions on prospective employers. This means avoiding extremes in all behavior without becoming just another conventional candidate, however difficult

this may be. Learn to _exceed_ expectations as well as satisfy
expectations.

EXPECTATIONS FOR INTERVIEWEES

   No single model of an interviewer is totally valid. Employers have
different sets of needs and expectations. Most have the same problem:
to find new personnel who are _competent_, _intelligent_, _honest_, and
likable (Stanat: 100)

   Whatever you can do to satisfy the interviewer's needs and expectations will be to your advantage. Furthermore, try to exceed the expectations of the interviewer. Or as Irish confidently advises you, "Go Hire
Yourself an Employer." Your talent, flair, qualifications, and time are
being offered in exchange for the interviewer's salary, position, and
benefits (Irish: 78). In other words, take as much control of the situation as possible without being too aggressive, threatening, or arrogant.
In the process, you will learn there are good interviewers as well as
bad interviewers, jobs which deserve your consideration and jobs which
should be avoided. Do not play the "I need a job--can you help me?"
game. Remember, the interview is a 50-50 business proposition.

   Our advice on conducting an interview represents a middle position.
Expectations of interviewers differ. Everyone has "hidden agendas."
Most employers want to hire individuals who possess a combination of
competence, intelligence, honesty, and likability, and most employees
would like to work for someone who holds such values. If the interviewer
is only concerned with your nonverbal dress and grooming behavior, find
a different audience with a more professional set of values. You want
to enhance your background qualifications, not overshadow them, with
your verbal and nonverbal behavior.

   Achieving balance requires an awareness of various social norms and
conventions of verbal and nonverbal behavior and a good deal of common
sense. It is true that how you dress, groom, sit, listen, and shake
hands makes a difference. A wet and limpy hand shake can communicate a
lack of confidence. Wearing brown shoes with blue plaid slacks and a
green-striped sport coat communicates that you are socially maladjusted!
Women who wear six rings, four bracelets, two necklaces, and a tight
fitting, low-cut dress may look fashionable and sexy, but such apparel
communicates that they may be applying for the bedroom rather than the
boardroom (Molloy, 1977: 21). Being late for the interview communicates
a lack of punctuality and responsibility. Untrustworthiness is communicated by failing to maintain sufficient eye contact--eyes roving over
the ceiling, walls, and floors. The list of nonverbal behaviors and
attendant negative communication goes on and on. Indeed, research shows
that nearly 65 percent of all face-to-face communication is nonverbal.

   Educators need to pay particular attention to how they dress. Most
educators dress in a very casual manner since educational environments
permit a certain degree of individuality to be expressed in dress and
mannerisms. Thus, if you are a casual dresser and are not keen at coordinating colors, patterns, and fabrics into acceptable business attire,
read a book or two on the subject. John Molloy's _Dress for Success_ (for

men) and *The Woman's Dress for Success Book* and Komar's *The Interview Game* are inexpensive starters.

You should always strive for a professional look when interviewing. Looking professional communicates competence, intelligence, honesty, and likability. Irish advises you to know "what you want to do is how you know what to wear" (116). In order words, dress according to the norms of your targeted work environment. But this is sometimes easier said than done. At the very least, wear a suit with the proper mixtures of colors and fabrics. Try to achieve a classic and conservative look by wearing a dark blue or gray suit. For women, the skirted suit from a medium range to dark blue or gray is best. Avoid double knit polyesters-- they look cheap and low class. Stay with wools, wool blends, or fabrics which have the look of a fine wool. Spend what is necessary on a new interviewing wardrobe. View this as an investment. After all, you will probably need to continue building a professional wardrobe suitable to your new job outside education, and your new salary should more than re-imburse you for this initial expense. But do not go to an interview looking like a stereotypical educator. This may mean getting a conser-vative haircut or shaving off a beard. One thing you must communicate to your prospective employer is the fact that he or she is not hiring a displaced educator who will use the company's time to do his or her "own thing." The transition into the non-educational world does not mean you will abandon your individual identity. On the contrary, con-forming means you will change from one set of institutional norms (shirt, slacks, or pant suit) to another (suit, sport coat, or skirted suit).

Other verbal and nonverbal considerations are equally important, and a great deal of literature is available to review these subjects. Be thoroughly prepared with your resume, a positive attitude, and know-ledge of the employer. Be on time for the interview. Look, feel, and generate confidence and enthusiasm. Ask intelligent questions and give intelligent answers. Be honest but selective with your answers. Don't talk too much or too little, and ask thoughtful questions. Relate your skills to the job. If necessary, role play with your spouse or a good friend prior to interviewing. Above all, use your common sense and a version of the Golden Rule: treat the interviewer as you would like to be treated.

MANAGING THE INTERVIEW

The *quality of the encounter* between you and the interviewer is one of the most important factors in getting a job offer. Employers inter-view numerous applicants, but only a few stand out as *individuals* and *professionals*. If you want to be an exception to the general rule, you must get the interviewer to deal with you as both an individual and a candidate. You must communicate your background information, strengths, and potential value as well as your personal qualities. You can strike this balance by (1) creating a psychological climate between you and the interviewer for acquiring accurate decision-making information, and (2) being positive about yourself by discussing your strengths rather than drawing attention to your perceived weaknesses. In the interview, then, *being yourself* requires being your *best* self.

Our career management principle of building and using strengths stresses basing a job search on your strongest competencies and interests. You want to achieve a good match between you and the employer when interviewing for a job. Knowing that employers need information on your performance in order to estimate your value, you can always help them by emphasizing your strengths. However, there is no need to communicate your weaknesses to employers. Since weaknesses do not contribute to getting the job done and they provide employers with good excuses to "screen out" candidates, avoid talking about your weaknesses to employers.

Interviews have an adversary quality which is understood by interviewers. While your purpose is to meet your needs, interviewers interview in order to satisfy their employer's needs. If an interviewer fails to do this, he or she may join you in looking for a job! Therefore, from the perspective of interviewers, a conservative approach to you is most rational because it minimizes the interviewer's risks. Not surprisingly, interviewers want to know about your weaknesses. They probe for weaknesses and usually find some, regardless of how well you present yourself. But do not help them find flaws by confessing your perceived weaknesses. While interviewers look for weaknesses, they also expect you to put your best foot forward. Don't disappoint them. The interview is *the* right time and place for you to be positive about yourself.

Both partners in the interview try to create positive images toward each other. While you put your best foot forward in the hope of being accepted for a job, interviewers put their best foot forward to you for certain reasons. First, rejected applicants may someday become the company's clients. Rather than alienate potential customers, interviewers try to promote goodwill toward their organizations. Second, interviewers attempt to generate interest because they feel a professional responsibility to present their organizations as a desirable place to work. Third, interviewers reconfirm their own value to the organization by advertising its positives to candidates. Therefore, interviewers are no more objective about their organizations than you are about yourself. They try to "sell" you on their organization in the same manner you attempt to "sell" yourself--by discussing strengths, assets, and goals. Interviewers, like you, avoid discussing their employer's weaknesses. Nothing is to be gained by doing so. In the end, both you and the interviewer play similar roles, but involving different stakes and goals.

Interviews should result in exchanging important information. Both you and the interviewer need detailed information about each other. As you develop a positive image, you must also gather job information. In so doing, you should view yourself as a "job analyst" who needs to (1) identify the specific *tasks*, *activities*, and *roles* relevant to the position, and (2) assess the abilities, skills, knowledge, and other performance criteria defining effective job performance.

A good way to gather and analyze this job information is to compare the performance requirements of the job to the components in your Motivated Abilities Pattern--abilities, subject matter, circumstances, relationship with others, and primary result. Based on this comparison, you should be able to determine the degree of congruence between the critical job requirements and your motivational pattern. However, do not expect a 100 percent match. This approach should help you make a decision to accept or reject a job offer. Furthermore, it may help you reconsider certain jobs which you ordinarily neglect but which are actually well suited for you. In the interview, then, you build upon your strengths and use your Motivated Abilities Pattern as a "management information system" for critiquing job requirements. This is a powerful method for selecting jobs which will lead to increased success and satisfaction for you as well as greater productivity and fewer problems for employers. However, using your MAP as an effective management tool requires practice. The informational interview, where the stakes are the lowest, is the ideal place to begin practicing. The job interview, where the stakes are the highest, requires perfection!

Gathering this job information requires open communication. However, do not mistake open communication with frank communication; the latter often places people on the defensive. You want to establish rapport and promote a positive climate in which the interviewer willingly volunteers useful information. You can accomplish this by relating to the interviewer in the following manner:

* _Be genuine_: Don't play games; a good interviewer will recognize this in no time. Feel comfortable with your feelings, values, and attitudes; don't be afraid to reveal your personality and humanity. Communicate from your level of experience while also focusing on your positives and strengths.
* _Be empathic_: Try to understand the interviewer's goals, perspectives, needs, and problems; he or she is facing risk and uncertainty with you. Recognize that the interviewer means well--is proud of his or her organization, wants to do a good job, and must often make decisions based upon incomplete and unreliable information. Assist the interviewer in achieving his or her goals by providing information on your goals, interests, and abilities.
* _Show positive regard_: Be accepting, positive, and warm toward the interviewer as a person.
* _Show respect_: Respect the interviewer's right to do his or her job, to have opinions, and to be different from you (Rogers and Stevens).

Good communication between you and the interviewer requires other behaviors too. You should describe your experience in concise terms, be articulate and clear, and project your voice appropriately. But don't go to extremes. Some candidates engage in verbal overkill when selling themselves. Effective communication is a two-way process which requires a balance between talking and listening. From the perspective of the interviewer, verbosity represents insensitivity. Indeed, some interviewees manage to talk themselves _out_ of an interview and job. Always try to strike a balance between talking and listening since you need to give as well as get information. Effective listening is an active, not passive, process. It requires the ability to seek clarification of information, be responsive to others' messages, and incorporate feedback. Furthermore, you should generate good attending behaviors, such as eye contact, posture, natural gestures, and facial expressions.

INTERVIEWING STRATEGIES

The columnist Joyce L. Kennedy once wrote that the first rule of effective interviewing is to project a favorable image; the second rule is to never forget the first! While we strongly agree with this per-scription, we also know it is easier said than done. For instance, how can you achieve the critical balance of being honest, genuine, and spon-taneous while also handling probing questions in a positive manner? So far, you should be prepared to deal with tough interview questions. Selecting certain interview strategies will be important to achieving this balance.

Provide positive information when answering questions. This is your most important interviewing strategy. Although simple in concept, it may be initially difficult to implement because you must respond to so many of the interviewer's questions. However, once you perfect this strategy as well as project your strengths, it will be very effective in analyzing the interview. This strategy should communicate both *substance* and *form*. The *content* conveyed and the *words* used should be positive. For example, such words as "couldn't," "can't," "won't," and "don't," may create a negative tone and detract from the positive and enthusiastic image you are trying to create. While you cannot eliminate all negative words, at least recognize that the type of words you use makes a differ-ence and therefore word choice should be better managed. To illustrate, compare your reactions to the following interview answers:

QUESTION: "Why are you leaving education?"

ANSWER 1: "I can't make ends meet any longer on an educator's salary and I don't see my circumstances getting any better."

ANSWER 2: "Although I have enjoyed my work in education, I am ambitious and feel that opportunities for growth and advancement would be greater elsewhere."

Which one has the greatest impact in terms of projecting positives and strengths?

In addition to choosing positive words, select *content information* which is positive and *adds* to the interviewer's knowledge about you. Avoid simplistic "yes/no" answers; they say nothing about you. Instead, provide information which explains your *reasons* and *motivations* behind specific events or activities (Krieder: 95-97). For example, how do you react to these two factual answers?

QUESTION: "I see from your resume that you taught at Smith High School. Are you one of the faculty being affected by the recent budget cuts?"

ANSWER 1: "Yes, that's correct."

ANSWER 2: "Yes. Like many others, I've been affected by the recent budget cuts. However, instead of looking at my situation as a crisis, I'm approaching it as an opportunity to explore several other strong interests of mine. I know my talents can be useful in any number of settings, and I'm particularly interested in the work your department does."

Let's examine this from another perspective. Think of the interview as a _learning situation_ where you are the "educator" and the interviewer is the "student." In order to make productive use of interview time, you should clearly define your "educational objectives" for the interview. Do this as you would in developing a lesson plan or preparing for an important class presentation. Similar to your resume work (Chapter VII), your interviewing "plan" should be thoroughly prepared in line with five general areas of information:

1. _Career Objectives_
   a. clearly define realistic objectives
   b. be prepared to relate objectives to position and employers
2. _Educational Background_
   a. outline and organize education
   b. select most relevant information
   c. be prepared to relate education as preparation for position
3. _Work Experience_
   a. outline and organize experience
   b. select relevant information
   c. be prepared to discuss specific work tasks and skills
   d. be prepared to relate work experience as preparation for position
4. _Abilities and Skills_
   a. review motivated abilities and skills
   b. be prepared to relate abilities and skills to position and organization
   c. use specific examples to support your presentation
5. _Knowledge of Employer_
   a. be prepared to demonstrate your knowledge of employer
   b. be prepared to give reasons for your interest in employer
   c. be able to relate your objectives to employers
   d. develop questions to give you the information you need to make a decision

You can further maximize your strengths by understanding the general concerns and questions of many interviewers. You will need to address them directly or indirectly during the interview. Some of the major questions include:

1. Do you have a _demonstrated, strong interest_ in a specific type of work?
2. Do your work history, education, and other experiences indicate a _sense of purpose, application of your energy,_ and _productive use of your time?_
3. _What can you do for me,_ i.e., what abilities, skills, and knowledge do you possess which I could use?
4. Generally speaking, what _kind of person_ are you in terms of your values, beliefs, early years, motivations, goals, and aspirations?
5. What _kind of employee_ would you be in terms of initiative, productivity, responsibility, loyalty, growth potential, supervision, and ability to learn?
6. Are you _genuinely enthusiastic_ and positive about the job and organization?
7. How well would you _fit_ into the existing people and work environment?
8. Have you provided _accurate and complete infor-mation_ on yourself?
9. How much will you _cost_ to employ?

The significance of managing these questions can be illustrated with some examples. Let's assume that you are a secondary English teach-er with ten years of public school experience. You now seek a position in the public relations field--a tough one to break into for anyone! As an educator, you gained some "extracurricular" experience in some public-relations type activities (served as the school's liaison with the PTA; coordinated fund-raising projects for senior plays; wrote and delivered speeches at student events; chaired district-wide committee which developed, designed, and printed new "PR" brochure for school system). In addition, you joined Toastmasters International, progressed steadily through their public speaking program, served as a club officer and recently were elected as a district representative. Furthermore, you chair your church's membership committee, recruit and welcome new members, and get them involved with church life. When you reviewed your achieve-ments, the public relations theme was obvious. Consequently, you decided to explore PR opportunities.

Your interests and related background information can be presented in a positive manner during the interview. This positive strategy is evident in the following interview dialogue:

INTERVIEWER: "Isn't conference promotion and coordination a major change for you?"
(concern: purpose, demonstrated interest, abilities)

YOU: "On the surface, it may appear like an abrupt change for me, but, in reality, it's a natural development from my career interests. For the past seven years, I have been involved in public relations-type

activities both within and outside education, and
I've found that I not only enjoy the work but seem
to have a flair for it. For example, I chaired a
district-wide committee which developed a new
public relations piece when staff were still being
recruited. I was involved in every aspect of the
project--conceptualization, design, writing copy,
layout, photography, and publication. It is still
being used today. In addition, I supervised several
fund-raising projects through which I worked with
local businesses, the media, parents, students, and
the school administration. Those required a lot of
selling and promotion. I've written and given
numerous speeches in several settings and I have
leadership experience at the local and district
levels with Toastmasters International, where I've
planned and conducted programs. Furthermore, I've
coordinated successful membership drives, welcomed
newcomers and got them involved with activities to
keep up their interest.

So, when I examine those activities which I
enjoyed doing and did well, public relations-type
work seemed like a natural choice. Over the years,
I learned how to coordinate people and events,
present ideas and activities in a way which projects
a positive image, and get people interested and involved in events. I enjoy the challenge of being
involved with a project from beginning to end,
working with different people, groups and organizations, promoting events, and meeting deadlines.
In addition, I'm very familiar with our city, its
attractions and its organizations. Through
Toastmasters and other activities, I've met key
business and civic leaders and know how to involve
others in a project."

INTERVIEWER: "What appeals to you about our position as
conference coordinator?"
(concern: enthusiasm for job, demonstrated interest)

YOU: "Well, there are a number of things. First, your
requirements call for skills and experience which
I have--ability to promote ideas and events; organize
and involve people; handle all aspects of publicity;
work with the media, advertising agencies, businesses,
and municipal officials; meet deadlines; work without close supervision; take initiative and solve
problems. Second, the position is very much in line
with my career interests, and because of related
past experience, I know that I'd enjoy doing the
work. It seems like a good match from my perspective. Third, I like what I see here. The staff
seems enthusiastic, friendly, and hard working.
The plans you have for developing new business are

exciting, especially the project to coordinate
conference events with the tourist bureau and
the Chamber of Commerce."

The most difficult challenge to your positive strategy comes when
the interviewer asks you to describe your negatives or weaknesses:

INTERVIEWER: "We all have our negatives and weaknesses.
What are some of yours?'

You can handle this question in five different ways, yet still give
positive information on yourself:

1. Discuss a negative which is not related in anyway
   to the job under consideration:

   "Well, to be honest about it, I've never
   particularly enjoyed repetitive tasks
   which are quantitative in nature. Perhaps
   that's one reason I've enjoyed my work
   and PR activities so much; they require very
   little in the way of math. Now, that's not
   to say that I can't perform quantitative
   tasks. For example, I think I do a good job
   in managing the family budget and deal real
   well in maintaining the financial records
   for Toastmasters. But neither one was my
   peak experience, if you know what I mean?"

2. Discuss a negative which the interviewer already
   knows:

   "As you see from my resume, most of my paid
   experience is in education. Although I've
   had considerable PR experience, I'm afraid
   that my job title as "teacher" will cause
   potential employers to stereotype me as
   another one of those educators who is react-
   ing to the hard times and problems in education
   and to not take a closer look at me as an individual. I am a realist and admit that times
   are tough right now in education, but things
   will turn around--they always do--and I'm
   sure I could survive until then. However, my
   exploration of career options is not simply
   a reaction to the problems in education. It
   is a result of a lot of soul searching and
   hard evaluation. When I carefully and honestly
   assess what I enjoy doing and do well,
   my public relations activities stand out from
   all the rest."

3. Discuss a negative which you have improved upon:

   "Well, like a lot of people, I sometimes get
   a little too wrapped up in my work, to the
   point of neglecting personal things. For
   example, with teaching, Toastmasters, and

some other commitments, I found myself working
all day, then running off to meetings several
evenings per week. With these commitments plus
my family obligations, there wasn't much time
left for me and I gave my physical fitness low
priority for awhile. However, I recognized
that, in responding to all these demands, my
life got a little out of balance. So, what I
did was assess priorities and adjust my schedule
to allow some time for me. Consequently, I've
put myself on a regular exercise program--3 days
per week--and feel like I've achieved that nice
balance again. Besides, I feel better, have
much more energy and seem to actually be able
to work more efficiently than before."

4. Discuss a "negative" which can also be a positive:

"I guess I'd have to say that I can become annoyed
by certain types of people. You know...there
are several teachers I work with who are always
complaining about this, that, and the other
thing. Nothing is ever right in their eyes.
Always complaining and negative, especially
when others present new ideas or try to make
improvements. Yet, they don't want to act or
follow through on any of their complaints.
You know the type--'Let Joe do it. It's not
my responsibility.' Then they criticize Joe
for trying. Well, I've always believed that
if anything positive is going to happen, a
person needs to assume some responsibility and
make a contribution, however small. If we all
waited around for 'Joe to do it', nothing would
ever get done."

5. Discuss a negative outside yourself:

"I don't feel that there is anything seriously
wrong with me. Like most people, I have my
ups and downs--that's normal--but overall
I have a positive outlook, feel good about
myself and what I've accomplished so far in
my life. However, I am somewhat concerned
how you might view my wanting to change occupations as a sign of instability. I want to
assure you that I'm not making this change on
a whim. I've taken my time in thinking through
the issues and taking a hard look at what I
do well and enjoy doing. If anything, this
change is a fine tuning of my career direction.
Like a lot of young people, I guess I didn't
have much life experience when I started my
career ten years ago, and I got into teaching
because I enjoyed that kind of environment.

However, as I got more experience and had
opportunities to become involved in different
areas, my interest in PR developed and I found
that I not only enjoyed those activities, but
that I had some natural talent for them. While
I've enjoyed my years in education, I am committed to finding work more in line with my
interests and abilities."

In all of our examples, we again return to our basic point about
effective interviewing. Your single best strategy for managing the interview is to emphasize your strengths and positives. Questions come
in several forms. Practice with these questions, especially the negative
ones, in order to best control your interview situation.

NEGOTIATING THE OFFER

The purpose of an initial interview is to get a second interview.
The purpose of a second interview is to get another interview and/or a
job offer as well as negotiate the terms of your employment. As you proceed through these interview stages, you should have "a professional
attitude and appearance, a knowledge of the company, a clear idea of
what you want to do, and a pitch" (Stanat: 169).

Of all aspects of your job search activities, the second interview
and negotiation are the most shrouded in mystery. This is due in part
to the American cultural reluctance to ask about others' salaries.
Hence, we tend to shy away from one of the most critical considerations
in the whole job search process: "How much are you going to pay me?"
You need to learn how to tactfully ask this question as well as arrive
at the highest possible salary figure for achieving initial job satisfaction.

Once you receive a job offer, finalizing the terms of employment
basically comes down to the art of negotiating your salary and benefits.
Knowing (1) how much to ask for, and (2) what figure to settle on are
important considerations relating to several dimensions of the job offer.
At this stage, you should have a clear understanding of your responsibilities and duties. Be sure you know about the amount of travel involved in your job. This can be an additional job benefit--especially
if you are young and single--or a burden, if you prefer being with your
spouse and children. These questions need to be raised and addressed
during the interview rather than negotiated on the job. Check into the
health insurance, vacation time, stock options, profit sharing, and retirement plans. You need some basic benefits for protection against the
dual disasters of bad health and old age. Most company benefits are
standard, and "standard" means they come with most comparable jobs, and
they are usually non-negotiable. Few of these benefits will offset the
appeal of "cold cash" (Irish: 147-148).

Go after the salary with a sense of purpose and tact. A simple
rule to follow is this: appear as if money is not really important to
you; however, "bargain for every penny you can get" (Irish: 164). You
are probably worth twice what you are being paid now. But don't overdo

it. You can price yourself out of the market as well as shock your prospective employer! In some instances, you may actually need to take a cut in income in order to enter a new career field. However, since most educators are low on the income ladder, expect to increase your present salary by 15-20 percent or more.

Always reserve the salary question until last, if at all possible. As Eisen advices, "Never talk money until you have a firm offer" and "never actually accept a job offer until the question of salary is settled" (205). Your task is to impress upon your prospective employer that you are worth every penny he or she is prepared to offer you--and probably much more. If you can do this, as well as engage in a profitable negotiating session, you will have a good chance of reaching your salary goal.

Although you avoid the question of salary until last, at least set a salary goal before you negotiate. This can be done through several means. First, determine the least amount you will take. Second, research what other individuals in comparable positions are being paid. Talk to three salary and wage administrators to get figures on the type of position you are considering. Also, since the government revises its salary schedule in reference to wage levels in the private sector, look at the federal government's General Schedule of salary ranges (Chapter XI). For example, if you have a Ph.D. and five years of teaching and administrative experience, you qualify for a GS-13 or GS-14 level; as of October 1980, salary at these levels ranged from $32,048 to $49,119 per year. Take the mid-point of these figures and consider yourself worth $40,678 per year. You may have done enough research on your targeted organization to find someone who knows what your interviewer is willing to offer. If you have this information, add 20 percent to his or her ceiling and compare this to your other calculations. Finally, it is also perfectly legitimate to ask the interviewer about the salary structure of the organization so that you can arrive at an accurate estimate of what the organization is prepared to offer.

After completing comparisons of these figures, again ask yourself what you are willing to settle for in order to make your career change. At this point you must consider other factors, such as where your salary will be two or five years from now. Do not project beyond five years with this organization since you probably won't be with them by then or inflation will have confused the picture; you may have further advanced your career by moving to another organization. You need to consider earnings now and in the immediate future.

The art of negotiating salary and benefits can be learned. You should begin with the following assumptions:

1. Most salaries are negotiable.
2. Level of salary generally predicts level of responsibility.
3. Your future earnings depend to some extent upon your next salary.
4. Most employers have a salary range in mind when they interview.
5. You can negotiate for the future as well as the present.

6. You want a salary reasonable for your ability,
    experience, and age.
7. Most employers will not try to exploit you.

When you actually begin negotiating salary, keep these guidelines
in mind:

1. To negotiate means to do business. How you nego-
    tiate salary indicates to the prospective employer
    how you will negotiate future business for him or
    her.
2. The interviewer's job is to hire you at the lowest
    reasonable salary. Your job is to be hired at the
    highest reasonable salary. The difference between
    these two points is the negotiable range.
3. You should negotiate salary in a friendly, pro-
    fessional, and firm manner.
4. Do not initiate discussion of salary. Allow the
    interviewer to raise the issue.
5. Do not be the first to give a figure. Once you
    do, you are locked into it. If asked about your
    salary requirements, try to turn the question
    around.

A typical salary negotiation may go something like this:

1. The interviewer asks what your salary requirements
    are.
2. You try to turn the question around to identify
    the range. For example, "I'm glad you raised
    the issue of salary. What is the salary range
    for this position?"
3. If the employer does not give you a range but
    turns it back to you by saying the salary is
    negotiable, you can then ask: "What is the salary
    range for comparable positions in the firm?" If
    he or she says that's not relevant and asks once
    more for your range, you probably should give it.
4. However, if the interviewer quotes a range, ignore
    the bottom figure and indicate to the interviewer
    that his or her top figure falls within your
    acceptable range. For example, if the interviewer
    quotes a range between $20,000 and $24,000, you
    might say that his or her $24,000 is within your
    range of $23,000 to $26,000. Try to obtain the
    highest reasonable salary possible.

These are only general guidelines; individual circumstances will
vary. However, if you approach salary negotiations in a business-like,
professional manner, you should improve your earnings potential.

Getting off on the right foot means getting your initial salary up
as high as possible. As we noted earlier, the job search is a 50-50
proposition: your talent, skills, and time for the employer's pay.
Reciprocity is in order.

CREATING COMPETITION

If you are fortunate enough to have more than one job offer or a potential for another job offer, it is common professional courtesy to give you a week or two to consider the job offer. Timing is important at this stage. Even without alternative job offers, it is best to sleep on all job offers. Don't appear too eager or too eager to please. Take your time and do some hard comparisons on all factors, especially the salaries. Do more research. Call potential employers to let them know you are being considered for a position. If need be, use an alternative offer as a bargaining tool. Let the competition know you have more than one job offer, and play one off on the other (Irish: 156). At least you will impress upon them that you are in demand and that their price is not the only one in town. This can be a risky game to play, but the payoffs are considerably higher with such competition.

You should handle competitive negotiations in a very professional manner. If you play hard to get, you may indeed find it hard getting started in your new job. Always remember that the way you negotiate your salary will most likely have an affect on your future within the organization. Indeed, as Bernard Haldane Associates have found over the years, "Employees who have handled themselves well during their salary negotiations were treated with greater respect and were given more opportunities to advance within their organization" (Germann and Arnold: 158). In other words, you may win the negotiating session but lose the larger game. As with most of your job search activities, "make sure that you are negotiating from a position of competence and compatibility, not need or greed" (Germann and Arnold: 159).

CHAPTER XI

PENETRATING GOVERNMENT BUREAUCRACIES

The job search strategies outlined thus far are valid for targeting employment in education, government, business, and industry. Even though you will encounter highly formalized personnel systems designed for hiring the best "qualified" candidates--especially in education and government--most jobs are filled through informal means. This informal hiring system becomes even more pronounced as the level of jobs increases.

In this chapter we examine the special case of government employment for two reasons. First, while many educators are interested in career opportunities with government, little information is available on how to conduct a job search in the public sector. Second, governments have elaborate formal recruitment systems which must be understood and incorporated into informal job search strategies. Failure to understand both the formal and informal systems will lead to an ineffective job search campaign.

Our examination of the public sector is confined to federal, state, and local bureaucracies of the executive branch of government. Other related sectors of government and the political system--legislatures, political parties, interest groups, and government consultants and contractors--are examined in Chapter XII on Washington, D.C.

STEREOTYPES AND OPPORTUNITIES

Government bureaucracies are often viewed in a pejorative sense-- red tape, inefficiency, dull work, limited career opportunities, poor pay, and incompetence. Some government agencies and officials indeed fit these images, but many do not. Viewed from the private sector, such stereotypes are equally valid for many business organizations. Except during periods of recession, when businesses are forced into periodic house cleanings, the public and private sectors probably have comparable degrees of deadwood and inefficiency (Irish: 214).

Another side of government bureaucracy consists of numerous exciting, challenging, and well-paid career opportunities. Government is the largest employer in American society. Consisting of 78,269 units, government encompasses 1 national, 50 states, 18,517 municipalities, 3,044 counties, 16,991 townships, 15,781 school districts, and 23,885 special districts. One-sixth of the American workforce, or approximately 15 million individuals, are employed directly by government. Millions of other individuals depend on government contracts and other forms of public largess for their livelihoods. While the government sector may seem large, it is relatively small when compared to many other countries. Furthermore, contrary to the campaign rhetoric of politicians, federal civilian government employment has actually decreased by 25 percent since the end of World War II and by 10 percent since 1967. At present the federal bureaucracy consists of 2.85 million civil servants. The major growth in government bureaucracy has taken place at the state and local levels. Since 1950, state bureaucracies increased by 209 percent to 3.3 million employees; local bureaucracies grew by 174 percent to 8.8 million people (Meier: 30-32).

Employment opportunities abound in government bureaucracies. Some bureaucrats fit the popular image of clerical paper-pushers, but most do not. Governments perform highly complex and technical functions which require a diversified workforce. They hire in almost every occupational category found in the private sector. For example, the federal government employs undertakers, movie directors, and realtors along with typists, accountants, policy analysts, and managers. The federal government's workforce includes approximately 150,000 engineers and architects, 120,000 accountants and budget specialists, 120,000 doctors and health specialists, 87,000 scientists, 45,000 social scientists, and 2,700 veterinarians. The Department of Defense, Veterans Administration, and the Postal Service together employ over two-thirds of the federal government workforce. The largest single category of employees at the state and local levels is educators. They constitute approximately 52 percent of the state and local government workforce or nearly 5.5 million employees; 2.6 million of these employees are teachers.

Government salaries and benefits at the lower and middle levels-- $10,000 to $30,000--are comparable to, if not better than, those in the private sector. Compared to education, federal government salaries are extremely generous. Take, for example, an assistant professor, with a Ph.D. and five years of teaching and administrative experience, who makes $20,000 a year. With the federal government, this individual would qualify for GS-13 or GS-14 positions which have a starting salary of $32,048 and $37,871 respectively for 1980-1981. In addition, federal employees do not pay into Social Security. Many city managers earn $50,000 to $70,000 a year. While few people get rich in the public service, few are ever poor.

Even within state and local governments, the public education workforce--including administrators, teachers, typists, and janitors--are placed under a separate bureaucracy which depresses individual earnings by providing relatively low salaries and benefits in comparison to other state and local employees. For example, a personnel director in a city school system may earn $10,000 a year less than a personnel director in city hall, even though the positions have comparable responsibilities. Indeed, the personnel director in education probably will have more responsibilities and seniority than his or her counterpart in city hall. Thus, compared to educators in both the public and private sectors, government employees are usually better paid.

Many people avoid government employment because they neither understand the opportunities available nor the formal and informal recruitment procedures for acquiring such employment. Some people believe you must have political "pull" to get a government job; others believe you must complete lengthy application forms, take examinations, and wait to be classified and chosen from someone's list of qualified candidates. Neither view is completedly true. Political patronage is still well and alive in America, particularly at the urban and county levels. Affirmative action and equal opportunity principles are acknowledged by most government units, but practices differ. Highly formalized merit personnel systems involving complicated examinations and selection procedures also operate, but moreso at the federal level than at the state and local levels.

Acquiring government employment requires understanding both the formal and informal employment systems. Thus, job search campaigns aimed at government bureaucracies should begin with this simple fact of life: learn both the formal and informal systems and how to integrate them into a successful campaign.

STATE AND LOCAL GOVERNMENTS

Most of the personnel and budgetary growth in the public sector during the past 30 years has occurred at the state and local levels. As the functions of state and local governments have expanded, so too has the demand for greater professional expertise to staff the higher-level judgment or management jobs. In many cases, state and local government salaries exceed those of the federal government. Despite a nationwide trend toward restricting the growth of state and local governments, especially in the aftermath of California's Proposition 13 tax revolt and President Reagan's threat to limit federal subsidies, opportunities for the high-level judgment positions abound in these governments. After all, demands for increased efficiency and effectiveness usually result in greater opportunities for highly trained managers and experts and correspondingly fewer opportunities for unskilled workers. Furthermore, opportunities always are available given normal personnel turnovers due to job-hopping, resignations, retirements, and deaths. Much of this natural attrition takes place at the highest levels of the bureaucracy--the judgment jobs you are interested in pursuing.

The major problem in discussing public sector employment opportunities and job search strategies at the state and local levels is the fact that there are so many separate and diverse units of government. Each governmental unit has a formal personnel structure as well as informal recruitment practices. Even within governmental units, separate personnel systems may exist for blue collar and white collar employees as well as for educators and other officials. And, despite attempts to control, centralize, and formalize hiring procedures, America's 78,269 governmental units have the same characteristics as other employers: decentralized, fragmented, and chaotic hiring practices. Given these characteristics, city and state governments cannot be approached with a universal job search strategy. Instead, you must research the structure, functions, problems, and practices of each governmental unit that interests you and then adjust your strategies accordingly.

Nonetheless, we can identify some general principles for orienting you to state and local government employment. First, political patronage still operates in many units of government. This is especially true in the case of rural county governments. Many state governments have reformed their personnel systems along the lines of the federal government's merit personnel system. Many city and urban county governments, especially large ones, also have developed highly formalized personnel systems with less and less emphasis on political patronage and the use of political connections. Contacting an elected state representative, mayor, city councilman, ward leader, or county commissioner for employment assistance may be an acceptable procedure in some communities. However, it may be tacky to do so in other areas. Political "pull" can, in some settings, have adverse effects on your job search campaign. Therefore, you should investigate hiring cultures of different units of government in order to learn what are both the proper and most effective methods for conducting a job search campaign.

Regardless of the prevalence of political patronage or a highly formalized "merit" recruitment system, you still need to use the informal strategies we outlined in previous chapters. Begin with the knowledge that personnel departments have little clout in the actual hiring process, even though they have a great deal of public visibility. After all, personnel departments are usually the weakest political units in state, city, and county governments. Furthermore, officials often move their deadwood into the Personnel Department where they are expected to do little damage to government operations. At the same time, political exiles or officials on the "outs" with others may get "promoted" to the Personnel Department.

Nonetheless, you should make contact with the Personnel Department, but do not expect it to be useful in your job search. Personnel departments usually hire people at the lowest levels, such as sanitation workers, janitors, and typists. This department does testing, processes the necessary papers involved in placing a new employee on the payroll, and engages in some training. Personnel departments also play an important gatekeeping function; they dissuade potential applicants from pursuing government employment with elaborate and complicated formal application and hiring procedures. Don't be discouraged with all the paper and personnel jargon thrown at you! This department is neither powerful nor particularly important. However, you may encounter exceptions to this general rule. Some governmental units have made special efforts to revitalize their Personnel Department by centralizing hiring decisions under an influential personnel director. Indeed, we know of a few city managers who have attempted to increase their overall control of the city bureaucracy by doing precisely this. Our best advice to you is: know thy organization!

The general pattern among state and local governments is to decentralize hiring decisions to the departmental or operating unit level. At this level personnel needs are first assessed, information on positions is most readily available, interviews are conducted, and hiring decisions are finalized. Knowing this pattern, your job search should consist of four major activities. First, research the governmental unit, beginning with an organizational chart, to identify who has the power to hire--usually the head of the unit. Second, conduct an informational interview with the head of the department, operating unit, or whomever you identify as important. Third, leave a resume, ask to be referred, ask to be remembered, and send a nice thank-you letter. Fourth, continue this same procedure throughout this and other governmental units. If and when a position opens or a new one is created, you should be one of the first to know. If you are interviewed, receive a job offer, and accept, the final step will be to contact the Personnel Department. At that stage you will initiate the necessary paper work to be placed on the payroll.

If you encounter a governmental unit with a highly formalized "merit" personnel system, position vacancies will most likely be widely advertised in adherence with affirmative action and equal opportunity principles. In this case you will compete with other applicants who are utilizing only the formal system. You will have an advantage over them, because you have made important informal contacts. Sometimes a position actually will be "wired" for you. This means the position description essentially is written around your specific qualifications so that you are, by definition, the best qualified applicant. "Wiring" positions is a notorious practice at all levels in government as well as in the private sector. Your informal prospecting, networking, and informational interview strategies may make it possible for you to be a subject of such "wiring." Again, you must know your particular organization, and this requires doing sufficient research on your targeted audience.

TAKING ON THE FEDS

Finding employment with the federal government is another matter. The federal government is a good example of unnecessary complexity. Its highly formalized personnel system and procedures are at best intimidating, and at worst misleading. Many people simply avoid the federal government because of the numerous barriers facing the prospective applicant. Moreover, politicians like to blame their inadequacies on the bureaucracy. New administrations usually intimidate agencies with talk about "freezes" and "cut backs." The bureaucracy grinds on nonetheless. Lack of knowledge about how the feds operate--rather than objective analyses of opportunities--is perhaps the single most important disincentive for individuals seeking federal government employment.

The federal government is shrouded in myths and mystery. Although federal employment has not expanded since World War II, an annual turnover of approximately 17 percent results in nearly 500,000 vacancies in the total civilian workforce of 2.85 million. Normally, the federal government hires approximately 1,500 employees each day. One of the largest turnovers takes place with the higher-level judgement jobs. Many senior level professionals in the GS-13 to GS-15 levels, as well as in the newly created super grade Senior Executive Service (formerly GS-17 to GS-18 positions), face a serious problem of premature career closure. Congress has placed a ceiling on federal government earnings. As noted in the federal pay scale in Table 5, once an employee reaches the magical $50,112.50 level--GS-15 Step Five--he or she cannot receive another salary increment until Congress raises the ceiling on all government salaries. Consequently, if you become a GS-15 at age 35, your government career suddenly ends in terms of future monetary rewards. Because of this situation, many high-level government employees leave government service each year for greener pastures with interest groups, consulting firms, contractors, and businesses. Others may move into the Senior Executive Service in the hope of securing yearly bonuses as well as encountering renewed prosperity. Thus, the federal government is

184

TABLE 5

GENERAL SCHEDULE PAY SCALE--October 1980

Time-in-Grade Step Increases

	ONE	TWO	THREE	FOUR	FIVE	SIX	SEVEN	EIGHT	NINE	TEN
GS-1	$ 7,960	$ 8,225	$ 8,490	$ 8,755	$ 9,020	$ 9,175	$ 9,437	$ 9,699	$ 9,712	$ 9,954
GS-2	8,951	9,163	9,459	9,712	9,820	10,109	10,398	10,687	10,976	11,265
GS-3	9,766	10,092	10,418	10,744	11,070	11,396	11,722	12,048	12,374	12,700
GS-4	10,963	11,328	11,693	12,058	12,423	12,788	13,153	13,518	13,883	14,248
GS-5	12,266	12,675	13,084	13,493	13,902	14,311	14,720	15,129	15,538	15,947
GS-6	13,672	14,128	14,584	15,040	15,496	15,952	16,408	16,864	17,320	17,776
GS-7	15,193	15,699	16,205	16,711	17,217	17,723	18,229	18,735	19,241	19,747
GS-8	16,826	17,387	17,948	18,509	19,070	19,631	20,192	20,753	21,314	21,875
GS-9	18,585	19,205	19,825	20,445	21,065	21,685	22,305	22,925	23,545	24,165
GS-10	20,467	21,149	21,831	22,513	23,195	23,877	24,559	25,241	25,923	26,605
GS-11	22,486	23,236	23,986	24,736	25,486	26,236	26,986	27,736	28,486	29,236
GS-12	26,951	27,849	28,747	29,645	30,543	31,441	32,339	33,237	34,135	35,033
GS-13	32,048	33,116	34,184	35,252	36,320	37,388	38,456	39,524	40,592	41,660
GS-14	37,871	39,133	40,395	41,657	42,919	44,181	45,443	46,705	47,967	49,229
GS-15	44,547	46,032	47,517	49,002	50,487	*51,972	*53,457	*54,942	*56,427	*57,912
GS-16	*52,247	*53,989	*55,731	*57,473	*59,215	*60,957	*62,699	*64,441	*66,183	
GS-17	*61,204	*63,244	*65,284	*67,324	*69,364					
GS-18	*71,734									

* Basic pay is limited by Public Law to the rate payable for Level V of the Executive Schedule, which is $50,112.50.

continually hiring people at the GS-13 to GS-15 levels and within the Senior Executive Service. You may well qualify for many of these positions, depending on your educational background and experience.

Another aspect of federal employment is the fact that 85 percent of the federal government is located outside Washington, D.C. Working for the feds, therefore, does not necessarily mean working in Washington. The federal government is divided into 10 administrative regions with headquarters in places such as Philadelphia, Boston, Chicago, Atlanta, St. Louis, Dallas, Denver, San Francisco, Seattle, New York, and Washington, D.C. However, the higher level GS-13 through GS-15 positions are disproportionately found in the Washington home offices.

Washington, as we stress in the next chapter, offers numerous opportunities for educators, two career families, and individuals wishing to fast-track their careers in both government and business. These opportunities are found within federal executive agencies as well as within the related congressional bureaucracy, congressional committee staffs, personal congressional staffs, interest groups, consulting firms, businesses, and universities. Indeed, more than 50 percent of the job opportunities in Washington now are found within the non-governmental "service" sector, which consists of "law and public relations firms and the trade associations where the paid lobbyists work" (Peters: 14). If you are considering federal employment as a career alternative, we strongly urge you to examine Washington. The next chapter will provide the necessary basics for getting you started on targeting a job search in Washington.

The higher-level positions with the federal government tend to emphasize skills many educators readily possess. GS-13 to GS-15 positions, for example, frequently emphasize analytical, planning, communication, organizational, supervisory, and interpersonal skills as well as some policy or technical specialties. The federal government also gives credit for educational achievements. M.A.s and Ph.D.s are considered equivalent to a predetermined number of years of experience. If you have a policy or skill specialty--anything from undertaking to speech writing-- consider yourself a good candidate for federal government employment.

In addition to the salaries in Table 5, the federal government provides several generous benefits which are not considered standard elsewhere. These include liberal vacation, sick leave, group life insurance, injury compensation, health benefits, and an excellent retirement program. Moreover, federal employees do not contribute to Social Security, because they have their own more viable program.

However, one major problem is evident with federal salaries and benefits. They are generous at the lower and middle levels, but there are few increasing monetary rewards as you move near the top. Once reaching the $50,112.50 level, you may need to redefine your career goals and plan for another career change. If you move into the private sector, you may enter into a $70,000 to $100,000 a year executive position or develop your own contracting and consulting business based upon your previous experience and contacts in government.

186

UNDERSTANDING STRUCTURE AND STRATEGY

You should begin your job search campaign with the understanding that there is _both_ a formal and informal system for getting a job with the federal government. Your success will depend on how well you relate the two systems. At the same time, you must understand that there is an incredible amount of decentralization, fragmentation, overlap, redundancy, and chaos within the federal government. For example, if your goal is a position in research and intelligence, the CIA is only one of many agencies performing these functions. The Defense Intelligence Agency in the Department of Defense, Intelligence and Research Bureau in the State Department, and the National Security Council in the Executive Office of the President essentially do the same type of work. Congress also gets in the act with its Federal Research Division within the Library of Congress. These agencies duplicate each other and contribute to the overall redundancy of the federal government.

Other occupations also are represented in numerous agencies which overlap and duplicate one another. If you are interested in investigative work, almost every department has its own police or investigative force--not just the FBI. If you are looking for personnel training opportunities, most agencies conduct training--not just the Office of Personnel Management. You will uncover this redundancy once you begin conducting informational interviews. Indeed, personnel at the CIA will tell you to talk to their friends at the Defense Intelligence Agency or the Intelligence and Research Bureau in the State Department--agencies they may have worked for prior to moving to the CIA.

Most people consider redundancy to be a waste of taxpayers' money. However, some observers view redundancy as a necessary and positive force; it contributes to the overall effectiveness of government by providing important internal checks and balances on policy (Landau). Whatever your interpretation, we recommend that you utilize overlap, duplication, and redundancy to your advantage by contacting several agencies for information and referrals on job opportunities.

Decentralization also should be used to your advantage. Your contacts should be developed with key personnel in the operating units. As previously noted, this is where most hiring decisions are made. Since units tend to be isolated from one another because of decentralization, you should conduct several informational interviews within and between agencies. In fact, it is not unusual to discover that one office does not know what another office is doing, even though it is in the same agency, housed in the same building, or located next door.

The formal structure of hiring in the federal government overlays an incredible amount of decentralization, fragmentation, and chaos. It presents a deceptive picture of a centralized, organized, coordinated, and efficient government personnel system. This image initially encourages people to apply but then intimidates would-be applicants sufficiently enough to dissuade many from following-through. Do not be intimidated or dissuaded from achieving your objective; understand the system, and use it to your benefit.

The Office of Personnel Management (OPM), formerly known as the Civil Service Commission, is an independent executive agency. It stands

at the apex of the federal government's merit personnel system. Many
people--including some working within OPM--believe you must apply for
federal jobs through this agency. This is true in many, but not most,
cases. Despite OPM, most government agencies are able to hire their own
personnel. Like most personnel departments or offices, OPM lacks political clout; it will most likely continue to do so in the foreseeable
future.

However, you cannot by-pass the Office of Personnel Management altogether, because it does have some power and performs certain useful roles.
OPM does engage in the normal personnel functions of testing, selecting,
classifying, and training employees. But it performs only some of these
functions for agencies. Since the federal personnel reforms of January
1980, OPM increasingly has been decentralizing these functions to each
agency. But decentralization has not been uniform. For example, some
agencies are capable of hiring whereas others are more dependent upon
OPM for assistance. In other cases, OPM's role increasingly is marginal
to the hiring process. Overall, OPM is likely to perform general support
functions for agencies, such as providing information and assisting in
the selection and training processes. Yet, even here, reality defies
simple explanation. As most insiders already know, the Department of
Agriculture conducts training programs for many agencies in competition
to OPM's training units. Indeed, if you are interested in training
positions, there are probably more opportunities in the Department of
Agriculture than in the Office of Personnel Management. This is another example of the ubiquitous decentralization, overlap, duplication,
redundancy, and bureaucratic politics which permeate the federal government and the executive and congressional bureaucracies.

OPM does perform one essential function for your job search campaign: dispenses information on procedures and opportunities. In addition to its 10 regional headquarters, OPM's Federal Job Information
Centers (FJICs) are located in 72 other cities which are considered sub-
regional centers or key geographical locations for dispensing federal
employment information. However, you should approach these FJICs with
some degree of caution and healthy skepticism. The major functions of
FJICs are to provide information on job opportunities in particular
agencies, hand out application forms (FS-171s), and conduct testing for
lower-level entry positions (GS-1 through GS-5). OPM representatives at
the FJICs will tell you to follow the formal procedures; most will deny
the existence of an informal system, or at best they will not endorse it.
This is understandable, because their job is to propagate the formal
system rather than help you learn the most effective methods for penetrating the bureaucracy.

OPM will outline the formal system by telling you that the best way
to get a federal job is to do the following:

1. Go to the FJIC for listings of job openings and
   information on procedures for getting a federal
   job. This results in a pile of literature and
   a FS-171 form.
2. Complete your SF-171--the federal government's
   version of an obituary resume or application
   form.

3. Take whatever examinations are required for your
level of qualifications (most positions you will
be interested in will be Mid-Level or Senior-Level,
which do not require examinations--only a completed
SF-171 for getting a rating).
4. Submit your application (usually the SF-171 and a
reference or performance evaluation) in response to
a position announcement.
5. Wait to be called for an interview and given a job
offer.

If you follow OPM's advice, your chances of getting a job are about as
good as applying to a newspaper want ad or standing in line at an employment firm--maybe five percent. However, OPM does not tell you about
one other mystery to this process. Remember, the federal government
hires about 1,500 people each day. But the FJICs only list a few of
these positions and usually only those positions available in their particular region or city as well as all positions classified as Senior-
Level (certain GS-13 through GS-15 positions) and a few Senior Executive
Service positions. In other words, the FJICs provide you with almost
worthless information on the availability of jobs in particular agencies
at your level of qualifications. There is a good reason for this. OPM
does not know what positions are available beyond the limited number
reported to OPM. In fact, no one in the federal government knows all
the positions vacant on a particular day, week, or month. The federal
government simply does not keep such information on itself.

Given OPM's lack of information on specific job openings, you must
contact the personnel offices of each agency for a complete listing of
vacancies. As incredible as this may sound, a private group--the Federal
Research Service, Inc.--every two weeks compiles and publishes a listing
of 2,500 to 3,000 vacant agency positions. While this publication is
relatively comprehensive, it misses many positions which are listed only
on the bulletin boards of agency personnel offices, circulated to a
limited number of government offices, or posted outside agency cafeter-
ias and snack bars.

Your alternatives to spending $4 for each issue of the "Federal
Career Opportunities Report" are most unattractice. The federal job information structure definitely favors individuals who physically are
located in Washington, D.C. and have the time and patience to walk from
one agency personnel office or cafeteria bulletin board to another. If
you live outside Washington, D.C., you encounter serious problems. You
can visit your FJIC every week or telephone every agency every week for
information on vacant positions. After spending $200 a week on long-
distance telephone calls, the $4 an issue for the "Report" will seem
cheap and convenient. Moreover, you can avoid having to travel to an
FJIC and stand in line for rather questionable information. The FJIC is
mainly designed to help people apply for the GS-1 and GS-5 entry-level
positions or for blue collar positions. Visit the FJICs, but beyond acquiring a copy of the FS-171, don't expect them to be useful in your job
search. Again, the federal government is highly decentralized and fragmented within and between agencies. Your job will be to centralize and
coordinate those aspects of the federal government job market that interest you. No one--including private employment and executive search
firms--can do this for you.

The informal federal hiring system is similar to the informal system we have discussed throughout this book. Since agencies continually face personnel problems because of normal turnover, they must recruit periodically. A personnel need is first identified in the operating unit and then communicated through the chain of command and eventually to a personnel office where it is formally announced in accordance with merit, affirmative action, and equal opportunity considerations. During the lengthy formal process of announcing the position, gathering SF-171s, and selecting candidates, agency personnel often try to hedge against uncertainty by looking for qualified personnel in the informal system. This means passing the information on the vacancy to friends and acquaintances in their networks in the hope of attracting qualified candidates. Fearing the unknown, officials often welcome an opportunity to meet informally with a candidate, especially in the format of an informational interview.

If your timing is right, you may uncover a pending vacancy in an operating unit. Again, the personnel office will be the last to learn about the vacancy in the agency. Furthermore, the position description may be written around your resume and SF-171 or the agency may assist you in customizing your SF-171 in line with the position description. If agency personnel send you to their personnel office to rework your SF-171, this is a good signal that you are under serious consideration for a position. Although we have no accurate figures on the phenomenon of "wiring" positions, it probably occurs in many GS-13 and above positions. Irish estimates that 95 percent of these positions are filled through agency "promotion" (Irish: 205). Such practices arise from certain personnel fears of agencies. Many agency heads wish to avoid leaving critical personnel problems to chance decisions of low-level officials in personnel offices. If many applicants knew about this informal system, they would be outraged. But, then, if taxpayers knew how much government officials earned, many of them, too, would be outraged!

The informal system consists of following the same general job search steps we outlined earlier as well as adapting them to the federal government setting:

1. Research federal agencies.
2. Focus on a few agencies for intensive research.
3. Conduct informational interviews with agency personnel--use your resume and SF-171.
4. Apply for agency vacancies with a customized SF-171.
5. Arrange interview with the hiring supervisor.

Revising Hawkins 1977 model of the federal employment process in Figure 15(Hawkins: 114), we outline the formal and informal systems of federal employment as well as the relationship between the two for positions at the GS-9 to GS-15 levels.

We believe it is best not to mobilize partisan political "pull" with agencies. Bureaucrats in general do not like to respond to blatant political pressures from elected officials. Such strategies may work wonders at the state and local levels where the "good old boys" are still powerful--but be careful with the feds. There are exceptions, however. Perhaps you know a congressman who is on a powerful budget or appropriations committee affecting a particular agency. The congressman

190

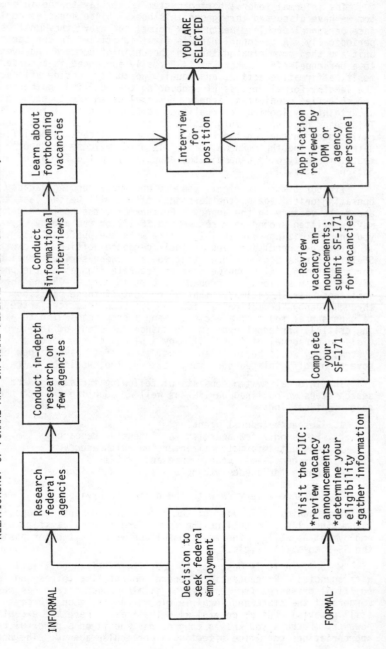

FIGURE 15

RELATIONSHIP OF FORMAL AND INFORMAL FEDERAL EMPLOYMENT PROCESSES, 1981

and his or her legislative assistants may know key people in the agency, and they will write you a standard constituent letter of introduction. But do not expect miracles to happen with such a letter or by dropping names of big shots. In fact, the President of the United States only directly controls 2,000 of 2.85 million civilian government positions. Even the President may not be able to help you with the relatively autonomous and resistant bureaucracy!

Federal bureaucrats understand and thrive on the informal system, but political patronage and political pull are considered tacky, if not illegal, these days. In this respect, government bureaucrats are no different from their counterparts in other organizations; the informal system continues to yield more reliable and trustworthy information than the formal system. Thus, the hiring goals of most government agencies are similar to those of the private sector: hire the most qualified person who is _competent_, _intelligent_, _honest_, and _likable_. Indeed, the 1980 personnel reforms, which are based upon the model of the private sector, already have decentralized many hiring decisions to the agency level. In this sense, conducting a job search with the federal government is remarkably similar to conducting a job search in the private sector.

RESOURCES AND RESEARCHING AGENCIES

Three books should be useful for planning your overall job search campaign targeted at the federal government. David Waelde's _How to Get a Federal Job and Advance_ (Washington, D.C.: FEDHELP Publications, 1980, $10) is the best "how to" book on federal government employment. He outlines both the formal and informal structure of federal employment, the role of OPM, how to complete the SF-171, and how to apply for a specific federal job. The book is based upon years of successful job search workshops and consulting activities sponsored by the Federal Research Service, Inc.

James E. Hawkin's _The Uncle Sam Connection: The Insider's Guide to Federal Employment_ (Chicago, Ill.: Follett Publishing Co., 1978, $4.95) is also a comprehensive treatment of both the formal and informal federal government employment processes. Compared to Waelde's book, this book says essentially the same thing, is a bit dated, and has less "how to" material on developing an effective SF-171. However, it is half the price of Waelde's book.

Patricia B. Wood's _The 171 Workbook_ (Washington, D.C.: Workbooks, Inc., 1979, $12.95), is by far the most comprehensive in-depth treatment of how to complete the SF-171. If followed carefully, this step-by-step guide should result in producing an outstanding SF-171 which would normally cost $100 or more if completed through a professional service or workshop.

Our final recommended resource is the "Federal Career Opportunities Report" which is published bi-weekly by the Federal Research Service, Inc. It lists approximately 2,500 to 3,000 job vacancies in agencies throughout the federal government. This is the only such listing available. In 1981, you could subscribe to it on the following plans: $4 per issue, $21 for 6 bi-weekly issues, $40 for 12 bi-weekly issues, and $78 for 26 bi-weekly issues. Write to the following address for subscription information:

> Federal Research Service, Inc.
> P.O. Box 1059
> Vienna, Virginia 22180
> Attn: Subscription Manager

The federal bureaucracy is an extremely large and complex organization consisting of departments, independent executive agencies, and indepent regulatory commissions. As we noted earlier, agency functions overlap and redundancy is well institutionalized throughout the bureaucracy. Understanding who does how much of what and where requires a major research effort on your part.

Your research should initially focus on the structure, functions, and problems of individual agencies. While conducting this research, you need to identify the names, addresses, and telephone numbers of key individuals within the agencies. For a good introduction to the federal government, start with the _U.S. Government Manual_ (Washington, D.C.: U.S. Government Printing Office). A new edition of this book is published each year and can be purchased for around $13. It presents organizational charts of each agency as well as brief summaries of federal agency duties and responsibilities. However, your best research tool will be the _Federal Yellow Book_ (Washington, D.C.: Washington Monitor). This is a loose leaf notebook published in revised form every six months. It breaks down all types of government agencies by listing the names, addresses, and telephone numbers of key agency personnel. Other useful research sources to consult are the _Federal Phone Book_ and copies of individual agency directories. If you write or call an agency for information on its structure, functions, and activities, you may receive a wealth of information including an annual report outlining specific accomplishments of the agency. Many agencies also have in-house journals or newsletters which you may be able to examine in a library or personnel office of an agency.

Another good source of information on an agency will be conversations with former or present employees of the agency or a congressional staff member or interest group representatives who have contacts with the agency. Ask these people about the functions and problems of the particular agency, and who might be the best person within the agency to target for conducting an informational interview. Acquiring key names, addresses, and telephone numbers should be your primary research goal.

COMPLETING THE SF-171

The SF-171 is to government what the resume, curriculum vitae, and application form are to the rest of the world. It is the most important marketing tool in your job search with the federal government. Criticized for being too long, and not particularly informative, and rumored to be replaced with a less intimidating form, the SF-171 lives on nonetheless. It probably will continue to draw similar criticism and live on into the foreseeable future.

The SF-171 can be intimidating, long, and less than revealing of your qualifications--but only if you let it become so. Despite the criticisms, you need to grin and bear the SF-171 and, in the process, restructure it to communicate much more than it was originally intended to communicate. If you complete the SF-171 according to our advice, you will overcome one of the major obstacles to acquiring federal employment. Remember, the purpose of a resume, curriculum vita, and application form is to advertise yourself. You must communicate as clearly as possible your qualifications to your prospective employer. This, then, is what you must accomplish with your SF-171.

The SF-171 is a four-page application form. It appears deceptively simple to complete, but it is an extremely complex document for those who know its value. Many people pay $100 or more to have professionals assist them in completing the SF-171. Others are able to complete the form in less than an hour by filling in the blanks in long hand. Those who know the importance of the SF-171 should spend hours--indeed a few days--in putting together an effective SF-171.

There are two keys to developing an effective SF-171. First, you should customize the SF-171 beyond its standard four-page length. Second, you should utilize a functional-skills vocabulary in describing your experience. If you describe your experience on the SF-171 in the same manner you describe it in a functional resume (Chapter VII), your SF-171 will conform to the best advice available on how to write an effective SF-171. At the same time, you may wish to consult the SF-171 sections of Waelde's and Wood's books for excellent step-by-step guidance in developing an effective SF-171.

Your SF-171 also should be customized. We recommend two customizing methods. First, expand the length of each section (experience, honors, special qualifications) in order to include more information. You can do this by clipping and pasting the section headings to separate sheets of paper. Copies of these new sheets become customized sections of your SF-171. Complete these expanded sections in as much detail as possible. The "experience" section is the most critical, and it requires your best creative writing effort. In this section you should stress your direct and transferable abilities, skills, and talents as you did when writing a functional resume.

Copies of the original SF-171 and our customized version appear in Appendix C. You may wish to make similar copies. Overall, try to keep the length of your customized SF-171 to ten pages or less. After completing this new form, you will have a generalized SF-171 which you can use for other federal applications. Be sure to keep a master copy--preferably the original--from which you can make additional copies to be sent to agencies. Leave items 1, 2, 13, "Signature," and "Date" blank on your master SF-171. When you submit a copy of your SF-171 in response to an agency vacancy, complete these vacant items at that time. It is best to use an IBM electric typewriter with a carbon ribbon so that your original and reproductions will look as professional as possible.

Another way to customize the SF-171 is to rewrite the "experience" sections to respond specifically to the qualifications outlined in a particular job vacancy announcement. Read each announcement carefully and then use similar skills terminology in your SF-171. If you customize your SF-171 in this manner, you must retype the "experience" sections for each vacancy announcement. While this is a time consuming process, it is the most effective approach for addressing the exact qualifications for

a particular position. Your alternative is to come close to the requirements yet to know someone else has customized their SF-171 in this manner.

If you need further assistance in completing the SF-171, examine
Waelde's and Wood's books on the subject. However, our advice on writing
functional resumes will substitute for most of their advice.

PROSPECTING AND NETWORKING

Conducting informational interviews within the federal government
should follow the same principles we outlined in Chapter IX on prospecting and networking. Begin with a list of desired agencies and positions
as well as the names of individuals who know people or who actually work
within your targeted agencies. Contacting these people for information
and referrals is the best way of gaining access to agencies and uncovering employment opportunities.

If you don't know people who know key agency personnel, the cold
turkey approach also will work relatively well. Consult the _Federal
Yellow Book_ or an agency directory for names, addresses, and telephone
numbers. Telephone or write key individuals for informational interviews
in your desired agencies. Request a brief meeting to discuss your professional interests. The approach letter should follow the guidelines
we discussed earlier.

When making an appointment for an informational interview, be sure
you do not ask someone for a job; instead, stress that you are gathering
information on opportunities in your area of interest and expertise.
You will probably flatter whomever you contact by the mere fact you are
asking for their advice; you are recognizing the person as an "expert"
who can assist you.

In most cases you will be successful in arranging an appointment
for an information interview. Moreover, most people will be gracious
and willing to assist you with advice and referrals. This is perhaps
one reason why federal officials often are criticized for being "too
accommodating" to the public as well as for developing their own interest
group clientele.

Informational interviews within government agencies should be conducted in the same manner as any other informational interview: ask for
advice, ask to be referred, and ask to be remembered. Within a few days
after the interview, send a thank-you letter in which you communicate
genuine gratitude for the assistance. Continue building your network of
new contacts by conducting several informational interviews. In so doing,
you will learn a great deal about the federal employment process--both
formal and informal. Accordingly, you should be one of the first persons
to learn of vacancies related to your qualifications in the agencies you
target.

MOVING IN, UP, AND ON

After you acquire a position within a federal agency, do an excellent job, and attach yourself to people who are moving ahead (Irish: 212).

At the same time, plan to move on to other positions within this or other agencies. Job-hopping within the federal government is a common practice--moreso in Washington, D.C. than elsewhere, as well as greater among individuals in the higher-level judgment jobs.

Always remember your friends and the importance of developing your networks both on and off the job. These networks will be the key to advancing your career within the government. At the same time, as we note in the next chapter, be sure to maintain and develop good relationships with agency clientele, particularly organizations doing contract work, interest groups, and congressional committee and staff members. Many of these individuals and groups may play critical future roles in advancing your career. If you reach the $50,112.50 annual salary ceiling before you are 50 years old, you may want to further advance your career by moving out of government into more lucrative and professionally rewarding private organizations. Be prepared to once again change jobs and perhaps explore a new and related career.

CHAPTER XII

TARGETING WASHINGTON AND THE PROVINCES

Our job search strategies are designed to be effective in most communities. So far we have examined several aspects of the general job search campaign, clarified public sector strategies, and touched upon how to conduct a long-distance job search. This chapter synthesizes previous chapters by examining how to target a job search campaign in Washington, D.C. Our purpose is not to unleash thousands of educators on this city. Indeed, Washington could not absorb so many new job seekers. Rather, we use Washington to illustrate general strategies for conducting similar campaigns in other communities.

POT LUCK AND TARGETING

Most people choose one of two strategies in looking for a job. We call the first approach "taking pot luck" or following-the-job. This approach involves looking for a particular type of position regardless of its location. Professional newsletters organize job listings along the lines of this approach. As such, a job seeker's major task is to locate positions wherever they may take him or her. This strategy may result in unexpectedly becoming employed in New York City; Cheyenne, Wyoming; or Kodiak, Alaska. Oil riggers and construction workers often use this approach. Many educators also follow this approach, particularly academicians who end up in small college towns they had never heard of previously.

The second approach involves targeting specific communities in order to conduct a community-based job search campaign. If you use this approach, you must first identify where you want to live and then research the community for opportunities relating to your job objective. We recommend this approach over pot luck for several reasons. Young, single, and adventuresome individuals, as well as single-career families, are best suited for the first approach. Relying on pot luck, they spread their much needed talents into relatively unexciting and isolated communities. However, we assume you are no longer so young, single, and adventuresome. Maybe you would like to settle into a community of your choice, particularly one which would give you greater career options. You may have two or three favorite cities you have selected because of their climates, topography, culture, or recreational opportunities. Why not focus your job search campaign on those communities?

It is also much easier to find a job directly related to your objectives and qualifications if you focus on a particular community. Our job search strategies, especially networking and informational interviews, are relatively easy to implement in particular communities. The pot luck approach is ideal for people who only respond to job listings rather than take the initiative to research the hidden job market. Furthermore, targeting a particular community may enhance your career in the long-run. Research communities to identify those which may provide good career opportunities for you.

Larger communities will have more opportunities because of their diversified populations and economies. However, many large communities should be avoided since their populations are declining. Avoid dying communities, unless you are a specialist on community decline. Take, for example, the changing population figures for the 40 largest metropolitan areas in Table 6. Based on these figures for the 1970-1980 period as well as continuing patterns into the 1980s, you should avoid cities such as New York City, Cleveland, Pittsburgh, Buffalo, Boston, St. Louis, Detroit, Newark, and Chicago. On the other hand, the most numerous job opportunities will be found in the metropolitan areas of Fort Lauderdale-Hollywood, Phoenix, Houston, Dallas-Fort Worth, Los Angeles, San Diego, Salt Lake City-Ogden,Miami, Portland, Sacramento, Tampa-St. Petersburg, Denver-Boulder, and Atlanta. Wherever you decide to target your campaign, be sure to begin with the name of a specific community. Focusing on a region or state is too broad and unmanageable for conducting a systematic job search campaign.

CENTER AND PERIPHERY

We chose Washington as our community target for several reasons. Washington is the center of political power, even though it is part of the overall fragmented, decentralized, and chaotic American political and governmental systems. Except for a few other cities, such as New York City, Chicago, San Francisco, Los Angeles, and Houston, the rest of the country can be viewed as many Washingtonians see it—the provinces. Washington, along with a few other key cities, is where the political, economic, cultural, and social action is. You may want to seriously consider moving to a "center" for a few years. You can later return to the provinces on the periphery.

A "center" provides numerous job opportunities for educators and two-career families. This is especially true in the case of Washington. Such opportunities generally are lacking at the periphery. Washington's opportunity structures include federal government agencies, Congress, interest groups, consultants, banks, law firms, the press, and thousands of related businesses. Although the cost of living is greater at the center, so too are salaries, benefits, and opportunities. Furthermore, it is much easier to fast-track your career in Washington than in most other cities. New York City, as Irish notes, provides similar opportunities for job seekers:

> Just living in New York, for instance, makes you worth twice as much as elsewhere because it *is* New York... Out in the provinces, in case you didn't know, New York has earned a bad name for itself. Being posted in New York by your company is roughly the corporate equivalent of a tough Peace Corps assignment or submarine duty. Accordingly, most firms are having a

198

TABLE 6

GROWTH OF 40 LARGEST METROPOLITAN AREAS, 1970-1980

Rank	Metropolitan Area	Population, 1980	Percentage Increase (+) and Decrease (-)
1	New York	9,081,000	-9
2	Los Angeles-Long Beach	7,445,000	+6
3	Chicago	7,058,000	+1
4	Philadelphia	4,701,000	-3
5	Detroit	4,340,000	-2
6	San Francisco-Oakland	3,226,000	+4
7	Washington	3,042,000	+4½
8	Dallas-Fort Worth	2,964,000	+24
9	Houston	2,891,000	+45
10	Boston	2,760,000	-5
11	Nassau-Suffolk, N.Y.	2,604,000	+2
12	St. Louis	2,341,000	-3
13	Pittsburgh	2,260,000	-6
14	Baltimore	2,165,000	+4½
15	Minneapolis-St. Paul	2,109,000	+7
16	Atlanta	2,010,000	+26
17	Newark	1,964,000	-5
18	Anaheim-Santa Ana-Garden Grove, Calif.	1,926,000	+35½
19	Cleveland	1,895,000	-8
20	San Diego	1,857,000	+37
21	Denver-Boulder	1,614,000	+30
22	Seattle-Everett	1,601,000	+12
23	Miami	1,573,000	+24
24	Tampa-St. Petersburg	1,550,000	+42
25	Riverside-San Bernardino-Ontario, Calif.	1,538,000	+35
26	Phoenix	1,512,000	+56
27	Milwaukee	1,393,000	-1
28	Cincinnati	1,390,000	+0.2
29	Kansas City	1,322,000	+4
30	San Jose	1,290,000	+21
31	Buffalo	1,241,000	-8
32	Portland, Ore.	1,234,000	+22½
33	New Orleans	1,184,000	+13
34	Indianapolis	1,162,000	+4½
35	Columbus, Ohio	1,088,000	+7
36	San Antonio	1,070,000	+20½
37	Sacramento	1,011,000	+26
38	Fort Lauderdale-Hollywood	999,000	+61
39	Rochester	970,000	+1
40	Salt Lake City-Ogden	935,000	+33

SOURCE: *The Miami-Herald*, March 8, 1981: 32A, from *American Demographics*.

devil of a time finding the right men and women to
staff their New York headquarters. The competition
for top jobs in New York is far less than legend
allows. While Americans like to move up in their
jobs, nobody wants to walk the plank. That's why
you double your income requirements the moment you
drive through the Holland Tunnel (Irish: 165).

Washington is an attractive city for many educators, and it lacks
many of the disadvantages associated with living in New York City and
other large metropolitan areas. Washington's public service orientation
and abundant career alternatives are appealing for people with specialized educations and skills relating to the higher level judgment jobs.
Washington also is a relatively charming city--it appears planned compared to the helter-skelter strip development of most American cities.
Its cultural complex is unparalleled, except for the live theater in New
York City. It does have its problems, such as a high cost of living,
congestion, and crime--but what big city in America doesn't? These problems become more or less apparent depending on where you live and work
in relationship to the city.

Washington is also a recession resistant city. The rest of the
country may collapse, but the banks and the government bureaucracy in
Washington will be the last to go. Regardless of what the politicians
say, there is little need to be afraid of hiring "freezes" or major budgetary cutbacks in government. While all presidents intimidate the
Washington workforce in this manner, the President and the elected politicians are always the first to lose their jobs and leave town. The
bureaucrats and their allies remain to keep the city safe from crazy
politicians. As Irish analyzes this situation,

there has been more or less a "freeze" on employment
since the second term of Grover Cleveland. It's
meaningless...There simply can't be a "freeze" on
employment. Too many civil servants are retiring
from government service, job-hopping from one agency
to another, dropping out from the job scene altogether,
returning to school, being reassigned--*all of which
means open slots for enterprising job-seekers* (Irish:
206-208).

Washington also provides a good illustration of how to successfully
target job search methods in a particular community. Charles Peters
characterizes Washington as a city operating on "survival networks"
(Peters: 5) and functioning in a "make believe world" (Peters: 17).
However, these characteristics may not be unique to Washington. In contrast to many other communities, Washingtonians talk openly about the
importance of utilizing networks, personal connections, and face-to-face
relationships. Although a sophisticated international city, Washington
also is a relatively parochial city where thousands of personal networks
function to integrate the city internally as well as with the provinces.
Consequently, if you understand how Washington really works and how to
penetrate its networks, you should be able to develop similar job search
campaigns in other communities.

MAPPING A CITY

Targeting Washington requires going beyond the standard approaches for conducting a long-distance job search campaign (Germann and Arnold; Bolles, 1980). These approaches, which mainly focus on getting a job, neglect several other equally important considerations. It is useful to view the city as a set of *opportunity structures* for employment purposes as well as a social, cultural, economic, political, and geographical entity in which you will live and work. Thus, you should research carefully numerous dimensions of the community. Focusing on jobs alone will be insufficient.

You should begin your research by mapping various community dimensions. Above all, a community has physical properties to which you must adapt. Buy a good detailed map of the area. We recommend the "Washington, D.C. and Vicinity Street Map" published by Alexandria Drafting Co. (6440 General Green Way, Alexandria, Virginia 22312, $5.95 plus postage). Washington sprawls over the District of Columbia as well as parts of Maryland and Northern Virginia. Since you will be living somewhere in the metropolitan area, you should contact two or three real estate agents who are licensed in the different areas. They can provide information on community characteristics relating to schools, shopping centers, restaurants, proximity to bus and Metro lines, costs of housing, and relative tax burdens.

Within a short period of time you will learn there are two life styles in Washington: inner city and suburban. Depending on where you will work, you must decide whether you want to live in the suburbs and make a lengthy daily commute to the city or live near your place of employment but in crime ridden, expensive, and congested sections of the inner city. Remember, Washington is not designed for driving a car to and from work. If you plan to drive to work, expect to be fighting traffic jams each day and parting with $80 a month in parking fees. Car pooling, buses, and the subway or Metro are the "in" ways of going to and from work. You should also know that the better elementary and secondary schools are located in the Virginia and Maryland suburbs. Lower property taxes are found in Virginia, and the housing becomes newer and less expensive the further you move from the city.

These differences are important. For example, you may be living in a 1,800 square feet townhouse worth $50,000 at present. The same townhouse may cost you $90,000 in a Virginia or Maryland suburb located 25 miles or a 50 minute commute from downtown Washington. This same townhouse may cost you $230,000 plus $200 a month maintenance fees in the exclusive Georgetown section of Washington. Here, you will be within walking distance of many government offices and businesses, live in one of the most socially and culturally fascinating and well-organized inner city communities in the nation, and make a bundle of money when you sell your much appreciated home--if the real estate market doesn't collapse!

However, you may not like living in the city, because of its poor schools, racial tensions, high crime rates, widespread poverty, and rising cost of living. If so, you need to reconcile yourself to the alternative life style and the headaches attendant with commuting to a job in the city. Since many government agencies, contractors, and businesses are located increasingly in the suburbs, living outside the city may actually result in living near your place of employment. Upon learning about these aspects of the community, and preferring neither life style, you may decide to drop the idea of moving to Washington altogether. If so, then this research was worth the time and effort. It is best to discover potential problems for both your personal and professional lives prior to making a move to a new community. Therefore, identify other communities and research them in the same manner until you find one which is most appealing.

Whatever the case, study the physical layout of the city and surrounding communities. Learn about the public transportation system. Washington's Metro is one of the best public transportation systems in the country. Price real estate, and compare property and income taxes. Ask questions about the schools and recreational facilities. For example, you will find that Washington has some of the finest state, national, and local parks in the nation. Baltimore and Annapolis, Maryland, as well as camping the the Blue Ridge Mountains and sailing on the Chesapeake Bay are only one to two hours away from downtown Washington. New York City and Philadelphia are nearby, and airplanes fly in all directions--just in case you need to get out of town occasionally.

If you are a lover of fine culture and foods, Washington will not disappoint you. Some of the finest museums, theaters, music, and restaurants in the country are found in and around Washington. Since the 1960s Washington has gone through a cultural renaissance. The quality of theater and art in Washington now rivals that of New York City's. Indeed, within the next two decades, Washington may become truly the nation's center for politics, culture, art, entertainment, and communication.

One of the best ways to acquaint yourself with Washington is to buy one or two standard guide books and subscribe to the _Washington Post_. This newspaper covers most important aspects of Washington life, and its quality is as good as, if not better than, _The New York Times_. Be sure to follow the employment section in the Sunday edition; the best real estate section is published in the Saturday edition. The _National Journal_ and the _Washington Monthly_ are good tabloids on politics and government in Washington; _The Washingtonian_ is the major community magazine. Through such sources you will learn that Washington has fewer than 10,000 millionnaires--not a city of the truly rich--and it is now entering the decade of a boom in high technology industries--previous decades saw booms in consumer hard goods (autos and appliances), retailing, and real estate (Glassman). Several other local journals, magazines, and newspapers may be worth examining. The Yellow Pages of the Washington, D.C., Northern Virginia, and Maryland Suburbs telephone books provide useful overviews of the business structure of the community. You may also want to examine a few of the hundreds of specialized directories and newsletters published on various aspects of government and business in Washington.

UNDERSTANDING AND UTILIZING NETWORKS

While you should research many aspects of the community, your most important goal is to acquire a job. This requires gathering information

202

on the political and economic structure of Washington.

Washington consists of literally thousands of networks involving
political, governmental, business, and media institutions. Ripley and
Franklin refer to the most powerful networks as "subgovernments" (Ripley
and Franklin: 5-7). These consist of clusters of individuals and groups
in a tripart relationship: congressional committees and subcommittees,
interest groups, and governmental agencies. Consisting of mutually supportive groups, together they shape the national policy process. This
subgovernment network is illustrated in Figure 16.

FIGURE 16

SUBGOVERNMENT PHENOMENON IN WASHINGTON

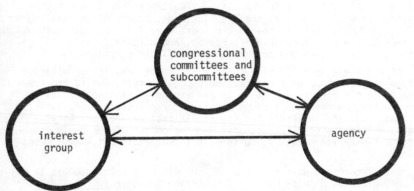

These networks have important implications for conducting a job
search campaign in Washington. Individuals working within the networks
know each other, cooperate regularly, and often utilize each other for
career advancement. For example, it is not uncommon for an agency official to resign and then acquire a new position with an interest group he
or she had dealings with while working in the agency. Another pattern
is for a government official to move into a congressional committee staff
position or on to a Congressman's personal staff. Even many defeated or
retired Congressmen utilize these networks in order to remain in
Washington as law partners, consultants, or lobbyists.

One other important group should be included in this subgovernment
network. These are the so-called "beltway bandits," or the ubiquitous
consultant and contracting firms, which do billions of dollars of contract work with the government each year. Such contracts involve doing
research and conducting programs for government agencies. Similar to
the employment dynamics of the tripart subgovernment network, these firms
also play an important role in the job-hopping phenomenon. Numerous individuals working for agencies, congressional committees and subcommittees, congressional staffs, and interest groups use their connections to
gain employment with the contracting and consulting firms.

Washington career opportunities relate to the use of these networks.
Depicted in Figure 17, this larger set of network relationships includes

FIGURE 17

INTERACTIVE WASHINGTON NETWORKS

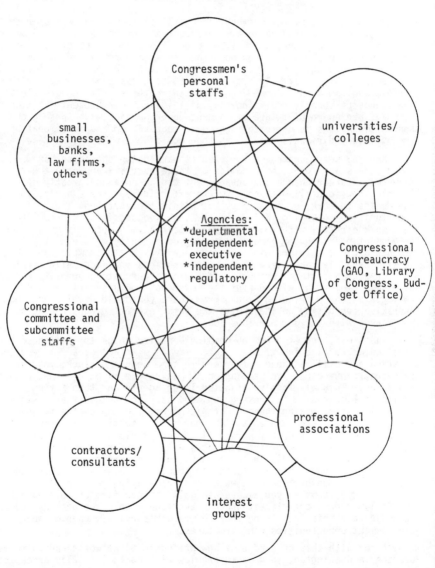

professional associations, the congressional bureaucracy, small businesses, banks, law firms, colleges and universities, and contractors and
consultants along with the more traditional interest groups, agencies,
and congressional staffs. Job-hopping takes place both within and between members of these networks.

Maintaining survival networks and gaining access are two major characteristics of jobs and careers in Washington (Peters: 5-7). Job-jumping
every two to five years, which takes place along the lines of our networks in Figure 17, is a common occurance in Washington. The nature of
government in Washington is such that interest group representatives and
contractors gain relatively easy access to congressional and agency personnel, who, in turn, accommodate each other. After all, congressional
and agency personnel, realizing they will leave their present positions
someday, are aware of future employment opportunities with these groups.
Hence, there is a much greater degree of cooperation and accommodation
among these individuals and groups than would otherwise be the case.

Any job search campaign targeted at Washington should be based on a
sound understanding of the dynamics of these survival and opportunity
networks. Career change and advancement can be enhanced greatly by
learning how to utilize these networks effectively. For example, you
may decide to work for an agency, but within two years you learn of
opportunities on Capitol Hill with the same congressional subcommittees
that work directly with your agency. Alternatively, you may resign your
government position for a more rewarding opportunity with a contractor
who has a close relationship with your agency. Whatever move you make,
it will probably take place through the contacts you made while working
in your agency-centered network. If you have graduate degrees, you may
also seek employment with one of the more than 100 universities and
colleges in the Washington area. From there you could develop your own
lucrative consulting business with the same interest groups and agencies
you worked with in your previous jobs.

The prevalence of such job-hopping behavior suggests that these survival networks also function as _career advancement networks_. If you understand and utilize these networks with some degree of luck, you can
fast-track your career in Washington by making the right combinations of
job-jumps. This may involve starting in an agency and then moving to
Capitol Hill, into an interest group, and back to an agency at a higher
GS level. After making these strategic moves, you may decide to join a
contracting firm and then establish your own consulting firm. From this
new base you may "raid" key personnel in the previous firm and compete
with your former employer for contracts with your former agency. Since
you know the right people in the agency, interest groups, and other consulting firms, your life in Washington should be relatively secure and
successful. However, you must work hard in managing your networks. If
your firm does poorly, you always can join another firm or move back to
the Hill, agency, or interest group. Everyone within the networks seems
to understand this "revolving door" of career survival, change, and
advancement opportunities and structures.

Armed with this knowledge of how professional networks and cultures
operate in Washington, your basic problem will be to initially break into
these networks. Once you get in, you can move around. While it is preferable to start in a government agency, other entry points should be

explored as well, particularly if federal opportunities are limited in your particular area of expertise. For example, several contracting and consulting firms should be examined. Although job security with contractors is limited because of the contract-to-contract nature of the business, working for one of these firms will result in making important contacts in government agencies and elsewhere. One of the easiest ways of identifying these firms is to go to the government agency you are interested in working for and ask for a list of their contractors. Copies of such lists usually are available; indeed, agency personnel often volunteer this information while giving you advice during an informational interview.

You should explore several possible employment entry points in anticipation of making strategic job moves for future career advancement. Getting a foot in the door, i.e., breaking into the networks at some point, may be more important than initially finding an ideal job. Thus, a Washington job search campaign should focus on several network entry points: government agencies, Congress (both personal and committee staff as well as the congressional bureaucracy), interest groups, professional associations, banks, businesses, and contracting and consulting firms.

THE PERSONAL TOUCH

Washington can be a closed world to outsiders seeking employment if not approached properly. It is a highly personalized world where career success depends on who you know as well as what you can do. You must make contacts by meeting and talking to people face-to-face and accumulating names and introductions to those people who can help you break into the networks. Targeting a job search campaign in Washington from a distance is difficult due to the importance of these personal relationships.

The job search strategies we have outlined in previous chapters ideally are suited to the personal world of Washington. If you choose to target Washington, follow the same advice as before: identify your objective, research organizations, write a one or two-page resume as well as complete the SF-171, prospect, conduct informational interviews, and wait for job interviews and offers. Your research activities and referral interviews will involve several types of organizations. Overall, targeting Washington requires a major investment of your time. After doing preliminary research and setting up appointments by mail and telephone, plan to spend two full weeks in Washington conducting informational interviews as well as learning more about other aspects of the community. Washingtonians understand networks and they will help outsiders who have a similar understanding. You may be surprised how easy it is to gain access to influential individuals. Your research and informational interviews will be keys to getting such access to job opportunities.

Always remember to send a thank-you letter to those who assist you. These people should be kept within your personal network even after you find a job. They will more than likely assist you again in your next job move, which may be within three years, and you may be able to assist them in turn. As soon as you find a job in Washington, it is common

206

practice to begin looking for another job for advancing your career.
When this happens, the networks need to be utilized again and again.
Although no one has precise figures, a large portion of individuals'
time is devoted to maintaining and expanding these personal networks for
career survival and advancement. In Washington you will probably learn
about, as well as join, this networking and job-jumping culture.

LIFE AFTER WASHINGTON

After Ronald Reagan defeated President Carter in the 1980 presidential election and hundreds of Democratic political appointees lost their
jobs, one former Washington-based Democrat advised the newly unemployed
that "there is life after Washington" (Kuttner: C1). We are uncertain how
unique Washington is when compared to other communities. Washingtonians
who have lived in other communities claim it isn't much different elsewhere. To them, America consistently has been a particularistic, ascriptive, and personal world. Unfortunately, many educators do not
understand this reality. However, there is one major difference in the
case of Washington. Congress, interest groups, and "beltway bandits"
are unique Washington-based institutions. As such, they create a more
complex system of networks as well as an expanded number of opportunity
structures for job seekers.

Other communities also have institutional networks which should be
utilized for job search purposes. As Norton Long observed many years
ago, the structure of communities is best viewed as an "ecology of games"
(Long: 252). Various institutions and individuals pursue their own
goals, but they also interact and cooperate with each other in this
process. Except in company towns, such as small university, mining, or
paper mill communities, no one game dominates the others. Banks, mort-
gage companies, brokerage firms, schools, churches, small businesses,
industries, hospitals, law firms, governments, and civic and volunteer
organizations play separate games as well as occasionally overlap with
one another for the purpose of achieving individual and common goals.
For example, city government is only one of many governors in the community. It needs bankers for maintaining the financial solvency of the
city. Bankers, in turn, need the city government for investment purposes,
and schools are dependent upon city government, bankers, and civic and
volunteer organizations for their continued support.

Long's perspective on communities in general is relevant to job
search campaigns. Although particular institutions and actors may differ,
all communities have networks comparable to those found in Washington.
Perhaps the major difference is that we are more aware of the dynamics
of networks in Washington than in New York City, Chicago, Atlanta, Dallas,
San Francisco, or other communities. Whatever city you choose, you should
begin by conducting a "mapping" operation similar to the one we outlined
here for Washington. You should thus be able to identify both personal
and professional opportunity structures for making your career change.

CHAPTER XIII

STARTING OVER AGAIN

We began this book with a definite purpose in mind: help educators
move out of education. Given the declining state of education today,
many educators need to seriously consider career alternatives. Many
teachers and administrators are increasingly finding themselves locked
into troubled institutions which are experiencing declining enrollments,
restrictive budgets, and the threat of terminating faculty and staff.
Others are beginning educational careers which will soon plateau and
stall. The trends are clear and the future for education is relatively
predictable. Overall, most educators are returning to the good old days
when they constituted an economically marginal class in society. Unfortunately, many educators will continue to be underemployed, underpaid,
and unappreciated. "High competition for low stakes" will continue to
characterize education as long as many educators remain to divide ever
decreasing resources.

Unless more educators face the truth about their future in education as well as explore their potential outside education, they will be
going nowhere over the next decade or two. There is life after education, and it can be extremely rewarding if you know how to identify and
relate your abilities and skills to alternative careers. Instead of
being defensive about retrenchment by seeking increased security within
education, we believe it is time for more educators to analyze their
present situations and plan to move out of education before more damage
is done to their careers. This book has provided the basic knowledge
and tools for you to begin making your move out and up from education.

CHANGING CAREERS

We have taken a no-nonsense approach to helping you develop a
realistic and successful job search campaign. These strategies are
based upon years of experience and are partly validated by social
science theory and research. If followed properly, our methods should
help you formulate and achieve your job objective. However, we also
recognize the complexity of reality. Our goal has been to equip you
with the basic concepts and approaches. You should adapt these to your
own job search campaign. The individual remains an important variable
in this whole process.

Success at changing careers and finding a job requires hard work,
planning, commitment, and perseverance. Many educators possess these
critical characteristics. In addition, they have flexible time schedules

which enable them to conduct a more extensive job search than people in other occupations.

Many myths about the job market and human behavior impede successful job search campaigns. These myths need to be challenged and replaced with reality-tested strategies. One of the most important myths is that the best qualified individual gets hired for a job. We live in interpersonal environments where who you are and what you can do are both important considerations in getting hired and moving ahead. Since the job market is highly personal, success in it requires job search strategies for communicating your abilities, skills, and personal characteristics. Building, maintaining, and expanding personal networks is central to finding a job best suited to your objective. We have outlined how you can accomplish this task in relationship to other important job search steps.

We acknowledge the role of luck and serendipity. Being in the right place and at the right time is always important to achieving success. Our goal is to put you in many places and at many times so that you can take full advantage of luck and serendipity. In this sense, our strategies attempt to optimize both planning and serendipity.

SUCCESSFUL ENTRY

This book assists you in making career and job changes; it does not tell you how to function in your new job. We assume you have the knowledge, intelligence, and sensitivity to also learn how to manage your new job and career. Pay particular attention to how you manage your networks on the job. If you need future guidance on this subject, Irish, Djeddah, Germann and Arnold, and several other writers provide useful advice on how to handle your new job as well as how to conduct an *internal career advancement campaign* as an alternative to job-hopping.

A vast amount of literature is also available on leadership and organizational behavior. This literature tells you how to become a good superior vis-a-vis your subordinates. Unfortunately, except for the career planning literature which tells you how to bail out of a job, there is no parallel "how to" information on how a subordinate can best handle a tyrannical or unreasonable superior. What do you do if your boss is an incompetent or a jerk? If you encounter such situations, we advise you to make a decision based upon an annual career and job assessment; this annual checkup should help you determine whether to stay in or get out. This assessment also should include an annual revised resume--just in case someone in your network is interested in knowing more about your qualifications. Since you never know when new opportunities may arise, always be prepared with your yearly resume.

Sometimes organizations get sick or you work for undesirable superiors. When this happens, you should analyze your situation and prepare to bail out for greener pastures if necessary. Doing internal patch work, such as having a frank discussion with your boss, may save your job, but it may well signal the beginning of the end of your career advancement within the organization. Thus, you also should face the truth about your new job and assess where you are going. If you are going nowhere, you may once again need to consider career and job alter- natives. Given the strategies outlined in this book, you should be well prepared for this change too. As we noted earlier, it is normal to un- dergo several career and job changes during your lifetime. In many sit- uations, the only way to advance your career is to change your job.

REMEMBERING YOUR NETWORKS

Our final advice for getting started in your new career and job is to work hard and remember your networks. A successful job search is a very personal experience. But don't mistake personal criteria for the good old boy, do-nothing system. Employers want _competent_, _qualified_, and _personable_ employees. Once you are hired, demonstrate that you are all of these things, especially your _competence_. Our strategies are not designed to help the incompetent and lazy get a free lunch. As you pull your own strings, you need to pull your own weight by producing results!

Always remember to build and nurture your networks. Family, friends, and acquaintances are the key to getting ahead. Most people want to give advice, want to help, want to be needed, and want recipro- city. Develop positive and mutually supportive relationships with others. Be thoughtful by sending thank-you letters and returning favors. Under no circumstances should you use, abuse, exploit, or forget friend- ships. If necessary, sharpen your interpersonal and communication skills so that you can better develop and utilize these networks.

REPEATING SUCCESS

Careers and jobs should not be viewed as life sentences. You should feel free to change jobs and careers whenever you want to. As Irish notes,

Most professional people today have four or five "careers." They feel free to leave a job they do well to take another. And there is no great secret why they do it; these men and women know what they _want_... Younger people stay at jobs they don't like because (a) they _panic_ at the thought of finding another job; (b) they don't know what to do _next_; (c) they feel "loyal" to the person or organization they work for; (d) they don't feel free to do what they _want_ (Irish: 218).

Once you make your career and job change, be prepared to repeat the change again. You should find this book useful for managing your other job and career changes. The strategies we have outlined for educators can be adapted to other occupational groups.

If you learn some things about career and job changes we failed to mention for educators, please let us know. We want to be as helpful as possible in seeing that you and others make the necessary breaks and find new careers and jobs which are more exciting, rewarding, and fulfilling than the ones you have previously experienced. We wish you well in your venture to move out of education.

APPENDIX A

UNDERSTANDING TRANSFERABLE SKILLS

Several studies stress the importance of occupational adaptability and transferable skills in today's changing job market. _Occupational adaptability_ refers to the capacity of individuals to adapt to work environments as well as adapt work environments to their motivations, abilities, and skills. _Transferable skills_ are the functional abilities individuals take with them from one job to another. Adaptability occurs when individuals transfer their skills to different occupational settings and adapt to new frames of reference (Ashley: 78-79). However, understanding your skills is important to effectively adapting to new occupational settings.

The concept of transferable skills is receiving greater research attention in attempts to better understand the dynamics of the job market. One of the leading researchers in this area, The National Center for Research in Vocational Education, has conducted extensive studies on what it terms "competencies" or transferable skills. In one study of the Transferable Skills program, they asked a national probability sample of 2,083 adults to classify and rank a list of 39 competencies. The eleven most important competencies are rank ordered in Table 7. Respondents further classified 28, or 71 percent, of the 39 competencies as having been learned primarily at work. These are presented in Table 8. Other competencies, as identified in Table 9, were judged to have been acquired essentially at home (10 percent) or in school (10 percent).

While the survey of the National Center for Research in Vocational Education presents the perspectives of _employees_, other research examines transferable skills from the perspectives of _employers_. Wiant's study of transferable skills, for instance, found that employers most frequently mention the skills outlined in Table 10 as best transferable to their occupational areas (Stump: 100). The studies of the Canadian Employment and Immigration Commission provide another comprehensive listing and classification of transferable skills and abilities. These are in basic agreement with several studies conducted in the United States (Neeb, Cunningham, and Pass; Mecham and McCormick). These skills are presented in Tables 11 and 12.

TABLE 7

MOST IMPORTANT COMPETENCIES
(in rank order)

Rank order	Competency/Transferable Skill	Percentage response N=2,083
1	Use the reading, writing, and math skills the job calls for	54
2	Use the tools and equipment the job calls for	52
3	Get along with others	51
4	Deal with pressures to get the job done	48
5	Follow rules and policies	48
6	Have a good work attitude	45
7	Follow job safety and health rules	43
8	Hold a job that matches one's interests and abilities	40
9	Get a job for which one has the training and background	39
10	Get information about what is expected of you when starting a new job	37
11	Work without supervision, if necessary	35

SOURCE: Ashley: 81.

TABLE 8

COMPETENCIES LEARNED AT WORK

Matching One's Personal Job Preference*

Hold a job that matches one's interests and abilities
Know if one wants to own a business or work for someone else
Use the tools and equipment a job calls for
Do parts of the job one may not like to do
Interview for different job positions when necessary
Fill out forms as required by law or by an employer
Use materials and the knowledge of other people to develop one's job interests

Traditional Job Values*

Get information about what is expected of you when starting a new job
Deal with pressures to get the job done
Tell others what you are doing or what you want done

TABLE 8--continued

Work without supervision, if necessary
Follow job safety and health rules
Deal with unexpected things that happen
Know one's rights as an employee
Follow rules and policies

Being Innovative--Taking Risks*

Figure out a better way to get things done
Get support from others to change things that need changing
    on the job
Do things at work in a new way when one gets the chance
Take chances that may result in rewards

Personal Benefit*

Be a member of a union or professional group
Know when one's own work is being done well
Learn new job skills to get a different job or position
Get promoted on the job
Ask for a raise in salary
Decide how and when to leave a job for another job
Use what one already knows to do a new or different job
Understand wages and deductions on one's pay stub
Understand the extras or benefits offered at work

* Group of competencies based on results of factor analysis
SOURCE: Ashley: 82.

TABLE 9

COMPETENCIES LEARNED AT HOME OR SCHOOL

Learned at Home

Get along with others
Dress and act properly
Have a good work attitude
Manage one's own time and activities

Learned at School

Know what kind of work one wants to do
Get a job for which one has the training and background
Use the reading, writing, and math skills the job calls for
Know where to look for information about jobs one has or would
    like to have

SOURCE: Ashley: 82.

TABLE 10

COMPOSITE LIST OF TRANSFERABLE SKILLS IDENTIFIED BY EMPLOYERS

Intellectual/Aptitudinal	Interpersonal	Attitudinal
Communicating (44)	Working with, getting	Diligence, or a positive
Problem solving (17)	along with, or relat-	attitude toward the
Analyzing/assessing (15)	ing to others (28)	value of work (11)
Planning/layout (14)	Managing, directing,	Receptivity/flexibility/
Decision making (13)	or supervising (13)	adaptability
Creativity/imagination/	Empathizing, or being	Determination/perse-
innovation	sensitive to others	verance
Problem identification/	Teaching, training, or	Acceptance/appreciation/
definition	instructing	concern for others
Managing ones own time	Counseling	Responsibility
Basic computation	Motivating	Willingness to learn
Logical thinking	Gaining acceptance, or	Ambition/motivation
Evaluating	building rapport	Self-confidence
Ability to relate common	Helping, or cooper-	Pride
knowledge or transfer	ating	Enthusiasm
experiences	Cultivating coopera-	Patience
Coping with the labor	tion	Self-actualization
market and job	Selling	Assertiveness
movement	Accepting supervision	Honesty
Understanding others	Delegating	Loyalty
Synthsizing	Instilling confidence	Reliability
Marshalling resources	Team building	Risk taking
Accommodating multiple		Compromising
demands		Kindness
Judgment		
Foresight		

Trouble shooting
Job awareness
Mechnical aptitude
Typing
Accounting
Implementing
Self-understanding, aware-
ness, actualization
Situational analysis
Assessing environments/
situations
Understanding human
system interactions
Organizational savvy
Conceptualization
Generalization
Goal setting
Controlling
Quantitative thinking
Dealing with work situa-
tions
Finance
Tool usage
Bookkeeping
Artistic ability
Business sense
Tolerance of ambiguity

SOURCE: Wiant.

TABLE 11

CONTENT OF CORE SKILL CLUSTERS OF NONSUPERVISORY OCCUPATIONS IN GENERIC SKILLS PROJECT

Skills Areas

Mathematics	Communications	Interpersonal	Reasoning
1. Read, write, and count whole numbers	1. Know plurals.	1. Attend physically.	1. Obtain information about takes, materials, equip.
2. Add and subtract whole numbers.	2. Know prefixes and suffixes.	2. Attend cognitively.	2. Obtain information about methods and procedures.
3. Multiply and divide whole numbers.	3. Contractions and abbreviations.	3. React to others.	3. Obtain information about sequence.
4. Solve word problems with whole numbers.	4. Use dictionary.	4. Elementary one-to-one conversation.	4. Obtain other job related information.
5. Round off whole numbers.	5. Synonyms, antonyms, and homonyms.	5. Task-focused conversation.	5. Recall theories or principles.
6. Read and write fractions.	6. Meaning from context.	6. Express point of view.	6. Sort objects.
7. Add and subtract fractions.	7. Use books.	7. Personable conversation.	7. Estimate time.
8. Multiply and divide fractions.	8. Comprehend oral communication literally.	8. Participate in group discussion.	8. Estimate weight.
9. Solve word problems with fractions.	9. Interpret oral communication.	9. Respond to information or directions.	9. Estimate distance.
10. Compute dollars and cents.	10. Pronounce words correctly.	10. Give instructions.	10. Sequence tasks.
11. Read, write, and round off decimals.	11. Use good diction and word choice.	11. Demonstrate.	11. Establish task priorities.
12. Multiply and divide decimals.	12. Speak fluently.	12. Monitor.	12. Get goals.
13. Add and subtract decimals.	13. Organize ideas while speaking.	13. Give directions.	13. Determine activities to reach goals.

216

TABLE 11--continued

Skills Areas			
Mathematics	Communications	Interpersonal	Reasoning
14. Solve word problems with decimals.	14. Ask the six W questions.		14. Decide about alternatives.
15. Read and write percents.	15. Give directions or information.		15. Set criteria.
16. Compute percentage.	16. Use the telephone.		16. Set priorities.
17. Determine equiva- lents.	17. Literal comprehension of reading.		17. Analyze situation.
18. Know order of operations.	18. Interpretive compre- hension of reading.		18. Make deductions.
19. Solve word problems (mixed operations).	19. Read forms.		19. See cause and effect relationships
20. Do quick calcula- tions.	20. Read notes, letters, memos.		20. Identify possible problems.
21. Compute averages.	21. Read charts and tables.		21. Set priorities in terms of diagnosis.
22. Read graduated scales.	22. Read manuals.		22. Explore possible methods.
23. Perform operations with time.	23. Write phrases on forms.		23. Ask probing questions.
24. Operate calculator.	24. Write sentences on forms.		24. Use senses.
	25. Write sentences.		25. Determine relevant informa- tion for problem solving.
	26. Write short notes.		26. Arrive at alternative statements.
	27. Take notes.		27. Select statement.
			28. Determine alternative solutions.
			29. Select alternative.
			30. Update plans.

SOURCE: Sjogren.

TABLE 12.

CONTENT OF CORE SKILL CLUSTERS OF SUPERVISORY OCCUPATIONS IN GENERIC SKILLS PROJECT

		Skills Areas		
Mathematics	Communications	Interpersonal	Reasoning	
1-24. Same as nonsuper-visory occupations.	1-27. Same as nonsuper-visory occupations.	1-13. Same as nonsuper-visory occupations.	1-30. Same as nonsupervisory occupations.	
25. Compute ratios.	28. Evaluative comprehen-sion in listening	14. Attend covertly or unobtrusively.	31. Sort data.	
26. Compute proportions.	29. Evaluative comprehen-sion in reading.	15. Persuasive conver-sation.	32. Rate objects.	
27. Compute rates.	30. Write paragraphs on forms.	16. Prepare group dis-cussion.	33. Rank objects.	
28. Compute principal.	31. Write paragraphs.	17. Present information or directions to group.	34. Develop classifications.	
29. Measure weight.	32. Write form letters.	18. Lead group discus-sion.	35. Esimate area.	
30. Measure distance.	33. Write single para-graph.	19. Maintain groups.	36. Estimate capacity.	
31. Measure capacity.	34. Write internal memos.	20. Prepare oral pre-sentation.	37. Estimate cubic measures.	
32. Know geometric forms and figures.	35. Write business letters.	21. Give factual infor-mation in oral pre-sentation.	38. Estimate costs.	
33. Computation on angles.	36. Write information reports.	22. Get attention and response to oral presentation.	39. Plan and coordinate activities and sequences.	
34. Draw/sketch geometric forms and figures.	37. Write recommendation reports.	23. Give a conceptual oral presentation.	40. Outline plans.	
35. Compute perimeters.	38. Write technical reports.	24. Give a persuasive oral presentation.	41. Identify resources.	

TABLE 12--continued

	Skills Areas		
Mathematics	Communications	Interpersonal	Reasoning
36. Compute areas.		25. Get reaction to oral presentation.	42. Estimate resources.
37. Compute volumes.		26. Establish training program.	43. Determine critical activities.
38. Read graphs.		27. Evaluate instructional communication.	44. Make a detailed plan.
39. Read scale drawings.		28. Demonstrate to others.	45. Make resource requisitions.
40. Read assembly drawings.		29. Give praise.	46. Monitor results.
41. Read schematic drawings.		30. Give discipline.	47. Determine standards of quality.
42. Draw graphs.		31. Prepare evaluation reports.	48. Determine standards of quantity.
43. Measure from scale drawings.		32. Prepare for interview.	49. Determine standards of completion time.
44. Draw to scale.		33. Ask closed questions in interview.	50. Establish priorities of standards.
45. Solve algebraic formulas.		34. Ask open questions in interview.	51. Exercise authority and responsibility.
		35. Deal with confrontation.	
		36. Interview customers/ clients.	
		37. Interview job applicants.	
		38. Negotiate.	

SOURCE: Sjogren.

APPENDIX B

RESUMES

(1) Standard Chronological Resume (Obituary Type)

(2) Improved Chronological Resume

(3) Functional Resume

(4) Combination Resume

(5) Resume Letter

220

Karen Jones (1)

Address: 1234 Main Street
          Norfolk, VA 23508

Telephone: Area Code 804, Number 440-4321

Marital Status: Divorced; 2 children; ages 10 and 12
Date of Birth: April 1, 1945
Health: Excellent
Height: 5 feet, 4 inches
Weight: 125 lbs.

Educational Background:

University of Virginia, Charlottesville, Virginia.
Bachelor of Arts Degree in English Literature with Certification
in Secondary Education, June 1967.

Old Dominion University, Norfolk, Virginia. Master of Science
Degree in Secondary Education, June 1972.

Work History:

1973 to Present - Norfolk Public Schools, Norfolk, VA.
English Teacher - I teach 11th and 12th grade English
composition and creative writing classes. I have also
served as co-director of the senior class play, coordinated
student fund raising activities, and chaired the school
committee which developed recruiting and public relations
materials. I have given speeches at student events and
helped write speeches for the school administration.

1969-1973 - Full-time Homemaker.

1967-1969 - Chesapeake Public Schools, Chesapeake, Virginia.
English Teacher - I taught 10th and 11th grade composition
classes.

Community Involvements:

Toastmaster's International. Since 1972, I have been very
active and have held a variety of chapter offices. During
the past three years I have served as a district representative
and officer.

Hobbies and Interests:

I enjoy physical exercise (running and racketball), sailing,
piano, theater, gardening, and gourmet cooking.

References:

Dr. James Smith, Superintendent of Norfolk Public Schools.
Mr. Robert Sinclair, Principal, Norfolk High School
Mr. Paul Amos, Governor, Tidewater District, Toastmasters International.

②

KAREN JONES
1234 Main Street
Norfolk, Virginia 23508
Telephone 804-440-4321

OBJECTIVE: A public relations position involving program planning and coordination which requires an ability to work with diverse publics, develop publicity and promotional campaigns, market services and benefits, and meet deadlines.

WORK EXPERIENCE:

English Teacher: Norfolk Public Schools, Norfolk, Virginia. Taught creative writing and composition. Organized and supervised numerous fund-raising projects which involved local businesses, media, parents, and students. Co-directed senior class plays. Wrote and gave several "keynote" speeches at special student programs. Served as school liaison to Parent-Teachers Association; designed a plan to increase membership and involve parents in school activities. Chaired city-wide public relations committee; coordinated development and production of promotional materials. Served as speech "ghost-writer" and editor for administrators. (1973 to present)

English Teacher: Chesapeake Public Schools, Chesapeake, Virginia. Taught English composition. Wrote, designed, and developed multi-media instructional programs to interest students in writing. Served as advisor to student newspaper. (1967-69)

ADDITIONAL EXPERIENCE:

Toastmasters International, Tidewater Chapter, Virginia.

District Representative: Elected to governing board of Southeast Virginia District. Served in liaison capacity between district officers and local chapter. Planned, organized, and publicized training workshops and regional competition. (1979-present)

Chapter Officer (President, Treasurer, Sargent-at-Arms): Developed a publicity plan which increased membership by 20 percent. Kept financial records and prepared budget reports. Acquired extensive public speaking experience and training. (1975-79)

EDUCATION:

M.S.Ed. in Secondary Education, 1972: Old Dominion University, Norfolk, Virginia.

B.A. in English Literature, 1967: University of Virginia, Charlottesville, Virginia.

③

KAREN JONES

1234 Main Street
Norfolk, Virginia 23508
Telephone 804-440-4321

OBJECTIVE: A public relations position involving program planning
and coordination which requires an ability to work with
diverse publics, develop publicity and promotional
campaigns, market services and benefits, and meet
deadlines.

AREAS OF EFFECTIVENESS

PLANNING
AND
COORDINATING

Organized and supervised several fund raising
projects. Designed and implemented membership
campaigns. Chaired public relations committee
for school system; coordinated development and
production of promotional materials. Served in
liaison capacity between different groups and
represented school to parents. Planned and
organized meetings, contests, and training
programs. Co-directed student plays.

PROMOTING,
PUBLICIZING,
MARKETING,
AND
WRITING

Developed promotional plan to attract new members
to organizations. Coordinated publicity of special
events with media. Wrote and edited speeches for
self and school administrators. Helped design and
produce promotional materials. Publicized special
events and programs to constituent groups. Developed
multi-media instructional package to facilitate
learning and involve students. Taught creative
writing.

COMMUNICATING
AND
INSTRUCTING

Gave numerous speeches over a seven year period
to a variety of audiences. Conducted meetings
and chaired committees. Coached administrators
in writing and presenting speeches. Taught
English for ten years in public schools.

EDUCATION: M.S.Ed., Old Dominion University, Norfolk, Virginia,
1972.

B.A., University of Virginia, Charlottesville,
Virginia.

(4)

KAREN JONES
1234 Main Street
Norfolk, Virginia 23508
Telephone 804-440-4321

OBJECTIVE: A public relations position involving program planning and coordination which requires an ability to work with diverse publics, develop publicity and promotional campaigns, market services and benefits, and meet deadlines.

AREAS OF EFFECTIVENESS

PLANNING
AND
COORDINATION

Organized and supervised several fund raising projects. Designed and implemented membership campaigns. Chaired public relations committee for school system; coordinated development and production of promotional materials. Served in liaison capacity between different groups and organized meetings, contests, and training programs. Co-directed student plays.

PROMOTING,
PUBLICIZING,
MARKETING,
AND
WRITING

Developed promotional plan to attract new members to organizations. Coordinated publicity of special events with media. Wrote and edited speeches for self and school administrators. Helped design and produce promotional materials. Publicized special events and programs to constituent groups. Developed multi-media instructional package to facilitate learning and involve students. Taught creative writing.

COMMUNICATING
AND
INSTRUCTING

Gave numerous speeches over a seven year period to a variety of audiences. Conducted meetings and chaired committees. Coached administrators in writing and presenting speeches. Taught English for ten years in public schools.

WORK EXPERIENCE:

English Teacher: Norfolk Public Schools, Norfolk, Virginia. Taught 11th and 12th grade creative writing and composition. (1973-present)

English Teacher: Chesapeake Public Schools, Chesapeake, Virginia. Taught 10th and 11th grade composition. Advisor to student newspaper. (1967-69)

EDUCATION:

M.S.Ed., Old Dominion University, 1972.

B.A., University of Virginia, 1967.

(5)

1234 Main Street
Norfolk, Virginia 23508
April 30, 198_

Mr. Dale Roberts, Business Manager
Virginia Beach Convention Center
Virginia Beach, Virginia 23519

Dear Mr. Roberts:

A mutual acquaintance of ours, Paul Amos, suggested that
I contact you about the new Virginia Beach Convention Center.
He remarked that you are developing a comprehensive public
relations and marketing plan to attract convention business.

As an officer of my local chapter and regional division
of Toastmasters International, I have acquired a substantial
amount of public relations, special events planning, and
program coordination experience. Along with my professional
work, my background includes working with diverse audiences,
developing publicity campaigns and promotional materials,
marketing services and benefits, recruiting new members,
handling financial records, and meeting important deadlines.
Furthermore, I have experience in writing and giving speeches,
chairing work groups, representing organizations, creative
writing, and teaching.

Since I have a strong interest in public relations-type
activities and have a thorough knowledge of our region and its
resources, I was quite interested to hear that your new marketing plan may utilize conference coordinators to work with your
sales staff. I would be very interested in learning more
about your plans and exploring future possibilities.

I plan to be near your office next week and wonder if we
could have a brief meeting? I'll give your office a call in
the next few days to see if a mutually convenient time could
be arranged.

Sincerely,

Karen Jones

APPENDIX C

Standard Form 171

Personal Qualifications Statement

IMPORTANT
READ THE FOLLOWING INSTRUCTIONS CAREFULLY BEFORE FILLING OUT YOUR STATEMENT

- You must furnish all requested information. The information you provide will be used to determine your qualifications for employment. DO NOT SUBMIT A RESUME IN LIEU OF COMPLETING THIS STATEMENT.

- If you fail to answer all questions on your Statement fully and accurately, you may delay consideration of your Statement and lose employment opportunities. See the Privacy Act Notice on the reverse of this sheet.

- So that it is understood that you did not omit an item, please write the letters "N/A" (Not Applicable) beside those items that do not apply to you unless instructions indicate otherwise.

GENERAL INSTRUCTIONS

- If you are applying for a specific Civil Service Commission examination:

    —Read the examination announcement or the Qualifications Information Statement for the position to be certain that your experience and education is qualifying.

    —If a written test is required, follow the filing instructions on the admission card.

    —If no written test is required, mail this Statement to the Civil Service Commission Area Office specified in the announcement or on the Qualifications Information Statement.

    —Be sure to include all other forms required.

    —If you have a change of name or address, notify the Civil Service Commission Area Office with which you filed this Statement.

    —You may want to make a copy of this Statement for your personal use.

INSTRUCTION RELATING TO SPECIFIC ITEMS
ITEM 13. LOWEST GRADE OR SALARY

- Enter the lowest grade or the lowest salary you will accept. You will not be considered for any lower grades or salary. You will be considered for all higher grades or salary for which you qualify based upon those specified in the examination announcement or the Qualifications Information Statement.

ITEM 16. OTHER GOVERNMENT & INTERNATIONAL AGENCIES

- The Civil Service Commission is occasionally requested to refer for employment consideration the names or eligibles on competitive registers to State and local government agencies, congressional and other public offices, and public international organizations. Indicate your availability by checking the appropriate boxes. Your response to this question will not affect your consideration for other positions.

ITEM 18. OVERNIGHT TRAVEL

- Indicate the number of nights per month you are willing to be away from home in a travel status. Some jobs require nearly constant travel of two or three weeks every month while others require infrequently short or occasionally extended periods of travel. You will be considered for positions requiring travel based on the number of nights per month for which you indicate travel availability.

ITEM 20. ACTIVE MILITARY SERVICE AND VETERAN PREFERENCE

- Five-point veteran preference is granted to veterans who receive an honorable or general discharge from the armed forces:
    - (a) after active duty during the periods April 6, 1917 to July 2, 1921 and December 7, 1941 to July 1, 1955;
    - (b) after more than 180 consecutive days of active duty, any part of which occurred after January 31, 1955 and before October 15, 1976.
        NOTE—Service under an initial period of active duty for training under the "6-month" Reserve or National Guard programs is not creditable for veteran preference; and
    - (c) after service in a campaign for which a campaign badge has been authorized.
    You will be required to furnish records to support your claim for five-point preference only at the time of your appointment.

- Ten-point veteran preference is granted to:
    - (a) compensably disabled veterans; and
    - (b) veterans awarded the Purple Heart.
    Ten-point veteran preference is granted in certain cases to:
    - (a) unmarried widows and widowers of veterans;
    - (b) spouses of compensably disabled veterans; and
    - (c) mothers of deceased or disabled veterans.
    If you claim ten-point veteran preference, submit Standard Form 15, Claim for 10-Point Veteran Preference, and the required proof with this application. Obtain SF 15 and information on provisions of the Veteran Preference laws at any Federal Job Information Center.

- A clemency discharge does not meet the Veteran Preference Act requirement for discharge under honorable conditions. Accordingly, no preference may be granted to applicants with such discharge.

PLEASE READ ADDITIONAL INSTRUCTIONS ON BACK OF THIS SHEET

ITEM 21. EXPERIENCE

- Allow sufficient time to fill in these experience blocks carefully and completely. A large part of your qualifications rating depends upon a thorough description of your experience and employment history.

- If you fail to give complete details, you may delay consideration of your Statement. Your description of duties may be verified with former employers.

- If you supervise or have supervised other employees, be sure to indicate the number and kind (and grades, if Federal Government) of employees supervised, and describe your duties as a supervisor under Description of Work.

- Volunteer Experience—You may receive credit for pertinent religious, civic, welfare, service and organizational work performed with or without compensation. Show the actual amount of time spent in such work (for example, average hours per week or month). Complete all the items just as you would for a compensable position.

- Use separate blocks if your duties, responsibilities, or salary have changed materially while working for the same employer. Treat each such change as a separate position.
  NOTE—Experience gained more than 15 years ago may be summarized in one block if it is not pertinent to the type of position you applied for.

- Include your military or merchant marine service in separate blocks in its separate order and describe what duty assignments.

- Indicate in each block of Item 21 the name under which you were employed if it was different from the name in Item 6 of this Statement. Show former name in parentheses after "Description of duties and accomplishments in your work."

- Indicate periods of unemployment exceeding three months and your address at that time on the last line of the preceding experience block.

- Block A—Describe your present position in this block. Indicate if you are now unemployed or if you have never been employed.

- Blocks B and C—Describe in block B the position you held just before your present position and continue to work backwards using block C.

- Enter the average number of hours per week you work. If you work part time, indicate the average number of hours per week you work.

- Description of work—Describe each job briefly, including required skills and abilities. Describe any specialties and special assignments, your authority and responsibility, your relationships to others, your accomplishments, and any other factors which help to describe the job.

- If your job contains experience in more than one type of work (for example; carpentry and painting, or personnel and budget) estimate and indicate the approximate percentage of time spent in each type of work. Place the percentages in parentheses at the end of the description of work.

- If you need additional experience blocks:
  —Use Standard Form 171-A, Continuation Sheet; or
  —A plain sheet of paper approximately 8 by 10½ inches in size. Be sure to include all of the information requested in Item 21.

  If you need additional space to describe a position held:
  —Continue in Item 35, Space for detailed answers; or
  —Continue on a plain sheet of paper.

ITEM 21. EXPERIENCE—(Continued)

- Identify each plain sheet of paper used by showing your name, birth date, examination or position title, and the block under Item 21 from which the description is continued.

- Attach all supplemental sheets to the top of page 3.

ITEMS 32 and 33. RELATIVES EMPLOYED BY THE UNITED STATES GOVERNMENT

- A Federal official (civilian or military) may not appoint any of his or her relatives or recommend them for employment in his or her agency, and a relative who is appointed in violation of this restriction cannot be paid. Thus it is necessary to have information about your relatives who are working for the Government. In listing relative(s) in answer to question 32 include: father; mother; son; daughter; brother; sister; uncle; aunt; first cousin; nephew; niece; husband; wife; father-in-law, mother-in-law; son-in-law; daughter-in-law; brother-in-law; sister-in-law; stepfather; stepmother; stepson; stepdaughter, stepbrother; stepsister; half brother; and half sister.

- Question 33 is needed because of restrictions in making a career or career-conditional appointment in the competitive service when a person is not entitled to veteran preference and two or more members of his or her family are already serving in the competitive service under a career or career-conditional appointment.

CERTIFICATION

- Be careful that you have answered all questions on your Statement correctly and considered all statements fully so that your eligibility can be decided on all the facts. Read the certification carefully before you sign and date your Statement.

- Sign your name in ink.

- Use one given name, initial or initials, and last name.

PRIVACY ACT INFORMATION

The U.S. Civil Service Commission is authorized to rate applicants for Federal jobs under sections 1302, 3301, and 3304 of Title 5 of the U.S. Code. We need the information you put on this form to see how well your education and work skills fit you for a Federal job. We also need information on matters such as citizenship and military service to see whether you are affected by laws we must follow in deciding who may be employed by the Federal Government. We cannot give you a rating, which is the first step toward getting a job, if you do not answer these questions.

We must have your Social Security Number (SSN) to keep your records straight because other people may have the same name and birthdate. The SSN has been used to keep records since 1943, when Executive Order 9397 asked agencies to do so. The Civil Service Commission may also use your SSN to make requests for information about you from employers, schools, banks, and others who know you, but only where that is allowed by law. The information we collect by using your SSN will be used for employment purposes and also for studies and statistics that will not identify you.

Information we have about you may also be given to Federal, State, and local agencies for checking on law violations or other lawful purposes. We may also notify your school placement office if you are selected for a Federal job.

PLEASE DETACH THIS INSTRUCTION SHEET BEFORE SUBMITTING YOUR STATEMENT

227

Personal Qualifications Statement
Read instructions before completing form

Form Approved:
O.M.B. No. 50-R0387

1. Kind of position (job) you are filing for (or title and number of announcement)

2. Options for which you wish to be considered (if listed in the announcement)

3. Home phone — Area Code — Number

4. Work phone — Area Code — Number — Extension

5. Preferred title (mark one)
☐ Mr. ☐ Mrs. ☐ Miss ☐ Ms.

6. Other last names ever used (e.g., Maiden)

7. Name (Last, First, Middle)

Street address or RFD no. (include apartment no., if any)

City | State | ZIP Code

8. Birthplace (City & State, or foreign country)

9. Birth date (Month, day, year)

10. Social Security Number

11. If you have ever been employed by the Federal Government as a civilian, give your highest grade, classification series, and job title.

Dates of service in that grade (Month, day, and year)
From | To

12. If you currently have an application on file with the Civil Service Commission for appointment to a Federal position, (a) list the name of the area office maintaining your application, (b) the position for which you filed, and (if appropriate) (c) the date of your notice of rating, (d) your identification number, and (e) your rating.

13. Lowest pay or grade you will accept:
PAY — $ per — OR — GRADE

14. When will you be available for work? (Month and year)

DO NOT WRITE IN THIS BLOCK
FOR USE OF EXAMINING OFFICE ONLY

Material ☐ Submitted ☐ Returned — Entered register:

Notations:

Form reviewed:

Form approved:

Option	Grade	Earned Rating	Preference	Aug. Rating
			☐ 5 Points (Tent.)	
			☐ 10 Points Comp. Dis.	
			☐ Other 10 Points	
			☐ Disal.	
			☐ Being Investigated	

Initials and date

ANNOUNCEMENT NO.

STATEMENT NO.

THIS SPACE FOR USE OF APPOINTING OFFICER ONLY
Preference has been verified through proof that the separation was under honorable conditions, and other proof as required.

☐ 5-Point ☐ 10-Point Compensable Disab. ☐ 10-Point Other

Signature and title

Agency | Date

---

15. Are you available for temporary employment lasting: | YES | NO
(Acceptance or refusal of temporary employment will not affect your consideration for other appointments.)
A. Less than 1 month? ....
B. 1 to 4 months? ....
C. 5 to 12 months? ....

16. Are you interested in being considered for employment by: | YES | NO
A. State and local government agencies? ....
B. Congressional and other public offices? ....
C. Public international organizations? ....

17. Where will you accept a job: | YES | NO
A. In the Washington, D.C. Metropolitan area?
B. Outside the 50 United States? ....
C. Anyplace in the United States? ....
D. Only in (specify locality):

18. Indicate your availability for overnight travel:
A. Not available for overnight travel ....
B. 1 to 5 nights per month ....
C. 6 to 10 nights per month ....
D. 11 or more nights per month ....

19. Are you available for part-time positions (fewer than 40 hours per week) offering: | YES | NO
A. 20 or fewer hours per week? ....
B. 21 to 31 hours per week? ....
C. 32 to 39 hours per week? ....

20. Veteran Preference. Answer all parts. If a part does not apply to you, answer "NO". | YES | NO

A. Have you ever served on active duty in the United States military service? (Exclude tours of active duty for training in Reserves or National Guard) ....

B. Have you ever been discharged from the armed services under other than honorable conditions? (You may omit any such discharge changed to honorable or general by a Discharge Review Board or similar authority.) ....
If "YES", give details in item 36.

C. Do you claim 5 point preference based on active duty in the armed forces? ....
If "YES", you will be required to furnish records to support your claim at the time you are appointed.

D. Do you claim 10 point preference? ....
If "YES", check the type of preference claimed and complete and attach Standard Form 15, "Claim for 10 Point Veteran Preference", together with the proof requested in that form.
Type of Preference: ☐ Compensable Disability ☐ Non-compensable Disability ☐ Purple Heart Recipient ☐ Spouse ☐ Widow(er) ☐ Mother

E. List dates, branch, and serial number of all active service (enter "N/A" if not applicable).
From | To | Branch of Service | Serial or Service Number

THE FEDERAL GOVERNMENT IS AN EQUAL OPPORTUNITY EMPLOYER — 171-106 — Standard Form 171 (rev. 12-77) U.S. Civil Service Commission

Page 1

228

21 Experience Begin with current or most recent work or volunteer experience and work back. Account for periods of unemployment exceeding three months and your residence address at that time on the last line of the experience blocks in order of occurrence.

May inquiry be made of your present employer regarding your character, qualifications, and record of employment?
(A "NO" will not affect your consideration for employment opportunities except for Administrative Law Judge positions.) ☐ YES ☐ NO

A

Name and address of employer's organization (include ZIP Code, if known)	Dates employed (give month and year)	Average number of hours per week
	From To	
	Salary or earnings	Place of employment
	Beginning $ per	City
	Ending $ per	State

Exact title of your position	Name of immediate supervisor	Area Code Telephone Number	Number and kind of employees you supervised

Kind of business or organization (manufacturing, accounting, social services, etc.)	If Federal service, civilian or military: series, grade or rank, and date of last promotion	Your reason for wanting to leave

Description of work (Describe your specific duties, responsibilities and accomplishments in this job.):

For agency use (skill codes, etc.)

B

Name and address of employer's organization (include ZIP Code, if known)	Dates employed (give month and year)	Average number of hours per week
	From To	
	Salary or earnings	Place of employment
	Beginning $ per	City
	Ending $ per	State

Exact title of your position	Name of immediate supervisor	Area Code Telephone Number	Number and kind of employees you supervised

Kind of business or organization (manufacturing, accounting, social services, etc.)	If Federal service, civilian or military: series, grade or rank, and date of last promotion	Your reason for leaving

Description of work (Describe your specific duties, responsibilities and accomplishments in this job.):

For agency use (skill codes, etc.)

C

Name and address of employer's organization (include ZIP Code, if known)	Dates employed (give month and year)	Average number of hours per week
	From To	
	Salary or earnings	Place of employment
	Beginning $ per	City
	Ending $ per	State

Exact title of your position	Name of immediate supervisor	Area Code Telephone Number	Number and kind of employees you supervised

Kind of business or organization (manufacturing, accounting, social services, etc.)	If Federal service, civilian or military: series, grade or rank, and date of last promotion	Your reason for leaving

Description of work (Describe your specific duties, responsibilities and accomplishments in this job.):

For agency use (skill codes, etc.)

If you need additional experience blocks, use Standard Form 171-A or blank sheets of paper
SEE INSTRUCTION SHEET

229

Attach Supplemental Sheets or Forms Here

22. A. Special qualifications and skills *(skills with machines; patents or inventions; your most important publications (do not submit copies unless requested); your public speaking and publications experience; membership in professional or scientific societies; etc.)*

B. Kind of license or certificate *(pilot, registered nurse, lawyer, radio operator, CPA, etc.)*

C. Latest license or certificate

Year   State or other licensing authority

D. Approximate number of words per minute

Typing   Shorthand

23. A. Did you graduate from high school or will you graduate within the next nine months, or do you have a GED high school equivalency certificate?

Yes | Month and year | No | Highest grade completed

B. Name and location *(city and State)* of last high school attended.

C. Name and location *(city, State, and ZIP Code, if known)* of college or university. *(If you expect to graduate within nine months, give MONTH and YEAR you expect to receive your degree.)*

	Dates Attended		Years Completed		No. of Credits Completed		Type of Degree (B.A., etc.)	Year of Degree
	From	To	Day	Night	Semester Hours	Quarter Hours		

D. Chief undergraduate college subjects

	No. of Credits Completed	
	Semester Hours	Quarter Hours

E. Chief graduate college subjects

	No. of Credits Completed	
	Semester Hours	Quarter Hours

F. Major field of study at highest level of college work

G. Other schools or training *(for example, trade, vocational, Armed Forces or business)*. Give for each the name and location *(city, State, and ZIP Code, if known)* of school, dates attended, subjects studied, number of classroom hours of instruction per week, certificate, and any other pertinent data.

24. Honors, awards, and fellowships received

25. Languages other than English: List the languages *(other than English)* in which you are proficient and indicate your level of proficiency by putting a check mark (✔) in the appropriate column. **Candidates for positions requiring conversational ability in a language other than English may be given an interview conducted solely in that language.** Describe in Item 35 how you gained your language skills and the amount of experience you have had *(e.g., completed 72 hours of classroom training, spoke language at home for 18 years, self-taught, etc.)*.

Name of Language(s)	PROFICIENCY							
	Can Prepare and Deliver Lectures		Can Converse		Have Facility to Translate Articles, Technical Materials, etc.		Can Read Articles, Technical Materials, etc., for Own Use	
	Fluently	With Difficulty	Fluently	Passably	Into English	From English	Easily	With Difficulty

26. References List three persons who are NOT related to you and who have definite knowledge of your qualifications and fitness for the position for which you are applying. Do not repeat names of supervisors listed under Item 21, Experience.

Full Name	Present Business or Home Address (Number, Street, City, State and ZIP Code)	Business or Occupation

Page 3

230

		YES	NO
	Answer Items 27 through 34 by placing an "X" in the proper column.		

27. Are you a citizen of the United States? .... ◄
If "NO", give country of which you are a citizen.

NOTE: A conviction or a firing does not necessarily mean you cannot be appointed. The nature of the conviction or firing and how long ago it occurred is important. Give all the facts so that a decision can be made. ◄

28. Within the last five years have you been fired from any job for any reason? .... ◄

29. Within the last five years have you quit a job after being notified that you would be fired? .... ◄
If your answer to 28 or 29 above is "YES", give details in Item 35. Show the name and address *(including ZIP Code)* of employer, approximate date, and reasons in each case. This information should agree with your answers in Item 21, Experience.

30. A. Have you **ever** been convicted, forfeited collateral, or are you now under charges for **any felony** or **any** firearms or explosives offense against the law? *(A felony is defined as any offense punishable by imprisonment for a term exceeding one year, but does not include any offense classified as a misdemeanor under the laws of a State and punishable by a term of imprisonment of two years or less.)* .... ◄
B. During the past seven years have you been convicted, imprisoned, on probation or parole or forfeited collateral, or are you now under charges for any offense against the law not included in A. above? .... ◄
NOTE: When answering A. and B. above, you may omit: (1) traffic fines for which you paid a fine of $50.00 or less; (2) any offense committed before your 18th birthday which was finally adjudicated in a juvenile court or under a youth offender law; (3) any conviction the record of which has been expunged under Federal or State law; and (4) any conviction set aside under the Federal Youth Corrections Act or similar State authority.
31. While in the military service were you ever convicted by a general court-martial? .... ◄
If your answer to 30A, 30B, or 31 is "YES", give details in Item 35. Show for each offense: (1) date; (2) charge; (3) place; (4) court; and (5) action taken.

32. Does the United States Government employ in a civilian capacity or as a member of the Armed Forces any relative of yours *(by blood or marriage)*? *(See Items 32 and 33 in the attached instruction sheet.)* .... ◄

33. Do you live with, or within the past 12 months have you lived with, any of these relatives who are employed in a civilian capacity? .... ◄
If your answer to 32 is "YES", give in Item 35 for such relatives: (1) name; (2) present address *(including ZIP Code)*; (3) relationship; (4) department, agency, or branch of the armed forces.
If your answer to 33 is "YES", also give the kind of appointment held by the relative(s) you live with or have lived with within the past 12 months.

34. Do you receive, or do you have pending, application for retirement or retainer pay, pension, or other compensation based upon military, Federal civilian, or District of Columbia Government service? .... ◄
If your answer to 34 is "YES", give details in Item 35.

Your Statement cannot be processed until you have answered all questions, including Items 27 through 34 above. Be sure you have placed an "X" to the left of EVERY marker (◄) above, either in the "YES" or "NO" column.

35. Item Number	Space for detailed answers. Indicate item number to which the answers apply.

If more space is required, use full sheets of paper approximately the same size as this page. Write on each sheet your name, birth date, and announcement or position title. Attach all sheets to this Statement at the top of page 3.

ATTENTION — THIS STATEMENT MUST BE SIGNED
Read the following paragraphs carefully before signing this Statement.

A false answer to any question in this Statement may be grounds for not employing you, or for dismissing you after you begin work, and may be punishable by fine or imprisonment (U.S. Code, Title 18, Section 1001). All the information you give will be considered in reviewing your Statement.

AUTHORITY FOR RELEASE OF INFORMATION

I have completed this Statement with the knowledge and understanding that any or all items contained herein may be subject to investigation prescribed by law or Presidential directive and I consent to the release of information concerning my capacity and fitness by employers, educational institutions, law enforcement agencies, and other individuals and agencies, to duly accredited Investigators, Personnel Staffing Specialists, and other authorized employees of the Federal Government for that purpose.

CERTIFICATION	SIGNATURE *(sign in ink)*	DATE
I certify that all of the statements made by me are true, complete, and correct to the best of my knowledge and belief, and are made in good faith.		

21. Experience Begin with current or most recent work or volunteer experience and work back. Account for periods of unemployment exceeding three months and your residence address at that time on the last line of the experience blocks in order of occurrence.

May inquiry be made of your present employer regarding your character, qualifications, and record of employment?
(A "NO" will not affect your consideration for employment opportunities except for Administrative Law Judge positions.) ☐ YES ☐ NO

A

Name and address of employer's organization (include ZIP Code, if known)	Dates employed (give month and year) From ___ To ___	Average number of hours per week
	Salary or earnings Beginning $ per Ending $ per	Place of employment City State

Exact title of your position	Name of immediate supervisor	Area Code	Telephone Number	Number and kind of employees you supervised

Kind of business or organization (manufacturing, accounting, social services, etc.)	If Federal service, civilian or military: series, grade or rank, and date of last promotion	Your reason for wanting to leave

Description of work *(Describe your specific duties, responsibilities and accomplishments in this job.)*:

For agency use *(skill codes, etc.)*

Name and address of employer's organization (include ZIP Code, if known)	Dates employed (give month and year)		Average number of hours per week
	From To		
	Salary or earnings		Place of employment
	Beginning $ per		City
	Ending $ per		State

Exact title of your position	Name of immediate supervisor	Area Code Telephone Number	Number and kind of employees you supervised

Kind of business or organization (manufacturing, accounting, social services, etc.)	If Federal service, civilian or military: series, grade or rank, and date of last promotion	Your reason for leaving

Description of work (Describe your specific duties, responsibilities and accomplishments in this job.):

For agency use (skill codes, etc.)

233

Name and address of employer's organization (include ZIP Code, if known)		Dates employed (give month and year)		Average number of hours per week
		From To		
		Salary or earnings		Place of employment
		Beginning $ per		City
		Ending $ per		State
Exact title of your position	Name of immediate supervisor	Area Code Telephone Number		Number and kind of employees you supervised
Kind of business or organization (manufacturing, accounting, social services, etc.)	If Federal service, civilian or military: series, grade or rank, and date of last promotion			Your reason for leaving

Description of work (Describe your specific duties, responsibilities and accomplishments in this job.):

For agency use (skill codes, etc.)

Name and address of employer's organization (include ZIP Code, if known)		Dates employed (give month and year)		Average number of hours per week
		From To		
		Salary or earnings		Place of employment
		Beginning $ per		City
		Ending $ per		State
Exact title of your position	Name of immediate supervisor	Area Code Telephone Number		Number and kind of employees you supervised
Kind of business or organization (manufacturing, accounting, social services, etc.)	If Federal service, civilian or military: series, grade or rank, and date of last promotion			Your reason for leaving

Description of work (Describe your specific duties, responsibilities and accomplishments in this job.):

For agency use (skill codes, etc.)

234

Name and address of employer's organization (include ZIP Code, if known)		Dates employed (give month and year)		Average number of hours per week
		From To		
		Salary or earnings		Place of employment
		Beginning $ per		City
		Ending $ per		State
Exact title of your position	Name of immediate supervisor	Area Code Telephone Number		Number and kind of employees you supervised
Kind of business or organization (manufacturing, accounting, social services, etc.)	If Federal service, civilian or military: series, grade or rank, and date of last promotion			Your reason for wanting to leave

Description of work (Describe your specific duties, responsibilities and accomplishments in this job.):

For agency use (skill codes, etc.)

Name and address of employer's organization (include ZIP Code, if known)		Dates employed (give month and year)		Average number of hours per week
		From To		
		Salary or earnings		Place of employment
		Beginning $ per		City
		Ending $ per		State
Exact title of your position	Name of immediate supervisor	Area Code Telephone Number		Number and kind of employees you supervised
Kind of business or organization (manufacturing, accounting, social services, etc.)	If Federal service, civilian or military: series, grade or rank, and date of last promotion			Your reason for leaving

Description of work (Describe your specific duties, responsibilities and accomplishments in this job.):

For agency use (skill codes, etc.)

Name and address of employer's organization (include ZIP Code, if known)		Dates employed (give month and year)		Average number of hours per week
		From To		
		Salary or earnings		Place of employment
		Beginning $ per		City
		Ending $ per		State
Exact title of your position	Name of immediate supervisor	Area Code Telephone Number		Number and kind of employees you supervised
Kind of business or organization (manufacturing, accounting, social services, etc.)	If Federal service, civilian or military: series, grade or rank, and date of last promotion			Your reason for leaving

Description of work (Describe your specific duties, responsibilities and accomplishments in this job.):

For agency use (skill codes, etc.)

235

22. A. Special qualifications and skills (skills with machines, patents or inventions, your most important publications (do not submit copies unless requested), your public speaking and publications experience, membership in professional or scientific societies, etc.)

236

24. Honors, awards, and fellowships received

REFERENCES

Abbott, Walter F.
    1980   "Commentary: When Will Academicians Enter the Ranks of the
              Working Poor? *Academe* 66:349-353.

Abert, Geoffry F.
    1979   *After the Crash: How to Survive and Prosper During the
              Depression of the 1980s*. New York: Bradford Press.

Abramowitz, Susan and Stuart Rosenfeld
    1978   "Setting the Stage," pp. 1-17 in Susan Abramowitz and
              Stuart Rosenfeld (eds.), *Declining Enrollments: The
              Challenge of the Coming Decade*. Washington, D.C.: U.S.
              Department of Health, Education, and Welfare.

Academe   Bulletin of the American Association of University
              Professors.

Ashley, William L.
    1980   "Occupational Adaptability: A Requirement for Future
              Careers," pp. 72-86 in Judith W. Springer (ed.), *Issues in
              Career and Human Resource Development*. Madison, Wisconsin:
              American Society for Training and Development.

Azrin, Nathan H. and Victoria A. Besalel
    1980   *Job Club Counselor's Manual: A Behavioral Approach to
              Vocational Counseling*. Baltimore: University Park Press.

Barnes, J. A.
    1968   "Networks and Political Processes," pp. 107-130 in Marc J.
              Swartz (ed.), *Local Level Politics: Social and Cultural
              Perspectives*. Chicago, Ill.: Aldine.

Biddle, Bruce J. and Edwin J. Thomas (eds.)
    1966   *Role Theory: Concepts and Research*. New York: John Wiley.

Blau, Peter M.
    1964   *Exchange and Power in Social Life*. New York: John Wiley.

Bolles, Richard Nelson
    1980   *What Color is Your Parachute?* Berkeley, Calif.: Ten Speed
              Press.
    1978a   *What Color is Your Parachute?* Berkeley, Calif.: Ten Speed
              Press.
    1978b   *The Three Boxes of Life: And How to Get Out of Them*.
              Berkeley, Calif.: Ten Speed Press.

238

Casey, Douglas R.
  1980   *Crisis Investing*. New York: Harper and Row.

CHE.   *The Chronicle of Higher Education*.

Congressional Yellow Book
  1981   Washington, D.C.: Washington Monitor, Inc.

Conn, Charles Paul
  1979   *The Winner's Circle*. Old Tappan, N.J.: Flemming H. Revell.
  1977   *The Possible Dream*. Old Tappan, N.J.: Flemming H. Revell.

Crozier, Michel
  1964   *The Bureaucratic Phenomenon*. Chicago: University of
          Chicago Press.

Crystal, John C.
  1975   "Life/Work Planning Workshop." Presented in Boston,
          Massachusetts, September.

Crystal, John C. and Richard N. Bolles
  1974   *Where Do I Go From Here With My Life*? Berkeley, Calif.: Ten Spee

Dalton, Melville
  1959   *Men Who Manage*. New York: John Wiley.

Davis, Russell G. and Gary M. Lewis
  1978   "The Demographic Background to Changing Enrollments and
          School Needs," pp. 19-45 in Susan Abramowitz and Stuart
          Rosenfeld (eds.), *Declining Enrollments: The Challenge of
          the Coming Decade*. Washington, D.C.: U.S. Department of
          Health, Education, and Welfare.

Dickhut, Harold
  1978   *Professional Resume/Job Search Guide*. Chicago: Management
          Counselors, Inc.

Djeddah, Eli
  1978   *Moving Up*. Berkeley, Calif.: Ten Speed Press.

Drucker, Peter
  1967   *The Effective Executive*. New York: Harper and Row.

DuBrin, Andrew J.
  1978   *Winning at Office Politics*. New York: Van Nostrand
          Reinhold Co.

Eisen, Jeffrey
  1978   *Get the Right Job Now!* Philadelphia and New York: J.B.
          Lippincott Co.

Etzioni, Amitai
  1967   "Mixed Scanning: A 'Third' Approach to Decision-Making."
          Public Administration Review 27:385-392.

Federal Yellow Book
1981   Washington, D.C.: Washington Monitor, Inc.

Ferrini, Paul and L. Allen Parker
1978   _Career Change: A Handbook of Exemplary Programs in Business_
           and Industrial Firms, Educational Institutions, Government
           Agencies, Professional Associations. Cambridge, Mass.:
           Technical Education Research Center.

Figler, Howard
1979   _The Complete Job-Search Handbook._ New York: Holt, Rinehart
           and Winston.

Fishlow, Harriett
1978   "Demography and Changing Enrollments," pp. 47-80 in Susan
           Abramowitz and Stuart Rosenfeld (eds.), _Declining Enrollments_:
           The Challenge of the Coming Decade. Washington, D.C.: U.S.
           Department of Health, Education, and Welfare.

Foster, George M.
1963   "The Dyadic Contract in Tzintzuntzan: Patron-Client
           Relationship." _American Anthropologist_ 65:1280-1294.

Fox, Marcia R.
1979   _Put Your Degree to Work._ New York: W. W. Norton Co.

Galambos, Eva C.
1980   _The Changing Labor Market for Teachers in the South._
           Atlanta, Georgia: Southern Regional Education Board.

Germann, Richard and Peter Arnold
1980   _Bernard Haldane Associates' Job & Career Building._ New
           York: Harper and Row.

Glassman, James K.
1981   "The Road to Riches in the '80s." _The Washingtonian_ 5:
           107-109.

Granovetter, Mark S.
1980   "The Strength of Weak Ties: A Network Theory Revisited."
           Paper presented at the annual meeting of the International
           Communication Association. Acapulco, Mexico. May 21.
1979   "Placement as Brokerage--Information Problems in the Labor
           Market for Rehabilitated Workers," pp. 83-101 in David
           Vandergoot and John Worral (eds.), _Placement in_
           Rehabilitation. Baltimore: University Park Press.
1974   _Getting a Job: A Study of Contacts and Careers._ Cambridge,
           Mass.: Harvard University Press.

Gross, Neal, Ward Mason, and Alexander McEachern
1958   _Explorations in Role Analysis._ New York: John Wiley.

Haldane, Bernard
   1974   *Career Satisfaction and Success: A Guide to Job Freedom.*
           New York: AMACOM.

Hawkins, James E.
   1978   *The Uncle Sam Connection: An Insider's Guide to Federal
           Employment.* Chicago: Follett Publishing Co.

Heclo, Hugh
   1978   "Issue Networks and the Executive Establishment," pp. 87-
           124 in Anthony King (ed.), *The New American Political System.*
           Washington, D.C.: American Enterprise Institute.

H.E.W.
   1973   *Work in America: Report of a Special Task Force to the
           Secretary of Health, Education, and Welfare.* Cambridge,
           Mass.: MIT Press.

Holland, John L.
   1973   *Making Vocational Choices: A Theory of Careers.* Englewood
           Cliffs, N.J.: Prentice-Hall, Inc.

Irish, Richard K.
   1978   *Go Hire Yourself an Employer.* Garden City, N.Y.: Anchor
           Press.

Jackson, Tom
   1981   *The Perfect Resume.* Garden City, N.J.: Anchor Books.

Jameson, Robert
   1978   *The Professional Job Changing System.* Parsippany, N.J.:
           Performance Dynamics.

Jencks, Christopher
   1979   *Who Gets Ahead? The Determinants of Economic Success in
           America.* New York: Basic Books, Inc.
   1972   *Inequality: A Reassessment of the Effect of Family and
           Schooling in America.* New York: Basic Books, Inc.

Kellogg, Mary Alice
   1978   *Fast Track: The Superachievers and How They Make It to
           Early Success, Status and Power.* New York: McGraw-Hill.

Kennedy, Marilyn
   1980a   *Office Politics.* Chicago: Follett Publishing Co.
   1980b   *Career Knockouts.* Chicago: Follett Publishing Co.

Keough, Jr., William F.
   1978   "Enrollment Decline: The Dilemma From the Superintendent's
           Chair," pp. 331-369 in Susan Abramowitz and Stuart Rosenfeld
           (eds.), *Declining Enrollments: The Challenge of the Coming
           Decade.* Washington, D.C.: U.S. Department of Health,
           Education, and Welfare.

Kirn, Arthur G.
1974   *Lifework Planning Workbook*, 2nd ed.   Hartford, Conn.: Arthur G. Kirn and Associates.

Kirschenbaum, Howard
1974   "In-service Training Program Workshop."   Presented to the Eastern College Personnel Officers, Mid-Atlantic Placement Association. New Paltz, N.Y. June.

Kocher, Eric
1979   *International Jobs: Where They Are, How to Get Them*.   Reading, Mass.: Addison-Wesley.

Komar, John J.
1979   *The Interview Game: Winning Strategies of Job Seekers*.   Chicago: Follett Publishing Co.

Korda, Michael
1977   *Success!*   New York: Ballentine Books.

Krannich, Ronald L.
1980   "Administrative Leadership of Mayors: The Politics of Mayor-Manager Relationships in Thailand." *Public Administration Review* 40:330-341.

Kreider, Paul T.
1976   *The Interview Handbook*. Alameda, Calif.: KCE.

Kuhn, Thomas S.
1970   *The Structure of Scientific Revolutions*.   Chicago: The University of Chicago Press.

Kuttner, Bob
1981   "Dear Democrats: Get Out of Town." *The Washington Post*, January 18:C1,C3.

Lakein, Alan
1973   *How to Get Control of Your Time and Your Life*.   New York: Signet Books.

Landau, Martin
1969   "Redundancy, Rationality, and the Problem of Duplication and Overlap." *Public Administration Review* 29:346-358.

Lande, Carl
1964   *Leaders, Factions, and Parties: The Structure of Philippine Politics*, Monograph No. 6. New Haven, Conn: Yale University--Southeast Asia Studies.

Lathrop, Richard
1978   *The Job Market*. Washington, D.C.: The National Center for Job-Market Studies.
1977   *Who's Hiring Who*. Berkeley, Calif.: Ten Speed Press.

Leinhardt, Samual (ed.)
1977   *Social Networks: A Developing Paradigm*. New York:
        Academic Press.

Levine, Charles H. (ed.)
1980   *Managing Fiscal Stress: The Crisis in the Public Sector*.
        Chatham, N.J.: Chatham House Publishers, Inc.

Levine, Charles H. and Irene Rubin (eds.)
1980   *Fiscal Stress and Public Policy*. Beverly Hills, Calif.:
        Sage Publishers.

Lin, Nan, Paul Dayton, and Peter Greenwald
1978   "Analyzing the Instrumental Use of Relations in the
        Context of Social Structure." *Sociological Methods and
        Research* 7:149-166.

Lindblom, Charles E.
1959   "The Science of Muddling Through." *Public Administration
        Review* 19:79-88.

Long, Norton
1958   "The Local Community as an Ecology of Games." *American
        Journal of Sociology* 64:251-261.

MacKenzie, R. Alex
1972   *The Time Trap*. New York: AMACOM, Inc.

McGuire, W. H.
1979   "Teacher Burnout: Symposium." *Today's Education* 68
        (November/December).

McLaughlin, John and Stephen Merman
1980   *Writing a Job-Winning Resume*. Englewood Cliffs, N.J.:
        Prentice-Hall.

Maslow, Abraham
1954   *Motivation and Personality*. New York: Harper and Row.

Mecham, R.C. and E. J. McCormick
1972   *Attitude Ratings and Profiles of the Job Elements of the
        Position Analysis Questionnaire (PAQ)*. West Lafayette, Ind.:
        Purdue University, Department of Psychological Sciences,
        Occupational Research Center.

Meier, Kenneth J.
1979   *Politics and the Bureaucracy*. North Scituate, Mass.:
        Duxbury Press.

Merton, Robert K.
1968   *Social Theory and Social Structure*. New York: The Free Press.
1957   "The Role-Set: Problems in Sociological Theory." *The
        British Journal of Sociology* 2:106-120.

Miller, Arthur F. and Ralph T. Mattson
    1977   *The Truth About You*. Old Tappan, N.J. Fleming H. Revell.

Molloy, John T.
    1977   *The Woman's Dress for Success Book*. New York: Warner
            Books.
    1975   *Dress for Success*. New York: Warner Books.

Neeb, R. W., J. W. Cunningham, and J. J. Pass
    1971   *Human Attribute Requirements of Work Elements: Further
            Development of the Occupational Analysis Inventory*, Center
            Research Monograph, No. 7. Raleigh, N.C.: North Carolina
            State University at Raleigh, Center for Occupational
            Education.

Nelson, Joan M.
    1979   *Access to Power: Politics and the Urban Poor in Developing
            Nations*. Princeton, N.J.: Princeton University Press.

Noer, David
    1975   *How to Beat the Employment Game*. Berkeley, Calif.: Ten
            Speed Press.

People Management
    1977   "Making Career Decisions: Practical Procedures for Those
            Who Have Discovered Their Motivated Pattern." Simsbury,
            Conn.: People Management Incorporated.

Perron, John D.
    1980   "The Ph.D. Cabbie: 'I Don't Miss It, Not Anymore'."
            The Chronicle of Higher Education. August 25:31.

Peters, Charles
    1980   *How Washington Really Works*. Reading, Mass.: Addison-
            Wesley.

Powell, John Duncan
    1970   "Peasant Society and Clientelist Politics." *American
            Political Science Review* 64:411-425.

Ricklefs, Roger
    1981   "Resume Floodtide Posing Problems in Job Market." *The Wall
            Street Journal*. February 23.

Riley, Robert T.
    1978   *How to Manage Your Time Successfully*. Dallas, Texas: The
            Drawing Board, Inc.

Ringer, Robert J.
    1974   *Winning Through Intimidation*. New York: Fawcett Crest.

Ripley, Randall B. and Grace A. Franklin
    1976   *Congress, The Bureaucracy, and Public Policy*. Homewood,
            Ill.: The Dorsey Press.

Rogers, Carl R. and Barry Stevens (eds.)
    1967   *Person to Person*. Lafayette, Calif.: Real People Press.

Ruff, Howard J.
    1979   *How to Prosper During the Coming Bad Years*. New York:
            Warner Books.

SCA (Speech Communication Association)
    1980   *Spectra*. April.

Scheele, Adele
    1979   *Skills For Success: A Guide to the Top for Men and Women*.
            New York: Ballantine Books.

Schwartz, David J.
    1965   *The Magic of Thinking Big*. New York: Cornerstone Library.

Scott, James C.
    1972   "Patron-Client Politics and Political Change in Southeast
            Asia." *American Political Science Review* 66:91-113.

Selznick, P.
    1949   *T.V.A. and the Grass Roots*. Berkeley, Calif.: University
            of California Press.

Shawn, K.
    1979   "Teaching: Why I Got in, Why I Got Out." *Media and Methods*
            16:12-13.

Simon, Herbert A.
    1977   *Administrative Behavior: A Study of Decision-Making
            Processes in Administrative Organization*. New York: The
            Free Press.

Simon, Sidney, Leland Howard, and Howard Kirschenbaum
    1972   *Values Clarification: A Handbook of Practice Strategies
            for Teachers and Students*. New York: Hart Publishing Co.

Sivy, Michael
    1981   "Putting Money into the Boom Regions." *Money* 2:74-84.

Sjogren, D. D.
    1977   *Occupationally Transferable Skills and Characteristics:
            Review of Literature and Research*. Columbus, Ohio: The
            National Center for Research in Vocational Education.

Smith, Jerome F.
    1981   *The Coming Currency Collapse and What to Do About It!*
            New York: Books in Focus.

Solmon, Lewis, Nancy L. Ochsner, and Margo-Lea Hurwicz
    1979   *Alternative Careers for Humanities PhDs: Perspectives
            of Students and Graduates*. New York: Praeger Publishers.

Stanat, Kirby W.
    1977   *Job Hunting Secrets & Tactics*. Chicago: Follett Publishing Co.

Steele, Addison
    1978   *Upward Nobility: How to Win the Rat Race Without Becoming a Rat*. New York: Quadrangle/The New York Times Book Co., Inc.

Stump, Robert W.
    1980   "Transferable Skills and Job Changes," pp. 87-111 in Judith W. Spring (ed.), *Issues in Career and Human Resource Development*. Madison, Wisconsin: American Society for Training and Development.

Today's Education
    1981   "How Changes in Enrollment Will Affect Higher Education." 1:54GS-59GS.

Travers, J. and S. Milgram
    1969   "An Experimental Study of the 'Small-World Problem'." *Sociometry* 32:425-443.

United States Government
    1981   *United States Government Manual*. Washington, D.C.: U.S. Government Printing Office.

Waelde, David
    1980   *How to Get a Federal Job and Advance*. Washington, D.C.: FEDHELP Publications.

Welch, Mary Scott
    1980   *Networking: The Great New Way for Women to Get Ahead*. New York: Harcourt Brace Jovanovich.

Wiant, A. A.
    1980   *Occupational Change and Transferable Skills: The Employers' Viewpoint*. Columbus, Ohio: The National Center for Research in Vocational Education.

Wildavsky, Aaron
    1964   *The Politics of the Budgetary Process*. Boston, Mass.: Little, Brown and Co.

Wolf, Eric
    1966   "Kinship, Friendship, and Patron-Client Relations," pp. 1-22 in Michael Banton (ed.), *The Social Anthropology of Complex Societies*, Association of Applied Anthropology Monograph #4. London: Tavistock Publications.

Wood, Patricia B.
    1979   *The 171 Workbook*. Washington, D.C.: Workbooks, Inc.

Yates, Douglas
    1976   "Urban Government as a Policy-making System," pp. 235-264 in
              Louis H. Masotti and Robert L. Lineberry (eds.), _The New_
              Urban Politics. Cambridge, Mass.: Ballinger Publishing Co.

Yeager, Dexter and Doug Wead
    1980   _Becoming Rich_. Ada, Michigan: Free Enterprise.

SUBJECT INDEX

AUTHOR INDEX

Abbott, 28-29.
Abert, 18.
Abramowitz, 17.
Academe, 34.
Arnold, 13, 45, 48, 51, 64,
  93, 97, 103, 107, 112,
  116, 134, 136, 141, 151,
  152, 153, 178.
Ashley, 90, 212-213.
Azrin, 69.
Barnes, 141.
Besalel, 69.
Biddle, 144.
Blau, 141.
Dolles, 13, 44, 45, 51, 60,
  61, 70, 80, 95, 96, 103,
  105, 131, 135, 152, 160,
  164.
Brown, 48, 141.
Casey, 18.
*The Chronicle of Higher
  Education*, 6, 7, 9, 19,
  24, 25, 26, 28, 30, 31,
  32, 33, 35, 36.
Conn, 43.
Crozier, 141.
Crystal, 51, 80, 92, 103,
  104, 105.
Cunningham, 211.
Dalton, 141.
Davis, 18.
Dayton, 52.
Dickhut, 128.
Djeddah, 140.
Drucker, 80, 81.
DuBrin, 7, 139.
Eisen, 7, 11, 139, 176.
Etzioni, 54.
Ferrini, 14.
Figler, 51, 129.
Fishlow, 19.
Foster, 141.
  14, 16, 163.
Franklin, 202.
Galambos, 19, 22.

Germann, 13, 45, 48, 51, 64, 93,
  97, 103, 107, 112, 116, 134,
  136, 141, 151, 152, 153, 178.
Glassman, 201.
Granovetter, 48, 55, 139, 141,
  142
Greenwald, 152.
Gross, 141, 144.
Haldane, x, 13, 45, 51, 69, 82,
  93, 97, 107, 133, 149, 153,
  178
Hawkins, 141, 189, 191.
Heclo, 141.
Holland, 51, 80, 83, 96.
Hurwicz, 91.
Irish, 7, 14, 46, 47, 60, 76, 96
  97, 139, 141, 149, 153, 162,
  165, 166, 175, 178, 179, 189,
  194, 197, 199, 209.
Jackson, 112, 128.
Jameson, 128.
Jencks, 55, 88.
Kellogg, 43-44, 55.
Kennedy, 7, 139.
Keough, 2.
Kirn, 106.
Kirschenbaum, 104.
Kocher, 74, 135.
Komar, 159, 166.
Korda, 43.
Krannich, 141.
Kreider, 169.
Kuhn, 54.
Kuttner, 206.
Lakein, 75.
Landau, 186.
Lande, 141, 163.
Lathrop, 13, 52, 96, 112, 114,
  116, 124, 126, 128, 159, 160.
Leinhardt, 141.
Levine, 5.
Lewis, 18.
Lin, 152.
Lindblom, 54.
Long, 206.

254

MacKenzie, 75.
Mattson, x, 83, 90.
Mason, 141, 144.
McCormick, 211.
McEachern, 141, 144.
McGuire, 6.
McLaughlin, 128.
Maslow, 88.
Mecham, 211.
Meier, 180.
Merman, 128.
Merton, 54, 141, 142.
Milgram, 141.
Miller, x, 83-90.
Molloy, 162, 165-166.
Neeb, 211.
Nelson, 141.
Noer, 65.
Parker, 14.
Pass, 211.
Ochsner, 91.
People Management, x, 109.
Perron, 6.
Peters, 141, 185, 199.
Powell, 141.
Ricklefs, 149.
Riley, 75.
Ringer, 43.
Ripley, 202.
Rogers, 168.
Rosenfeld, 17.
Rubin, 5.
Ruff, 18.
Speech Communication
  Association, 8.
Scheele, 60.
Schwartz, 42-43.
Scott, 141.
Selznick, 141.
Shawn, 6.
Simon, H., 54.
Simon, S., 103.
Sivy, 34.
Sjogren, 90, 216-218.
Smith, 18.
Solmon, 91.
Stanat, 137, 160, 162, 165,
  175.
Stevens, 168.
Stump, 90, 139.
Thomas, 144.
Today's Education, 1, 23, 26,
  27, 31.

Travers, 141.
Waelde, 141, 191.
Wead, 42.
Welch, 69.
Wiant, 90, 214.
Wildavsky, 54.
Wolf, 141.
Wood, 191.
Yates, 54.
Yeager, 42.

AUTHORS

<u>WILLIAM J. BANIS</u> is Director of Career Planning and Placement at Old
Dominion University, Norfolk, Virginia, where he is responsible for
program development, office management, employer relations, teaching,
and career/job search counseling. He was previously Director of Career
Development and Placement and Director of Housing at the University of
Hartford, and Assistant Staff Coordinator in the student affairs
division at the Pennsylvania State University as well as a teacher,
counselor, and salesperson. He has a B.S. in vocational rehabili-
tation and business, and a M.A. in speech communication, counseling,
and student personnel administration from Penn State University and
is currently pursuing doctoral studies in human resources management.
His career development training includes: Group Approaches to Career
Counseling, College Placement Council; Lifework Planning Workshop and
leader's training, Arthur Kirn/Lifework Planning Associates; Lifework
Planning and Job Search Course, Crystal Associates of New England, Inc.;
career workshops with Richard Bolles, John Crystal, and Richard Irish;
Professional Internship, Bernard Haldane Associates; clinical and
management applications of the System to Identify Motivated Abilities,
People Management, Inc.; and numerous professional development workshops
with professional placement groups. He has designed and conducted
programs on career development, job placement, work planning, and time
management for professional associations, cummunity groups, government
agencies, colleges, and corporations. He recently authored with
Ronald L. Krannich, _High Impact Resumes and Letters_ (1982).

<u>RONALD L. KRANNICH</u> is President of Progressive Concepts Incorporated.
He received his Ph.D. in political science from Northern Illinois
University where he specialized in public administration, local government, and comparative politics. A former Peace Corps Volunteer in
Thailand and a high school teacher in Rock Falls, Illinois, he previously was associated with Old Dominion University where he taught
public administration and political science as well as developed a
career planning module for social science students. He has conducted
workshops and seminars on career planning and internships and holds
offices in international and state professional associations. He has
conducted several research projects in the United States and abroad on
career planning, internships, role theory, planning, public policy,
and local government. At present he is developing training materials
and conducting workshops on outplacement and human resources development. His books have been published by the University of California
at Berkeley and Ohio University, and his articles appear in major
professional journals: _Administration and Society, Asian Profile,
Asian Survey, International Journal of Public Administration,
International Journal of Women's Studies, Public Administration Review,_
and the _Urban Affairs Quarterly_. He recently authored with William
J. Banis, _High Impact Resumes and Letters_ (1982) as well as completed
Moving Out of Government (1982).

RESOURCES FROM PROGRESSIVE CONCEPTS INCORPORATED

────────────── OUTPLACEMENT IN EDUCATION ──────────────

Reshaping Faculty Careers. By W. Todd Furniss, 178 pages, ISBN 0-8268-1449-2, 1981. $16.25 ($15.00 prepaid).

Published by the American Council on Education, this book reviews the problems of faculty careers, questions traditional assumptions about the "one life, one career" pattern, and recommends a new approach to faculty careers. Develops both philosophical and policy perspectives for administrators and faculty in the 1980's.

────────────── NEW CAREER OPTIONS FOR EDUCATORS ──────────────

Expanding Faculty Options: Career Development Projects at Colleges and Universities. By Roger Baldwin *et. al,* 116 pages, 1981. $7.95 ($6.95 prepaid).

A new report on faculty career mobility problems published by the American Association for Higher Education. Includes 26 case studies of campus career development programs and three essays on designing career programs.

How to Teach School and Make a Living at the Same Time. By Patrick H. Crowe, 159 pages, ISBN 0-8362-2605-4, 1978. $10.95 ($9.95 prepaid).

Designed specifically for educators who plan to remain in education but who seek additional financial rewards. Offers teachers on-the-job career alternatives with special emphasis on developing part-time businesses. Especially valuable for secondary and elementary teachers who are anticipating career changes but who wish to test the waters before making a major career change. "This is the best book written about teaching in the last 30 years" — Literary Critic, Doug Campbell.   "Covers everything that a neophyte entrepreneur could want to know" — *Change Magazine.* "Practical guide for the dedicated teacher" — *Richmond Times Dispatch.*

────────────── NEW FOR 1982 ──────────────

High Impact Resumes and Letters. By Ronald L. Krannich and William J. Banis, 138 pages, ISBN 0-940010-01-1, 1982. $8.95 ($7.95 prepaid).

A unique career planning book. Placing resumes and letters in the larger career development process, this book incorporates proven methods for setting objectives, identifying transferable skills, networking, and marketing. The book is designed as a general self-directed guide as well as a standard reference book and classroom text for both undergraduate and graduate students. Includes worksheets and examples of resumes and letters printed on high-quality paper — a first for such a book!

The Career Connection. By Ron Petit, 180 pages, 1982. $6.95 ($5.95 prepaid).

Based on interviews with more than 5,000 individuals, this book has received excellent reviews: "the best book of its kind" — Maron Corporation. It is a comprehensive job hunting guide with special emphasis on interviewing strategies, including the critical telephone interview. The book is the subject of a six-part public television series which airs in Fall 1981 and Spring 1982.

ORDER FORM

SEND TO: PROGRESSIVE CONCEPTS INCORPORATED
2541 Lakewood Lane, Chesapeake, Virginia 23321

(804) 467-9248 / 465-0646

Quantity	Publication	Invoiced Price	Prepaid Price	Cost
	Moving out of Education: The Educator's Guide to Career Management and Change (Krannich and Banis)	$16.70	$14.95	
	Reshaping Faculty Careers (Furniss)	$16.25	$15.00	
	Expanding Faculty Options (Baldwin et al)	$ 7.95	$ 6.95	
	How to Teach School and Make a Living at the Same Time (Crowe)	$10.95	$ 9.95	
	High Impact Resumes and Letters (Krannich and Banis)	$ 8.95	$ 7.95	
	The Career Connection (Petit)	$ 6.95	$ 5.95	

Virginia residents add 4% sales tax

TOTAL

☐ Invoice me personally   ☐ Invoice my institution   ☐ Payment enclosed

Name _____   Title _____   Phone _____

Address _____

☐ Send me information on PCI's training materials and consulting services.